# JEAN TOOMER, ARTIST

*Jean Toomer in the mid-to-late 1920s*
*Courtesy of Fisk University*

# Jean Toomer
## ARTIST

A Study of His Literary Life
and Work, 1894–1936

NELLIE Y. MCKAY

The University of North Carolina Press

Chapel Hill and London

Manufactured in the United States of America

Library of Congress Cataloging in Publication Data
McKay, Nellie Y.
Jean Toomer, artist.
Bibliography: p.
Includes index.
1. Toomer, Jean, 1894–1967. 2. Authors, American—
20th century—Biography. I. Title.
PS3539.O478Z78 1984   813'.52 [B]   83-21570
ISBN 0-8078-1583-7

Material from "The Blue Meridian" is reprinted from *The Wayward and the
Seeking*, edited by Darwin T. Turner, copyright © 1980 by Darwin T. Turner and
Marjorie Content Toomer, with the permission of Howard University Press,
Washington, D.C.

The quotations from *Cane* by Jean Toomer are reprinted by permission of Liveright
Publishing Corporation. Copyright 1923 by Boni & Liveright. Copyright renewed
1951 by Jean Toomer.

Selected materials from the Jean Toomer Special Collection at Fisk University are
used by permission of Marjorie Content Toomer.

*For the memory of my Ancestors—for those who
survived and for those who did not;
and
For my parents, who dared to dream beyond survival;
and
For Nicholas, whose dreams are in all our hearts*

# CONTENTS

# Contents

# PREFACE

This book, an interpretive study of Jean Toomer's published literary works and their intersection with his life, is the result of a two-pronged analysis of his early years and his important working years, 1894–1936. In the first place, I examine and evaluate Toomer's major literary writings as contributions to black and American literature. In the second, I look at some of the elements in his personal life in order to determine how his life and literary output affected each other. *Cane* (1923), a book of indefinable genre, which brought him praise and recognition from writers and critics in his time, and which continues to do so in our time, marked the beginning of his literary career. "Blue Meridian" (1936), a long poem, stands at the opposite end of his career. Although less celebrated than *Cane*, it is also a work that reveals its author's continued dexterity with language and literary form. *Cane* commands attention for both its aesthetic and philosophical merits, and it remains one of the finest representations of the black American experience. It is a vision of that experience which dissipates the shame of the slave past without indulging in self-glorification or denying the pain that has been a prominent factor in black life in white America. "Blue Meridian" represents more than twenty years of Toomer's working toward an artistic resolution to the problems of racial differences in America.

Much of my discussion focuses on materials drawn from Toomer's autobiographical writings, which were not among his published credits during his lifetime, nor has a full-length "autobiography" of Jean Toomer yet appeared. These writings are thus especially appropriate for this study, which seeks to link the man to his public achievements. Toomer was particularly attracted to the autobiographical form, and his literary corpus includes a substantial number of autobiographical documents, which he used as the basis of many of his other works.

With the analysis of *Cane* as the heart of my study, I explore the growth, development, and decline of Jean Toomer as a literary artist through the publication of "Blue Meridian." I believe that Toomer's desire for a unified self was the most pronounced organizing principle of his life, and I attempt to show how it affected his artistry. I connect his writings to his life and his literary imagination to his lived experiences, and I analyze them in the context of black and American literature and of the writer and society. The result is a special kind of reading of a selected period of this author's life and career, one that is viewed through the peculiar lens of his lifelong search for personal internal harmony.

I decided to study Toomer in this way, and during this particular period of his life, because I was curious about the brevity of his literary career. Shortly after *Cane* was published, he disappeared, somewhat mysteriously, from the literary world, and nothing was heard from him for several decades. The publication of "Blue Meridian" in 1936 did little to revive interest in him. Later, in the 1960s, scholars discovered that he had continued to write for many years following the publication of *Cane* but that, after the middle of the 1930s, he had abdicated his ambition to be a man of literature. Early research revealed that he had abandoned literature for personal interests, which eventually outweighed his creative needs. I was interested in how and why this had happened, in the part that American racial attitudes had played in his decision, and in how he had perceived himself as an American writer during the years in which he strove to be a man of letters. Such questions were later subsumed within the larger issue of the role and function of the artist in society.

These interests led me to see the importance of Toomer's autobiographical documents for this study. I have used selections from them for their historical value, but more so because they represent an imaginative rendition of parts of his life. I suspect, along with other scholars, that he created an idealized self-portrait and that his self-analysis lacks some degree of objectivity. At the same time, it is my opinion that these writings reveal much about how he perceived his life and about how, as an artist in search of internal harmony, he used those perceptions to describe his experiences. Although I have found these materials useful, I have not allowed them to persuade me to distort or compromise the facts of Toomer's life.

Because Jean Toomer's works are an important part of the black and American literary canon, the life of the man is important to the study of American lives, black and white, and, in particular, to the lives of artists. His personal story is as interesting as anything he might have imagined. His career in letters was truncated at the moment of its most brilliant promise, but his achievement has earned him a distinguished place in literature, and his success and failure as an artist is a story worthy of literary consideration. Thus I hope that this book will provide readers with a useful interpretation of Jean Toomer's literary life and work between 1894 and 1936.

# ACKNOWLEDGMENTS

The limitations of this space make it impossible for me to recognize everyone who has contributed to the birth of this book. To each unnamed person, I apologize, and I offer you my sincere thanks for your part in whatever is positive in the outcome of this venture. For its shortcomings, I take full responsibility.

First, I acknowledge the faith and confidence that my family has had in me, and I tender my appreciation of their love.

I also wish to express special thanks to the following people: to Nell Irvin Painter, whose warm affection, abiding faith, wise counsel, and not-always-gentle prodding hovered unfalteringly over the manuscript from its beginning to its end, always close by even when far away; to William L. Andrews, friend *extraordinaire*, for his encouragement, critical eye, and the generosity of spirit with which he read the manuscript in draft and offered suggestions for its improvement; to Claudia Card, Marilyn Frye, Kathy Fishburn, and Barry Gross, for their part in helping me to secure a Humanities Grant from Michigan State University, which enabled me to complete the manuscript under optimum conditions; to Herbert Jackson, who discussed ideas in Eastern religions with me and thus made the Gurdjieff philosophy more comprehensible; to Pat and David McConnell and their mothers, who took me into their family at a much needed time; to Warner Berthoff, Robert Kiely, Larry Langer, and Wylie Sypher, who in different but crucial ways nurtured the idea of this book when it was no more than a faint hope of mine; to Houston Baker and David Levin, who always believed in it; to Mark Coburn, who introduced me to Jean Toomer's *Cane* in 1969; to Preston Williams, Cornell West, and my associates at the DuBois Institute and the Warren Center at Harvard University in 1977, from whom I learned that scholarship need not be an isolating endeavor; to my friends and former colleagues at Simmons College, who missed no opportunity to celebrate the signs of progress; to the chairman, department members, and staff of the English Department at Michigan State University, who made my stay with them in 1981 one that began with my being a welcomed guest and ended with my having made vital new friendships; to my friends and colleagues at the University of Wisconsin, Madison, and especially to those in the Afro-American Studies Department, the English Department, and the Women's Studies Program, who more than any others bore the direct burdens of my frustrations as the manuscript moved into its final stages of preparation and who, in that time, offered me patience and loving kindness beyond my ability to thank them; to Pam Bromberg, Robert Grant, Arnold Rampersad, and Joyce and Donald Scott for their expressions of concern, their encouragement of this project, and the assurances of their special friendships over time and miles of separation; and to my Sisters, Thadious Davis, Roberta Logan, Marilyn Richardson, Andrea Rushing, Barbara Smith, Hortense Spillers, and Mary Helen Washington, partners in a marriage of true minds, for the inexhaustible bounty of their supportive love in the best of times as well as in the worst of times.

I owe a debt of special acknowledgment to William Van Deburg, chairman, and to the staff of the Afro-American Studies Department at the University of Wisconsin, Madison, for the many ways in which they offered their cooperation during the preparation of the manuscript. Special thanks goes to Lytton Davis, who not only typed a part of it during its early stages of revision but who also gave me useful criticism on Jean Toomer's women; to Laurie Huggett, for her helpful editorial comments; and to Linda Gorman, Susan Linehan, Kathy Page, and Jo Ann Smith, who at various times typed parts of the manuscript.

I wish to thank Anne Allen Shockley, Sue Chandler, Beth Howse, and Samuel Cameron of the Fisk University Special Collections Archives, and Clifton Johnson of the Amistad Research Collection at Dillard University for the help and cooperation I received from them during the time that I was doing research for this book. Also, I am very grateful to Mrs. Marjorie Content Toomer, who was always ready to offer whatever help she could to advance this work.

And I thank my editor, Sandra Eisdorfer, who for a long time has believed in me, in Jean Toomer, and in the rightness of this project.

Finally, I am grateful to the Graduate School of the University of Wisconsin, Madison, and to Michigan State University for grants that enabled me to spend two summers and one semester in full-time work to complete this book.

# JEAN TOOMER, ARTIST

One ever feels his twoness,—an American, a Negro; two souls, two thoughts, two unreconciled strivings; two warring ideals in one dark body, whose dogged strength alone keeps it from being torn asunder.

Through history, the powers of single black men flash here and there like falling stars, and die sometimes before the world has rightly gauged their brightness.

W. E. B. DU BOIS
*The Souls of Black Folk*

# INTRODUCTION

## I

**J**ean Toomer was born in Washington, D.C., in December 1894, and he died in Pennsylvania in 1967. In 1923, he published *Cane*, a work that proved to be of major significance to both black American and American literature. Toomer's friends and associates, during the time that he was writing the book, were the men and women who were in the vanguard of new trends in American literature—Waldo Frank, Sherwood Anderson, and Hart Crane were part of this group—and *Cane* was an achievement within their ranks. At the same time, the book also won accolades from and brought more recognition to the writers and critics of the incipient Harlem Renaissance. This was the first work by an American writer to present an artist's vision of the Afro-American experience, even though Toomer never identified himself or his writings with that experience. However, because most readers associated Toomer with his Afro-American heritage, *Cane* is still the first important book to emerge from the black movement of the 1920s. The nature of the work defined the small audience it reached, but both black and white writers and critics praised it as the herald of a new day in Afro-American letters, and they called Toomer the "most promising Negro writer" on the American horizon. It was a brilliant beginning for a new writer.

However, the promise never materialized. By 1930, Jean Toomer was no longer an up-and-coming prominent personality on the landscape of arts and letters, and, after 1930, he remained almost unknown for more than forty years. During those years, *Cane* was out of print and relegated to an unfortunate obscurity.

Toward the end of the 1960s, a new black movement reached out to embrace all areas of the cultural life and history of Afro-America, and *Cane* and Jean Toomer were rediscovered. In that era, a fresh generation of critics, most of whom were not born when the book was first published, assumed the task of reinterpreting the work and finding answers to the enigma of its author's brief literary career. They expected to find their insights in the writer's un-published manuscripts, which had recently been placed in the ar-chives of Fisk University in Nashville, Tennessee, mainly through the efforts of the late Arna Bontemps, who was then head librarian there. Those who made the early pilgrimage to Fisk were the first to know that Toomer had not stopped writing after *Cane* was published. He had pursued that course for another twenty years, but changes in his philosophy toward life led to certain changes in his style, as a result of which publishers rejected almost every-thing that he produced thereafter. The skeletal facts of his life and literary ventures were not difficult to assemble, and they became widely known in a very short time.

Jean Toomer was a fair-skinned man from a mixed-blood family. His grandfather, the controversial P. B. S. Pinchback of Louisiana post-Civil War political fame, had claimed that he was not a white man, even though his physical appearance belied that fact. In Washington, the city to which he moved his family in the early 1890s, he maintained a way of life that included relationships with black and white people of the middle classes. For a large part of his early life, Jean Toomer lived in all-white communities in Washing-ton and in New York.

As a young man, Jean Toomer had taken a long time to decide on a career. He had attended the University of Wisconsin in Madison in the fall of 1914, then left for reasons that now seem to us as readers and critics unreasonable, inappropriate, and a demonstra-tion of his inability or unwillingness to face challenge. Between 1914 and 1918 he enrolled in and spent some time at five other institutions of higher education, but he never earned a degree. He always left when he thought he perceived difficulties ahead that were beyond his power to surmount. In 1919, after a period of intensive and extensive reading in the literatures of Eastern and Western civilizations, and after meeting many young writers who lived in New York at the time, he decided he wanted to become a writer.

Success was not immediate, but he worked hard at this new resolve. Part of his struggle centered around his need for internal harmony. From the time that Toomer had been a teenager, he had believed that the human being could be happy and successful only if the mind, the body, and the intellect worked together in har-mony. His earliest acceptance of a means to that end came at the University of Chicago, one of the colleges he attended. There he encountered socialism and embraced it in the hopes that it would provide a system around which he could conduct his life as a harmonious whole. But socialism proved disappointing in this respect. It did not offer him internal unity, and he soon grew disillusioned with it. Yet his need for harmony increased, and his search for it became the single most important issue around which his life revolved.

In 1921, he was back in Washington, taking care of his aged, ill grandparents and trying to write without much success. That fall he accepted a brief appointment at a rural black school in Georgia as a respite from the frustrations of his divided life. That was his first trip to the South, and the black folk culture made an immediate impact on him. Living close to it, he felt magnetically attracted to its spirit, and the disparate parts of him came together into a unity he had not experienced before. He began to write, even while he was there, with the assurance that he had found his own voice.

*Cane*, in three parts, is a slim volume of prose narratives, poetry, and one dramatic piece. The first section of the book, in which women are the major characters, is set in Georgia; the second, where men are more prominent, is in the North; and the third, which features men again in the important roles, returns to the South. This is the dramatic setting, and the poet is the principal actor. In brief, the whole is made up of two portraits, one of southern folk culture and the other of black urban life. They merge into one when North meets South. So overwhelmed was Toomer by his experiences that fall that he began to write the narratives of the southern section of his book while he was on the train returning to Washington two months later. The achievement of this work is in the quality of its portrayals, which represent the black situation in America without resorting to apology, sentimentality, or propaganda. A combination of lyrical language, powerful symbols (especially in the women), vivid imagery, and realism fill in the details that are painful and tragic but also beautiful, spiritual, and transcendent at the same time. With the help of his friend, Waldo Frank, then prominent in American letters, Toomer saw his manuscript win easy acceptance, and it was published in September 1923. Nothing like this had ever been done with black American culture before this book.

Difficulties arose from two sources, and they began almost immediately. As soon as the book was done, Toomer had ambivalent feelings toward it. He had not found personal liberation and unity in its meaning and could not accept, for himself, the identity that had caused him to write it. Toomer had claimed for many years that racial groups in America were in a state of dissolution and that all Americans belonged to the American race. He became upset that everyone around him considered him a "Negro" writer on the basis of the content of this book. He wanted to be no more than an American writer, whose work reflected one part of the American experience. Racial designations were divisive factors among Americans, he felt, and should be abolished. All Americans were a mixture of many groups, and the mixture was continually becoming more complicated. He, for one, was not a Negro, he claimed, because he had at least seven bloodlines running through his veins, and his African heritage was a matter of hearsay information based on his grandfather's assertion of it. If in fact he did have African blood, it had been so diluted over time that it was of little consequence to the person that he was. These were his arguments.

His ambivalence toward the book and the controversy over his racial identity contributed to new states of internal disharmony for Jean Toomer. He saw that literary art, which he had worked so hard to achieve, was not the answer to his search for harmony. By the fall of 1923, he separated himself from his friends of several years and turned his back on the literary world, which he realized had brought him only transient satisfactions. He began to look around for a new system.

Shortly after, in the spring of 1924, he decided he had found it in the movement headed by the Eastern mystic George Gurdjieff. Toomer had read and studied Eastern philosophies earlier, and in his attitudes to life and the universe he was already a visionary mystic. Gurdjieff's movement promised internal harmony through a system of activities that involved the mind, body, and intellect, and it was very appealing to Toomer at this time. He accepted it unhesitatingly. As a result, he gave up the kind of writing he had done in *Cane* and focused his creative energies on works designed to advance the tenets of this newfound source of unity. This proved to be the bane of his literary career.

Between 1926 and 1930 Toomer published four prose pieces and a couple of poems. All were on nonracial topics. In 1936, his final work appeared. A long poem called "Blue Meridian," it documents the various racial groups in America as they evolve into "raceless" Americans. Toomer's name, as the author of the successful *Cane*, never created any special interest in his later works, which went unnoticed by critics. Toomer, as writer and as a figure of some controversy, faded from view, and his place was taken by a publicly inconspicuous man. For the last three decades of his life, it is doubtful that any of the people who knew him were aware that the issue of race had ever been a concern in his early life, or that he had given up an important career in the world of letters.

From 1924 until 1934, Toomer was an avowed Gurdjieff follower and one of the most successful American teachers of the system. In 1931, he married Margery Latimer, a midwestern writer with New England ancestry that went back to Anne Bradstreet. But in the following year, he experienced great sorrow when she died in childbirth. Three years later he married again, and Marjorie Content, a New Yorker from a wealthy family, provided him a new mother for his daughter, financial security, and a thoughtful and sympathetic life partner who has outlived him. The Toomers bought a farm in Bucks County, Pennsylvania, which was their home from 1936 until his death.

But the Gurdjieff movement did not hold Toomer's loyalties beyond 1934, although he trained himself to accept many of its ideas long afterward. However, this work too had failed to satisfy his need for internal harmony, and by the middle of the 1930s he had embarked on another new search toward that end. In 1936 and 1937, he read the works of A. E. (George William Russell), the Irish poet and mystic, and Aldous Huxley for the first time. He liked Russell for his emphasis on individual development, and he admired Huxley's *Means and Ends* because it focused on the achievement of higher consciousness. As a result of this influence, he began a new phase of thinking and writing and started to compose what he called "Psychologic Papers." As he moved away from literature, he saw psychology doing what his own methods had failed to accomplish in his life.

In the wake of patterns set by Gurdjieff and some of his earlier disciples, in the late 1930s Toomer decided that he needed to go to the East. He was convinced that sources existed there, especially in India, from which he could learn the secret of tapping larger amounts of universal energy than Western man was capable of doing. He was propelled to this action by weak spells and lack of energy from which he began to suffer in the 1930s and which he felt were manifestations of his emotional disharmony.

The trip to India lasted from June 1939 to March 1940 and was particularly tedious because he traveled with his family, including his seven-year-old daughter by his first wife. It also did nothing to improve his health or increase his expertise in harnessing universal energy as he had hoped it would. He was extremely disappointed with the outcome. Mostly, he was appalled at the dire poverty of the natives. Two unfinished plays, "Colombo Madras Mail" and "Pilgrims, Did You Say?," are records of his disillusionment. He concluded that such poor living conditions created an overconcern for material possessions and diminished the spiritual lives of the people. The separation between the religious and the ethnic groups in the country was an indication of this impoverishment. Both plays are pleas for a return to a simple spiritual life in harmony with the elements of the universe.

Still in pursuit of internal harmony, in 1940 he joined the Society of Friends. He felt he had always shared their basic faith and was in agreement with their "way of life . . . arising from free association, with a minimum of organization."[1] He became a good Quaker, who traveled and lectured for the society.

Perhaps the relationship that Jean Toomer developed with the Society of Friends helped to ease the bitter disappointments he must have felt by 1940 over his inability to reach the public through his efforts in writing. In any event, in the 1940s and 1950s, in addition to his Psychologic Papers, which it is doubtful he ever tried to publish, he wrote essays on the beliefs of the Quakers and on various social subjects, including race, which were published in the *Friend's Intelligencer*.

As World War II came to an end, his relationship with the Friends helped him to define his feelings about that conflict. He believed that this war was the result of a failure within modern civilization and that everyone should take serious cognizance of the causes and attempt to eliminate them.[2] An enduring peace would come only when all people achieved internal harmony, he continued to say. During Christmas 1944, he and anthropologist Margaret Mead met in New York for a public discussion of the issues surrounding the end of the war.[3] He used the opportunity to state his wish that the Quakers take a public stand against the increasing mechanization of life, the growing centralization of economic, financial, and political power, all forms of prejudice, and the causes and instruments of warfare. He felt that such a stand could be an example to the world. His last public words for the harmonious development of man were in the cause of world peace.

For most of the years between 1936 and 1940 Toomer continued to write in various literary forms. Having rejected the fame that might have come to him as a Negro writer, he addressed himself to universal issues, particularly man's alienation in an industrial, technological world. He proposed answers that would come from seeking the truth about the meaning of human existence through the Gurdjieff method. He wrote a great deal—novels, short fiction, autobiographies, poetry, and plays—and he submitted his work to publishers, but the results were almost always negative. His style, they said, disqualified his work as literature; he had grown doctrinaire. The voice of the philosopher-teacher was not an acceptable substitute for that of the literary artist who had created *Cane*. Gradually, *Cane* and Toomer were forgotten.

His post-1936 creative writings include a long prose narrative entitled "The Angel Begoria," completed in 1940, and a collection of thirteen poems. In the former, the central theme is the value of religion as a unifying force between man and God. Using the life-threatening uncertainties that World War II had created for most people, Toomer argued that in times of universal crisis there was a greater-than-ever need for a strong religious faith to restore stability to the world at large. He postulated that America had a splendid opportunity to lead the world in that direction.

The poems of this period also have their basis in religious faith. They were written between 1936 and 1939 in connection with a Gurdjieff-like group that Toomer led during that time known as the Mill House Experiment.[4] The poems are invocations, personal and spiritual. Their message concerns the integration of the inner and outer parts of the human being. In addition, they express a strong religious belief in individual potential, which is linked with the higher Being of the universe, and confidence in the Gurdjieff doctrine of Reciprocal Maintenance.[5]

**I I**

The editors and publishers who rejected Toomer's manuscripts for fifteen years did not do so capriciously, or with malice aforethought. The stories that issued from his pen during this time were turned down because they were tedious and described uninteresting people around whom he was unable to develop dramatic plots. This is even more unfortunate a circumstance when we realize that, as he developed over the post-*Cane* years, he deliberately put himself at the center of the action of his work and seemed unable to write about anything or anyone else. The aim of these works was to lead readers to develop themselves according to the tenets of Gurdjieff's thought, and Toomer was unable to separate his artistic self from this philosophy. To understand and appreciate these writings one needed to believe, as he did, that the first duty of conscious man was to be on a continual journey toward an integrated development of mind, body, and intellect. In pleading for the publication of a particular manuscript in 1933, he made this perspective very explicit. He stressed the importance of getting "the materials and the forms of this book" out so that they could become available to large numbers of people in the world. That year he expressed the conviction that he had been on a "far journey into strange lands of experience" since 1923 and that he had returned a new person. He was then writing with the intent of putting new things into literature, which had become his "mission."[6] Toomer wrote, and publishers rejected his writings; finally, after 1943 he began to realize that his efforts were futile.

Still in search of internal harmony, in 1943 Jean Toomer met with Edgar Cayce, the mystic, but received no help from him. Six years later, he went into Jungian psychoanalysis. It was a "real adventure" for him, a chance to "explore the unconscious and its symbols—painful at times, but all in all quite an adventure."[7] Psychoanalysis led him into another path of exploration. In June 1950, he began to read L. Ron Hubbard's *Dianetics*, which is the study of scientology. His enthusiasm about this work was equal to his early discovery of socialism or Gurdjieff. He remarked at the time that "no one else in any book I've ever read, of the East or of the West, has been this definite, and as helpful in as specific a way."[8] He became an associate at the Hubbard Foundation in 1951. That year he wrote to a friend that he felt dianetics could enable people to live the "religious life," especially as Christ outlined it, and particularly in a world in which it was so desirable to reduce violence and improve the feelings of kinship between individuals and groups.[9] However, he was critical of the laxness of the foundation in permitting insufficiently trained people to engage in the practice. Yet he was certain that the spread of dianetics emphasized the urgent need that people had for a direct and effective but inexpensive way to deal with their problems.

In 1954, Jean Toomer made his final effort in favor of the theory of the achievement of internal harmony as he had pursued it for all of his life. He met with a group of friends who had been Gurdjieff disciples, and together they discussed the issue in a series of eight meetings. His ideas, although never published, were collected in a group of essays entitled "The Re-Integration of Man." In that work, he asserted that the unity of all mankind was based on the individual's awareness of his potential and limitations for growth and on his understanding of the meaning of life. After 1954, although he made efforts to remain in contact with old friends and continued to talk about his philosophy, the confinements of ill health put an end to his participation in activities in which he might otherwise have been engaged.

Jean Toomer's search for internal harmony had been long and thorough, but in the end, for him, unsuccessful. He came closest to the fullness of his goal only twice in his life. It came to him unexpectedly during the brief period when *Cane* was a living experience for him, and then through the early years of his involvement with the Gurdjieff work. These episodic interludes of fulfillment were frustrating, because Toomer was in search of a way of life in which his mind, body, and intellect would be in harmony consistently. Yet in his teachings, Gurdjieff had insisted that higher consciousness was not a permanent condition except for those who had reached the highest levels of conscious behavior; for others, it was an occasional experience that could be neither willed nor avoided, and it occurred periodically along the way to higher regions of consciousness. If higher consciousness and internal harmony are either identical or contiguous, then perhaps Toomer lost the war because he overlooked the importance of fully understanding the battle. Perhaps it is because of this misunderstanding that he rejected the various systems he explored; each, in turn, proved inadequate as an answer to his goals of completeness and harmony. Strangely enough, he was never interested in social or political solutions to his or to the world's problems, and except for his brief embrace of socialism in his early adulthood, he appears to have conducted his life above their considerations. For instance, there is no record of his response to such a world-shaking phenomenon as the rise of Nazi fascism, nor did he seem to have any interest in the civil rights struggle in America from the early 1950s into the 1960s. Few thoughtful, sensitive people who lived through these times and situations have not had strong reactions to them. His concerns remained with the concept of the mystical union between humankind and the natural universe. He would have argued that all political systems and governments are sources of disharmony and that the world can only be made better by each person turning all of his or her efforts toward the goals of higher consciousness.

Toward the end of his life, ill health forced Jean Toomer to withdraw more and more from any outside activities. As the 1940s progressed, he became increasingly disabled, and he took his last vacation with his family on a trip to Mexico in 1947. He continued to believe that his physical symptoms were a manifestation of his unresolved internal tensions. Later he suffered from painful arthritis and had difficulties with his eyes. After 1954, he periodically entered a nursing home for care and treatment. His final years were sad ones for him. He was a disappointed man, and his failed expectations doubtless hastened the process of his physical deterioration. On March 30, 1967, he died, and the cause of his death was given as arteriosclerosis. It is ironic that his old friend, Waldo Frank, American man of letters, who, in the time of his eminence, had written and published fourteen novels, eighteen social histories, and over a hundred articles on literary and political subjects and whose name had stood for the radical, cultural, and aesthetic aspirations of a generation of American writers, had died in obscurity equal to Jean Toomer's on January 9, 1967, in New York City.

# The Long Climb, 1894–1921

I

When America was in winter I was born the day after Christmas 1894," begins Jean Toomer's "Outline of an Autobiography."[1] There is no record of this event but no reason to doubt the accuracy of the date. The son of Nathan Toomer and the former Nina Pinchback, he was named Nathan Eugene, and spent his early years in Washington, D.C., where he was born.

His mother was the daughter of Pinckney Benton Stewart Pinchback, a charismatic figure who, although sufficiently light-skinned to have been taken for a white man, early in his life chose to claim African heritage and champion the cause of black Americans. He was a commissioned officer of the Corps d'Afrique, a black regiment in the Civil War, and he went on to gain political eminence in Louisiana in the Reconstruction era that followed.[2] During that time, Pinchback and his family lived in a large house in New Orleans, a kind of southern mansion, surrounded by ample grounds, flowerbeds, and many trees. Although his activities marked him as a political rebel, by nature he was a conservative man. His family life was separate from the political violence that rocked the city and in which he was an active participant, and in his home the genteel conventions and traditional moralities were religiously observed. His wife, the former Nina Emily Hethorne, a white woman of English and French descent, was an appropriate partner for him, sensitive and conservative. Fearing the loss of position and prestige, the Republican Pinchbacks moved to Washington in the early 1890s in the aftermath of the Democratic return to political power in the South during the latter part of the nineteenth century.

Nina Pinchback was born in 1868, the only daughter in a household of four children. It is doubtful that she attended public schools; most likely she was tutored at home. She learned music and those accomplishments considered the female arts—needlework, embroidery, how to run a house and how to manage the servants—for the Pinchbacks belonged to the affluent class.

Pinchback cared deeply about his daughter and was very strict with her. She, on the other hand, admired him, but this did not prevent her from being critical of him. In 1885, she was sent to Auburndale, Massachusetts, to attend the Riverside School for Young Ladies, where she remained for two years, did well in her studies, and made many friends. Her three brothers were carefully educated. Pinckney went to Andover and later to the College of Pharmacy in Philadelphia; Bismarck, who became a Quaker, and with whom Jean Toomer shared a warm relationship for many years, was a lawyer; and Walter, the youngest, followed his brother's footsteps to Andover and later became a doctor.

Nathan Toomer, Jean Toomer's father, was born in 1841 in North Carolina but lived for most of his life in Georgia. Nathan's father was a prosperous southern planter of English, Spanish, and Dutch ancestry, and his mother was believed to have been of mixed-blood heritage, probably from African and Native American forebears. Toomer sometimes called himself a farmer, but it is doubtful that he ever engaged in that profession. There are stories that Nathan's father had left him substantial financial holdings, which he squandered mainly through gambling.[3] In appearance and mode of living, he was a gentleman: attractive, conventionally handsome, and with all the mannerisms of the upper class, said Jean Toomer.

Nina Pinchback and Nathan Toomer met in Washington and fell in love early in 1894. Pinchback strongly opposed the match, mainly on the grounds of rumors of Toomer's involvement in unscrupulous business deals. In addition, Toomer was a good deal older than Nina. She rebelled against her father's wishes, and in the clash of strong wills she emerged the winner. Of the aftermath of the clash, Jean Toomer wrote: "[Pinchback] took Nina in his arms and shook hands with Toomer, wishing them happiness. . . . There had been a struggle. It had been waged by upright people on both sides, cleanly fought. The power of love had won. Now the contestants were reconciled, and all, even her father, were happy."[4] The wedding took place in March of that year, and the Toomers set up their home in Washington close to the Pinchbacks. But the alliance was short-lived. During the course of the first year that followed, Toomer made three unexplained trips to Georgia, and in October 1895, when Jean Toomer was ten months old, and while his father was away on another mysterious trip, Nina Pinchback-Toomer gave up her home and returned to her father's house. In September 1898, she filed for divorce, which was granted in January 1899. She resumed her maiden name, and for many years her son was called Eugene Pinchback and the name of Nathan Toomer was seldom spoken in the Pinchback family.

Jean Toomer wrote that 1422 Bacon Street, N.W., where he spent his early years, was a "glorious playground." He remembered the neighborhood as almost rural in quality. There was a farm still in operation down the street, and nearby fields held weeds, wild-flowers, and insects. It was a delightful blend of city and country, of the urban and the rural, of civilization and nature. The families were predominantly white middle and upper class, and they produced a tone of fineness and refinement. As a child, Jean loved all the natural things, but he was also aware of the buildings going up around him, paralleling his own growth. "While I myself [was] growing, I had pictures of constructive activity, the symbol of building, impressed upon me."[5]

At an early age he took a position of leadership among his peers. He loved games and athletics, showed interest in machines, automobiles, and bicycles, and had a passion for electricity. He was aware that his mother had difficulties with her father, and as time progressed he saw less of her, while his grandfather became more like a father to him and his grandmother took on more of the duties of his mother. He recalled the summer of 1905 as the "Dark Summer," the one in which he tried, often unsuccessfully, to gain special attention from his mother. Even so, she did not willfully neglect him, and in later years he would credit his love of music to her having played the piano to him often in his early childhood. However, she was occupied with her own problems and gave him less of her time than he desired. To compensate for her lack of attention, he turned to his friends and "enjoyed playing with them more than [he liked] to eat,"[6] until an illness, presumably growing out of bad eating habits, deprived him of play for a long time. For several months, he was confined to the house, and when he returned to the street, he discovered that he had lost his leader's position in his group. His response was to withdraw from his playmates, and with this action he began to develop an interior life and to grow introspective. He claimed "inner things [became] more real and interesting than outer [things]."[7] This inner life actively served as a protective layer of emotional stability during the break with his familiar environment that came when his mother remarried in 1906 and he moved with her from Washington, first to Brooklyn, New York, and shortly after to New Rochelle, New York.

In Brooklyn, he had his first contact with a complete city life and was particularly aware of its developing commercialism, its industry, and its politics. Bacon Street had been a friendly world; by contrast, Brooklyn was indifferent and sometimes hostile. But while he did not wholly like it, he found it stimulating. Here he lived in an apartment rather than in a house such as he had previously been accustomed to, but soon he made new friends and for the first time he met "tough" boys. In this new environment, he had his initial experience with emotions created by the tension between excitement and displacement, but he concealed his feelings from those around him. He lived in two worlds: an inner world that was sensitive to the conflicts and ambivalences of new experiences and an outer world from which the inner emotions were excluded.

Toomer left only sparse information about his stepfather, who three years after he met him would pass completely out of his life. In his unpublished "Autobiography," he expressed the belief that the man had misrepresented his financial standing to the Pinchbacks and that his mother was unhappy in this marriage. He did not sympathize with her unhappiness because he had always felt that she had entered an unsuitable alliance.[8] But he admitted that the man had tried to be kind to him. He, in turn, had refused to respond favorably to his stepfather's advances.

In the fall of 1906, Jean Toomer, along with his mother and his new stepfather, moved from Brooklyn to New Rochelle. Here he had more difficulty in forming new friendships and consequently became even more withdrawn and introspective. But he discovered the public library, and the building of a rich private life accelerated as he began reading intensively. His main love was for novels and books on knighthood and chivalry—books about King Arthur and the Knights of the Round Table, Sir Galahad and Sir Lancelot, and the quest for the Holy Grail. He was also a good student, and in time he made new friends. His social life improved. He was elected president of the Current Events Club at school and received honorable mention for a paper he wrote on the life of Lincoln.

In addition to school and books, he loved to bicycle, swim, fish, and sail. He had his own boat, learned the harbor along Long Island Sound very well, and developed a new passion for the sea. Reading and boating became his main pursuits. One very exciting experience that he recalled was having been caught in a heavy gale while he was alone on the Sound. He later used material from this period of his life in his early attempts at writing fiction.[9]

But, in a short time, change was to come to his life again in the form of a great loss. In June 1909, his mother died from an attack of appendicitis.[10] This was his first experience with death, and it affected him profoundly, for with it came his initial realization that it "comes to those we love." His recollections of this period were that to the world he turned a face that was agreeable; inwardly, he felt depressed and he ached with misery.[11] He had never known his father; now he was fully orphaned, with an aging grandmother the only person for whom he felt real affection. He blamed his grandfather for his mother's death, maintaining that Pinchback's tyranny at home had driven her to her second marriage. Thus began the open and often bitter fights between Jean Toomer and his grandfather that lasted until the older man's death in 1921.

In 1910, he returned to Washington and to the home of his grandparents. He was fifteen years old. The Pinchbacks were living in a different section of the city now, and Toomer perceived that it was the world of an aristocracy—a world midway between the white world and the black world—and for the first time in his life he had real contact with the colored world. It was different from anything in his earlier experiences, although when he was very young, and living in Washington, he had attended a Negro school. He had resented it then, because the school was outside his neighborhood, and, as a result, he missed several hours of play with his friends each day. At age fifteen, however, he saw that the racially mixed Washington neighborhood had more emotion, more rhythm, more color, and more gaiety than the other places in which he had lived. At the same time, his enthusiasm was tempered because he was aware that his grandfather, still active in politics, was growing less physically able. His grandmother too, never a strong woman, was getting weaker, and there was a noticeable loss of family affluence. But he did well in school, especially in history and algebra. He was given the leading role in *The Merchant of Venice* and wrote that he loved the sonorous lines. He read Charles Dickens and learned that there were novels that described actual life conditions. Thus in spite of inner tensions, his first year back in Washington went well. He graduated from the eighth grade with honors and looked forward with great anticipation to high school.

His first year at Washington's M Street High School (1911–12), later renamed the Paul Laurence Dunbar High School, was also enjoyable. Among other things, he made a close friend with a boy whom he described as more rebellious and radical than the other youngsters around. He loved and enjoyed parties, dances, and girls. He loved and had a special aptitude for algebra and physical geography. At the end of the year, his grandfather, who had supported Republican William Taft during the presidential campaign, received a political appointment in New York, but Toomer and his grandmother remained in Washington and moved out of their home into a small apartment.

During his second year in high school he faced a new personal crisis. He was eighteen years old. For the previous three years, he had lived with his grandparents and had not felt sufficiently close to them, any other adults, or his peers to be able to discuss his adolescent sexual concerns. His relationship with his grandfather was strained. Because he blamed his mother's death on the older man's tyranny, he had cut off all avenues of effective or open communication between them. There was mutual goodwill and sympathy between himself and his grandmother, but he was unable to communicate his anxieties and uncertainties to her. He was at a loss and considered himself alone, trapped in a private world of conflicting emotions regarding sex and growing up.

His studies fell off, he grew listless and restless, and he began to experience acute depression, which became even more severe in the following year. It did not help matters that at this time he and his grandmother moved into his uncle's house, both as an economy measure and because of her failing health. By then she was quite feeble, and he retreated from almost all social activities by spending most of his free time taking care of her. This withdrawal exacerbated his depression, and he later wrote that he felt as though he had suddenly been "hit by an avalanche of sex problems," that he was "falling apart," and that he consciously worked hard to "hold on." Fearing actual physical disintegration, he submitted himself to a program of rigorous self-imposed disciplines. He exercised at home, took correspondence courses in muscle building and health promotion, practiced with dumbbells, lifted weights, wrestled and tried special diets, and conducted a silent and solitary struggle. Others saw only that he was becoming exceptionally strong and healthy (he grew strong enough to lift one hundred and twenty pounds with one arm), but on his part there was only a great compulsion to gain control over himself, to find a way to deal with the problems of personal discipline, body development, and relationships with people. In time he thought he found a suitable system in the works of Bernarr MacFadden[12] and decided to follow his teachings.

In 1913, P. B. S. Pinchback finally retired from active public life, and Jean Toomer and his grandparents moved to another new apartment. The Pinchbacks were now on a swift decline into poverty.

High school graduation signaled the time for him to enter a new world, the adult world that offered alternatives and required decisions on his part. Toomer was aware that the choices and decisions he now made were important to his future. This was a serious time, especially since he was not attracted to any of the professions about which he knew anything. He later said: "They all seemed dull: office jobs, teaching, law, medicine. They were routines that appeared deadly and most people seemed folded up."[13] He decided to go to the University of Wisconsin, a school far from the "beaten track" of the people he knew, to study scientific agriculture and to make a "clean break" with his past life.[14]

The months immediately preceding college were full of a new anxiety about the problem of race. Although nothing in the records of his early life indicate that he had thought about this problem seriously before the age of twenty, Jean Toomer had always been aware of racial distinctions, and he knew they were significant in an individual's life. His earliest awareness, which he claims he accepted with indifference, came when he noticed that he was darker than most of his childhood playmates. Not long after that discovery, on his grandfather's insistence, he began attending a Negro school outside of his neighborhood. This could only have reinforced for him, perhaps unconsciously, the sense of separateness caused by race. In New Rochelle, he had lived in a predominantly white world, and now in Washington, in the years just prior to college, his world was predominantly black.

However, through all the changes, Jean Toomer had lived outside of and above the discomforts of racial discrimination and inequality. His grandfather looked like a white man, no matter what his claims of African blood, and Pinchback was not above exploiting that. His grandmother was a white woman. They lived for most of their lives in a manner befitting the white American middle class, including vacationing in places like Saratoga Falls in New York and Harpers Ferry in West Virginia, where Pinchback indulged his love for horse racing. Although it would have been difficult or almost impossible for Toomer not to know about the murky side of the black experience, his own life, until this time, had not been assaulted by it, or limited by the economic, social, and psychological deprivations experienced every day by the larger number of black people in America.

Years later, Toomer denied that he was a Negro and blamed his grandfather's political ambitions for having misrepresented the nature of the racial problem. Of Pinchback's racial stand, his grandson claimed that it was a well-designed ploy to give him reason to champion an unpopular cause, to be daring, and to foster his political motives. Few people would consider it to their advantage to claim Negro blood, but Pinchback thought otherwise, and he was correct. It gave him the advantage of securing the Negro vote when he lived in the South and joined the fight for Negro rights.[15] Among his recollections of the Washington years between 1910 and 1914, Toomer noted that Pinchback was a man of wide and varied contacts, who enjoyed many people around him, black and white, and who had goodwill toward everyone except his personal enemies. From his observations as well as from the things he heard, the young Toomer learned of the racial situation, and he later claimed they had no effect on his life at that time. He wrote:

> Among the items that came to me were items concerning the racial situation; but they seemed unrelated to my life. Nevertheless, of course, my mind stored them up. I heard of the color line. I heard of segregation. I heard that colored people were barred from white hotels, theatres, and restaurants. I heard of social inequality. I heard of passing. I heard that the white world was the world of opportunity, that the colored world was limited. I heard that if a person was known to have Negro blood, no matter how little, he was called Negro. I was more than curious about these items. Some seemed unfair. Some seemed untrue. But it never occurred to me that this might have some personal bearing on my personal career. . . . It was not until my last year in high school that I came face to face with the race question in a personal way.[16]

His decision to enter the University of Wisconsin turned his thoughts for the first time to a direct, serious consideration of race as a factor affecting his own life.

Implicit in his precollege racial concerns was the question of the nature of the reception he would receive in a predominantly white college when it became known among his peers that he had attended a high school with a black student body. The fair-complexioned Toomer knew that he would be categorized as Negro and that, regardless of his physical appearance, he would be vulnerable to all the harassments and limitations of such a classification. He pondered the matter for a time, and after he had made his choice to go to Wisconsin, he told himself that he would hold to the position that he was an American, neither white nor black. He was a person of many bloodlines, some of them dark. He had lived in both the white and the colored worlds, and he would make no special claims to either.[17]

Arriving in Wisconsin for the summer school session in 1914 on his first adventure away from home, his initial homesickness soon gave way to the gaiety of his surroundings, and Toomer became the center of an admiring group of young students. His studies went well, especially in English; he made friends, and with one in particular, Rose Hahn, he went sailing and swimming, played tennis, and danced a great deal.

When the fall term came, he entered the freshman class and his popularity increased. He was invited to sorority parties and was seen often with senior girls. His social star was rising. He decided to run for class president, but he discovered, to his distress, that because he was not a member of a fraternity, he lacked the strength of certain important political connections. In what may have been an overreaction to that impediment, he withdrew his candidacy before the elections were held, a move that from his point of view resulted in a diminishing of his popularity. Although his room remained the gathering place for beer parties and for meetings of small groups, the joy of the college experience was lost to him. He began to feel extremely lonely for the love and warmth that he had known in Washington and to think that his fellow students lacked strong emotions and feelings. He wrote that he found them uncritical and fickle, "attracted to glitter, never examining the worth of their idols, merely following the shifting winds of popularity."[18] Soon after, he lost interest in his studies and decided that he was unsuited for a career in farming, scientific or otherwise. Yet, in spite of Toomer's negative pronouncements toward his university life at this time, the situation was not as gloomy as he suggests. Through the interest of an English teacher, he became acquainted with the *Nation*, the *New Republic*, and the *Manchester Guardian*. During his earlier life in Washington, his

Uncle Bismarck had introduced him to literature. Now he became aware of the possibilities of a literary career. Although this discovery intrigued him, he had no particular interest in following such a career, for, at this time, he was less enthusiastic about the intellectual aspects of college life than he was about athletics and the social life of the community. He returned to Wisconsin after Christmas vacation but remained for only a brief time. By the middle of January he was back in Washington.

His grandparents were predictably shocked and disappointed when he left the university, and because of their disapproval he began to feel that people whose good opinion he valued were already beginning to see him as a failure. During this very difficult period, he struggled with the issue of his right to individuality at the same time that he seriously questioned his values and ideals. Later he wrote of that period:

> I saw myself as if on a boat which the nations would allow to put up at no port. I could come in for food and supplies. This done, I'd have to put out to sea again, and again, never having a harbor which I could call my own, never knowing a port in which I could come to rest. . . . [I] was always at sea, knowing there was land and port and cities; at sea, crossing and re-crossing, stopping at many places, staying at none by the order of the government of the universe.[19]

The long stay in Washington over the spring and summer of 1915 gradually restored his sense of self-worth. He spent most of his time reading and seeing Phyllis Terrel, a girl with whom he had fallen in love the previous Christmas. From a fall and winter of unhappiness, he moved to a summer that he later described as "one of the most lyric and joyous periods of my life."

In the fall of 1915, he returned to college life at the Massachusetts College of Agriculture in Amherst. He arrived there much earlier than necessary, liked the place, and enjoyed the companionship of his fellow students. He lived in a fraternity house, started training for football, and was chosen temporary captain of the team. But when difficulties developed over the transfer of grades from Wisconsin, he became angry and impatient, and he left. Like his Wisconsin experience, this one had begun in a burst of exuberance; then something had gone wrong, and, confronted with possible hardship or defeat, he withdrew, this time even before the fall semester was fully under way. On the return to Washington, he stopped in New York City and remained there until his money ran out. Then he went home to face even sterner disapproval on the part of his family.

He did not remain in Washington long. Early in 1916, he left for Chicago, where he enrolled at the American College of Physical Training and also took courses at the University of Chicago. Again, the beginning held great promise. He liked the people and the work and did well physically and academically. During that spring, he developed as a gymnast, and he became a basketball star and almost an expert in anatomy. His adviser, a doctor, encouraged him to prepare for and apply to medical school. He was doing very well.

But he never completed his courses, for that fall he discovered socialism, and everything he previously believed about life and philosophy underwent a metamorphosis. He struggled hard to hold on to the Republican capitalist notions of his upbringing, but they went down to defeat in his conviction about the rightness of this new and compelling way of looking at the world. For the first time in his life, he thought, he was seriously looking at society as a unit, and he began reading the literature in sociology. The result was that he soon announced himself a believer in socialism:

> I [had] been, I suppose, unconsciously seeking—as all men must seek—an intelligible scheme of things, a sort of whole into which everything fits, or seems to fit, a body of ideas which hold [sic] a consistent view of life and which enables one to see and understand as one does when he sees a map. Socialism was the first thing of this kind that I had encountered. I responded accordingly. It was not so much the facts and ideas, taken singly, that aroused me—though certainly I was challenged and stimulated by them. More it was the *body*, and *scheme*, the order and inclusion. These evoked and promised to satisfy all in me that had been groping for form amid the disorder and chaos of my personal experiences.[20]

Toomer first neglected then dropped his formal studies. Because of this new insight he saw no need for them. Instead, he attended lectures on naturalism and evolution and heard Clarence Darrow on Darwin and Ernst Heinrich Haeckel, the German biologist and natural philosopher. Although his early training had no strong doctrinal religious emphasis, his grandmother had given him certain Christian ideas and beliefs that were by now an integral part of his faith and thinking. Until that fall, he had believed in God and a religious premise of the universe; now those beliefs had come in collision with and lost the battle to ideas in direct opposition to them. He read, thought, and listened, for his world had collapsed, and in the new world in which he found himself there was no Christian God; he felt that the very foundations of his existence were pulled out from under him. He was emotionally and intellectually stunned and broken, and he felt betrayed and bereft of good reason for living. With one blow, his political and religious structures were demolished.

Devastated by these feelings, he responded by withdrawing from all interaction with the world around him so that he might "pull himself together." Such an experience of complete loss, necessitating complete rebuilding, occurred many times in his life. In time, he ventured through science, philosophy, history, and literature, embracing each in turn without cynicism or critical awareness, thinking that he had discovered the "intelligible scheme" he was determined to find; and although he became aware of the pattern, he was powerless to change it. Each new experience of loss was followed by a period of painful readjustment, and then by the exhilaration of the new discovery. In his words, "each stripping away occasioned something of an inward revolution and an opening of my eyes to new views of the world around," and he believed that each time he was "not studying as in college, but growing, expanding, contending with fundamental questions, drawing near to the best findings of mankind through the ages, coming abreast of great men and great minds, feeling them companions."[21]

Of the Chicago experience with socialism, he wrote that while he immersed himself in the works of men such as Victor Hugo and Herbert Spencer, at the same time he felt a great need to write and lecture. He was able to secure a lecture room at the college and proceeded to speak on Hugo, evolution, society, the intelligence of women, and the origin of the universe. With a new commitment, despair evaporated in the glow of action. He was inspired and excited, and he enjoyed the role of teaching immensely. But the lectures were soon discontinued, he said, as a result of pressure from women students and administrators, who disagreed with his concepts on the intelligence of women.

In the spring of 1917, Toomer returned to Washington, but this time his spirits were high. To avoid another confrontation with his grandfather, he pretended he had completed college. His grandparents were happy, and he said he was happier than he had ever been. He was full of strength—physical, moral, and mental—and he had discovered a hitherto unknown zest for living and a good deal of self-confidence. One of the works he read at this time was Lester

Ward's *Dynamic Sociology*, a massive three-volume tome published in 1883, when the discipline of sociology was still very new. Ward claimed that all human intent and all moral and religious systems are based on the fundamental desire to be happy and that these traditional systems fail to bring man happiness because he is ignorant of nature. Ward asserted that dynamic sociology is the philosophy of human progress through which scientific education, as the replacement for religion and other dogma, offers "the organization of feeling," removes the hindrances to the course of natural feeling, increases what is favorable toward that end, and rewards humankind with an enlarged sense of happiness. From this reading Toomer gained a new ambition: the desire to complete his formal education, to earn a Ph.D., and to devote his life to scholarship.

That summer he went again to New York City, where he registered in a sociology course at New York University and in a history course at City College. The sociology course was a disappointment, so he transferred all his energies to history and did well in it.[22] It was a good summer for him. He worked in the college library and discovered the writings of George Bernard Shaw. He played tennis and had an active, full, intensive social life, and his physical strength seemed inexhaustible.

Shaw had a powerful influence on Toomer for the next two years. Shaw, who called himself a creative evolutionist, had developed his philosophy from Darwin's *Origin of Species*, from Lamarck's idea that species changed by willing themselves to do so, and from Ibsen, who he thought used theater in a more creative and productive way than any other dramatist by making people think and by illuminating the disparity between the way life is and the way it ought to be. Shaw believed that the creative force could inspire men to evolve and improve, and he made this idea the fundamental theme in *Man and Superman* (1903), a play that Toomer probably knew well. Other Shaw plays that may have impressed Toomer and helped to crystallize his thinking at this time probably included *Candida* (1895), with a heroine reminiscent of Nora in Ibsen's *A Doll's House; The Devil's Disciple* (1897), with an antihero who, in spite of himself, is trapped in his own soul and goes on to save another man; and *Caesar and Cleopatra* (1906), which explores the theme of contrast between the really great man and others around him who are small and petty in comparison.

In the fall of 1917, Toomer enrolled again in courses at City College and continued to work in the library. He was sought after for the basketball team and pledged a fraternity. In the face of this academic and social success, and because of the absence of any clear statements by him regarding his motivation, it is impossible to understand the reasons for Toomer's next move: he once again left college, this time to enter military service. He explains only that toward the end of the fall he was overtaken by a desire to serve in the war, though not from any special feelings of patriotism, for he was not convinced of right on one side and wrong on the other. In truth, he admits, he felt some ghastly mistakes had been committed on both sides and that millions of ordinary people were being dragged in to bolster opposing sides, to fight and to die. But he was attracted to it as a terrible adventure, one in which he wanted to participate and yet from which he also shrank in great horror. As it turned out, he was rejected for active duty because of poor eyesight and an injury suffered years before. He attempted to enlist in noncombat service, but failed in that too. The result of the rejections was another bout of depression. He could not return to school.

Years later, looking back over the four years of his life that followed high school, he explained that in 1917 the world seemed a "tougher nut to crack" than he had anticipated, and during that time he discovered that he had less force and fewer possibilities than he had previously estimated. He felt a new gravity in life— danger as well as challenge—and many times he experienced enormous disruption of spirits and felt personally threatened with chaos.

In his words, he weathered the emotional crisis of 1917 by alternating between moods of despair and hope. He describes high moments when he had visions in which he saw that the ends ordinary men sought did not measure up to the worth and dignity of the lives of human beings, and he longed for the unnamed things that did. He also had low moments when he felt on the verge of folding up. He experienced frustration, defeat, and failure. He had started out to attain a "greater life," but he found himself "increasingly *out* of life." He had set forth to gain freedom but seemed to become more entrapped:

> I climbed small hills and plunged into abysses. I built, I let fall, or wrecked. I loved. I forgot. I was intense, or nothing. Now and again I'd be of some real service to others. Most often I was selfish, the more so the more desperate my personal needs became. I was honest. I also bluffed. Indeed I came to be

more of a bluffer than I knew. I struggled for myself. I indulged myself. By turns I was sensitive or incredibly callous. . . . I hurt myself and I grew. I grew and outgrew. I outgrew friends and occupations, places and interests, and passed on.[23]

A short stay in Washington preceded a move back to Chicago early in 1918. There he took a job as a car salesman, but he was an abysmal failure at it and suffered acutely from the cold weather and lack of funds. He next took a one-month position as a physical education director in a school in Milwaukee. It turned out to be a year in which he lived in many different places. The road to Chicago and Milwaukee led back to Washington, to Ellenville, New York, and to New York City. The kinds of jobs at which he worked were as numerous as the number of places in which he lived. In Ellenville, he recuperated from strain and worked as a physical education instructor; in New York City, he worked in a settlement house and for a business firm, Acker Merral Conduit Company. To his readings in Shaw that year, he added the works of Walt Whitman. He liked Whitman for having, like Shaw, shown him that creative literature can be used as a vehicle for philosophical expression. A return to Washington late in 1918 was marked by a painful confrontation over money matters with his grandfather.

Toomer returned to New York in the spring of 1919 and lived on East 13th Street, where he had an opportunity to meet first radical, then literary, New York. At this time, he considered himself a socialist politically, economically, and socially, and for the first time he seriously considered a writer's career. He worked, took piano lessons (he was interested in music and wanted to study harmony and composition for an alternate career), read (especially Ibsen and Shaw), wrote, and engaged in physical gymnastics. Two of the more interesting people whom he met at that time were Elmer Rice, the playwright, and Moses L. Ehrlich, who introduced him to the works of Santayana and Goethe and to Carnegie Hall concerts.

This was a significant year for would-be writer Toomer to be in New York and to be living in Greenwich Village. The war in Europe, which had only recently ended, had deeply affected the lives of many of the young men who had come of age between 1914 and 1918. A number had seen active duty. The aftermath proved an exciting, if sometimes confusing, period for numbers of Americans, which included the group that later became known as the writers of the Lost Generation. Malcolm Cowley has written that many of these Americans went to New York because it was the only city where young writers could expect to be published or where they could live cheaply. They lived in Greenwich Village and "belonged to the proletariat of the arts." They were the young men and women who felt uprooted, who put Freud's ideas at the center of their thinking, and who were experiencing a historical period of shifting values. They were prepared to respond to the call for a literary renaissance. They saw themselves as rebels against their society and had arrived in New York for the "long adventure of the 1920s," which proved to be a shining era in literature. In 1919, Jean Toomer began to associate with these young artists.

Toward the end of the year, with a zeal similar to that of his 1916 Chicago lecture days, he took a job in the New Jersey ship-yards, intent on spreading socialist ideas among the dock workers. His plans never bore fruit, for he found his co-workers uninterested in political education. Their work was hard, and they seemed to care only for drinking, playing cards, and sex. The new apostle of socialism made no converts among them. He left the job in disgust, questioning the validity of the doctrine he preached.

Back in New York, he resumed a more cultured way of life. He read a great deal, including Goethe's Wilhelm Meister novels—studies in how the individual finds his place in the world and how a youth becomes an artist. Toomer appreciated Goethe's argument for a morality based on the human being's natural inclinations rather than on abstract moral principles. The novels seemed to pull together Toomer's "scattered parts," and he felt lifted from a pedestrian state into Goethe's aristocracy of culture, of spirit and character, of ideas, and of true nobility. Reading these novels strengthened Toomer's will to become a writer.

Of this year, 1919, he records that he read all that Walt Whitman had written. He also met several of the leading writers of the period, including Edwin Arlington Robinson, Witter Bynner, Sco-field Thayer, and Waldo Frank, as well as editor Lola Ridge. Many years later, in his *Memoirs*, Frank would recall that at the beginning of the 1920s Toomer was seen by many as a Negro writer of great promise. Both Frank and Ridge played significant roles in the young writer's life, having introduced him to Greenwich Village's artistic society in 1919.

Through the sale of some Washington property that had belonged to his mother, Toomer was able to support himself without working during the first half of 1920, but the sum was less than substantial and by the summer of that year he was back in Washington, again facing an angry and disappointed grandfather. This time Toomer was successful in working out a financial agreement with Pinchback. His grandparents were old and in need of constant personal care and attention. He agreed to stay with them in return for a weekly allowance of $5 for taking over the management of the household chores.

This arrangement had obvious drawbacks for the young man who by now had committed himself to explore a career in writing. Yet aside from his immediate financial needs, there were other compelling reasons for making this decision. He realized that his grandparents were dying, and he was deeply moved. After all, they had been more like parents to him than his own parents had been, and now they needed someone to care for them. He felt a need to do this, even if, in so doing, the physical care of the home was to be solely his responsibility at this crucial time in his own development. On one hand, he hungered to explore, unhindered, ideas that suggested new approaches to literary materials and to personal growth; on the other, he felt a moral responsibility toward the old people.

Although it was difficult, for the next several months he took care of his grandparents, ran the house, cooked, and cleaned; and he read and wrote. He recalled that during this period he read the works of Waldo Frank, and he read Dostoevski, Tolstoy, Flaubert, Baudelaire, Sinclair Lewis, Theodore Dreiser, and some of Freud, as well as such current magazines as the *Dial*, the *Liberator*, the *Nation*, and the *New Republic*. He also began to write and settled down to it as he had done to nothing before in his life. He wrote essays, articles, poems, short stories, reviews, and a long piece between a novel and a play. Long before *Cane* had been conceived he claimed that he had a trunkful of manuscripts. But he found it difficult to express his ideas suitably, and nothing he wrote satisfied him; he desired excellence and experienced only frustration. He had a great deal to say and a great need to express himself, but he felt that his life's experiences exceeded his ability to write these things down. He was disorganized and despaired of achieving order and form.

Toomer linked his inability to capture his own literary voice at this time with a more fundamental problem—a lack of harmony between his mind, his emotions, and his body. This state of disorder within himself had been a problem for him since early adolescence, and by this time he had come to believe firmly that he would have to achieve personal harmony if he were to experience success and happiness.

Early in 1920, he discovered Buddhist philosophy, Eastern teaching, occultism, and theosophy. They seemed extraordinary to him and he spent eight months reading nothing else, captivated by their suggestion that it is possible for men to comprehend the universe through a higher consciousness, or an all-inclusive reality. Through this body of ideas, he also began to comprehend the role of the "great man" in a new light, to see the function of the teacher, to understand the meaning of disciples and discipleship in a different way, and to feel the need to become the pupil of a great teacher.

He returned to Western literature and to the Christian Bible as literature with a new excitement for the study of religions. He now had the concept of an Ideal Man—a complete and whole individual—who was able to function physically, emotionally, and intellectually as a unit. He read Robert Frost, who gave him ideas on how a writer can express the qualities of his specific environment, and Sherwood Anderson, who incorporated psychological notions in his work. Of these two writers, he said: "Their insistence on fresh vision and on the perfect clean economical line was just what I had been looking for. I began feeling that I had in my hands the tools for my own creation."[24]

By 1920, Robert Frost had published two volumes—*A Boy's Will* (1913) and *North of Boston* (1915)—and he had won a *Poetry Magazine* prize for "Snow." Although Frost confined himself to writing about the New England he knew and loved, using the simplest diction and words that seldom exceeded two syllables, the lyric quality of his verse, his use of psychological drama, and his perceptions of profundity in the lives of rural, unsophisticated people constituted the brush strokes of a master. Perhaps most important for Toomer was Frost's explorations of the themes of loneliness, loss, psychological disturbance, and his insistence that the language of poetry can be a significant tool in understanding the human condition.

Two works by Sherwood Anderson helped Toomer particularly in his own formulations of a literature of social analysis. In a letter to Anderson in 1922, he wrote: "[T]he beauty and full sense of life that these books contain are natural elements, like the rain and sunshine of my own sprouting. . . . Roots have grown and strengthened. They have extended out. I sprang up in Washington. *Winesburg, Ohio* and *The Triumph of the Egg* are elements of my growing. It is hard to think of myself as maturing without them."[25] The close thematic relationship between the sketches in *Winesburg,*

*Ohio,* the sympathy and understanding that the author brings to the portrayal of the lives of defeated people, and the growth and maturity of George Willard are aspects of this book that can be compared with Toomer's *Cane.* In his book, Toomer struggled with the problems of the cultural failure of a society that is unable to facilitate meaningful relationships between people in the same way that Anderson does in both *Winesburg, Ohio* and *The Triumph of the Egg.* Despair, human isolation, frustration, and hopelessness are vividly portrayed by both men, and the hope for richer, fuller possibilities in human experience is also expressed in the work of both Anderson and Toomer. Like Anderson, Jean Toomer was interested in understanding the ills and strengths of the human heart—the essence of human character—and the older writer made an important contribution to the thinking of the emerging artist in Jean Toomer.

Although he mentions no titles and identifies no writers, Toomer records that he read some books on the American race problem during these years of his creative gestation. He had had the advantage of living within and without the black community, and he had also been able to shed his Afro-American identity in some situations. For these reasons he felt that he understood the dynamics of race relations in ways that it was not possible for most other people to do. Compared with his own insights, most of what had been written was nonsense, he believed, and he wanted to write on the subject as a way of offering an objective opinion to the discussion. He wrote several fragments of essays and did a lot of thinking on the matter. Once again he evaluated his own philosophical position and "formulated it with more fulness and exactitude."[26] He wrote a poem, "The First American," in which he introduced the idea of the American race—a group of people made up of all the nationalities who have come to live in America and now constitute a new race—and Toomer saw himself as the first conscious member of that race. A decade and a half later, after several revisions, the poem became "Blue Meridian," which was published in the *New Caravan* in 1936.

**I I**

As 1921 wore on, and as Jean Toomer struggled with the problems of a would-be writer and tried to keep his bargain with his grandparents, the demands on his time became more frustrating for him.

He wrote that he felt sapped and imprisoned, torn between what was expected of him and his literary ambitions. He envied those people who lived ordinary lives, who did not suffer acute swings from high to low, those who were not concerned with the problems of the "big climb."

Early that fall he was rescued from his domestic burdens by an offer to be a substitute teacher in a rural school for black children in Georgia. The regular teacher was on a mission in the North to solicit funds for the institution. Although he had never been to the South, Toomer accepted the offer without hesitation. In October, he left Washington and arrived in Sparta, Georgia, to confront rural, poor black people for the first time in his life. What he saw made a lasting impression on him:

> No plot of ground had been like this or so moved me. Here the earth seemed part of the people, and the people part of the earth, and they worked upon each other and upon me, so that my earth-life was liberated from the rest of myself. The roots of my earth-life went down and found hold in this red soil and the soil became a shining ground.
>
> I had seen and met people of all kinds. I had never before met with a folk. I had never before lived in the midst of a people gathered together by a group spirit. Here they were. They worked and lived close to the earth, close to each other. They worked and loved and hated and got into trouble and felt a great weight on them. . . . And what I saw and felt and shared entered me, so that my people-life was uncased from the rest of myself. The roots of my people-life went out to those folk, and found purchase in them, and the people became people of beauty and sorrow.[27]

The school was several miles from the village. All the teachers lived there. Toomer had a little shack off on one side. He noted that the setting was crude and strangely rich and beautiful—it was a valley of cane, smoke wreaths during the day, and mist all night. There for the first time he heard the folk songs and spirituals sung by "back country Negroes," and he realized how rich and sad, joyous and beautiful they were. However, he also recognized that he was experiencing something that was quickly coming to an end, for blacks too were heading toward the towns and the cities, as industry, commerce, and machines became more important to twentieth-century living: "The folk spirit was walking in to die on the modern desert. Its death was so tragic. And this was the feeling I put into 'Cane.' ... On the train North, I began to write the things that later appeared in that book. . . ."[28]

But there were other lessons to be learned in the South. Aside from the positive rhythms of black life, he observed the tensions surrounding any discussion of race. He noticed the bitterness and strain in racial attitudes and the violence of the southern racial situation. This was also the section of Georgia from which his father had come. He made discreet inquiries about Nathan Toomer and learned he had died in Augusta in 1906.

Jean Toomer spent only two months in Georgia. After his teaching appointment ended, he returned to Washington in November, anxious and excited about the prospects of turning his recent experiences into literature. Before he left, however, he sent a poem, "Georgia Dust," to the *Liberator*, and on the train north he began to write the sketches that later appeared in the first section of *Cane*. By the end of the year, they were almost completed. The southern experience had touched his soul as nothing else had done before, and it inspired him to the lyrical presentation of the harshness, cruelty, strength, and beauty of black reality in America. *Cane*, when it was completed, was his song of celebration to the elements that constitute the Afro-American experience. His contact with the folk and the folk culture had provided the medium that brought together all the hitherto "scattered parts" of his artistic yearnings. And the proof was immediate. During the winter of 1921–22, he also wrote the plays, *Balo*, which was presented by the Howard University Repertory Company during its 1923–24 season, *Natalie Mann*, and "Kabnis," all concerned with the Afro-American experience.

When Toomer left for Georgia in the fall of 1921, he placed his ailing grandfather in a hospital and secured a woman to stay with his grandmother. When he returned to Washington, he brought the old man home, noting that his condition was "too pitiable . . . to bear." Pinchback sank rapidly after that, and in December, the day after his grandson had completed his first draft of "Kabnis," he died. His body was taken back to New Orleans and buried in the family vault, beside that of his daughter. The bitter fights between Jean Toomer and the once-forceful and dominant P. B. S. Pinchback came to an end at the time when the young man was at the beginning of a new life. It had been a long hard climb for him, but the view from the top was splendid.

*P. B. S. Pinchback, Toomer's maternal grandfather, in the early 1900s
Courtesy of Marjorie Content Toomer*

*Emily Hethorne, Toomer's maternal grandmother,
taken in the mid-to-late 1880s in a New Orleans studio
Courtesy of Marjorie Content Toomer*

*Nina Pinchback, Toomer's mother, in the late 1880s
or early 1890s in Boston
Courtesy of Marjorie Content Toomer*

*Toomer as child in Washington, D.C., in the late 1890s*
*Courtesy of Marjorie Content Toomer*

*Toomer at about age 12*
*Courtesy of Marjorie Content Toomer*

*Toomer at about age 13*
*Courtesy of Marjorie Content Toomer*

*The Pinchback house on Bacon Street in Washington, D.C.,
built in the late 1880s
Courtesy of Marjorie Content Toomer*

*Toomer and an unidentified friend at
the University of Wisconsin in 1914
Courtesy of Marjorie Content Toomer*

*Toomer and his Uncle Bismarck in the 1920s*
*Courtesy of Marjorie Content Toomer*

# The Artist in the Making,

## 1921–1922

**I**

Nineteen hundred and twenty-two was the year in which Jean Toomer felt his greatest confidence in his potential as a writer. His childhood, punctuated by parental loss and constant movings from one community to another, had led to an adolescence of emotional upheavals, which in turn was followed by a host of personal and professional conflicts and uncertainties during his young adulthood. In 1914, when he was twenty, he had unequivocally rejected those professions in which most of the people he knew were engaged, and it was not until 1919 that he felt a sufficiently keen interest in writing as a vocation. It is not surprising that he chose the making of literature as a life's work at this time. Love of the well-told tale had by then become the single visible persistent thread of continuity among his many changing interests—a thread that linked his enjoyment of the stories of knights and tales of chivalry that he had read in early childhood to his appreciation of the works of Shakespeare and Dickens during his teen years and then to his respect for Dostoevski, Shaw, and others, who gave a measure of emotional stability to his thinking during the turbulent period of his young adult life.

Toomer had attended half a dozen colleges but had remained at none long enough to achieve even minimum success. He had acquired no salable skills, and by now monetary pressures were also a prime consideration for speeding up his choice of a profession. During these years, he had engaged in only occasional employment and had depended mainly on his almost impoverished grandparents for support. He had spent a great deal of his time reading in quest of a "form" for living, and in 1919 he began to feel that he could adapt his own writing to express his personal form of self-discovery.

He noted that his family and friends, by this time, were confused by his vacillating behavior. He had spent his money and that of others; he had spent his energies; and he was spending his life but not producing anything that was of value in the marketplace. The writings of Whitman and Goethe appear to have supplied the "mysterious connection" that he had been seeking. In these writers, although he could not define it, he felt he had found "something." His contact with the living writers of American literature such as Lewis Mumford, Lola Ridge, Waldo Frank, and others also opened a new world for him—a world of human values that he had not previously considered and of cultural values that were expressed in art and writing. This dual world was connected vitally to America and to his own experiences.

In 1919 he began to learn to write. In his "Autobiography," he recalls that he felt the germinating of a seed deep within himself, a seed that he said was reached and stirred by the brokenness of his outward life, watered by Whitman's largeness, and made fertile by ideas implicit in Whitman's life, ideas that demonstrated that higher consciousness was possible for man. He found, in reading Whitman, that the purpose of life is development and that the meaning of life is to be found in progress toward the attainment of cosmic consciousness. He was convinced that he could consciously reach this goal through writing. But techniques were necessary to writing and he had yet to learn these. He read more books and sought to make his objective more definite, more vivid, more desirable.

Several aspects of Toomer's disposition further explain his gravitation toward writing as a means of defining himself in relation to the world. He had a need to be heard, to be a leader. In reviewing his early life as he records it in the "Outline of an Autobiography," we see that the childhood needs of the six-year-old to be the leader among his playmates developed into the young man's need to be president of his freshman class at Wisconsin, the captain of the football team at Amherst, and a star basketball player at Chicago. In Chicago in 1916, after his conversion to socialism, one of his first impulses was to become a teacher, an impulse that led to his abortive efforts to lecture on subjects about which he had no or only very limited knowledge. It was a similarly presumptuous impulse that carried him to the New Jersey docks to spread the gospel of socialism among people he considered exploited because of their ignorance. Later, when he read Eastern writers in 1920, he was particularly attracted to ideas concerning the roles of the master and the disciple, the leader and the follower, the teacher and the pupil. And, except for one brief moment, Jean Toomer saw himself always as the leader, as the teacher. This aspect of his personality was recalled by Gorham Munson, a member of the New York literati of the 1920s, who met Toomer in 1922. In an interview in New York in 1969, he described Toomer's behavior after Toomer had become involved with the Gurdjieff movement in the mid-1920s. He thought that Toomer had a great ambition to "outstrip" old friends and to become a leader in the movement. In the end, this need to surpass others might have been his undoing.[1]

Toomer also had a sense of mission. Both the lectures in Chicago and the desire to inform the dock workers are manifestations of the missionary zeal that overcame him first in 1917 and that stayed with him for most of the remainder of his life. The early ventures had failed, but writing, if he could succeed at it, could open up wide new doors to carry his voice and opinions to the world.

Toomer's writings of the time between early 1919 and 1921 no longer exist, but his accounts of that period, taken from his extant autobiographical writings, suggest that he applied himself assiduously to the development of the writer's craft. His assessment of that time was that he searched for a perfection which eluded him and left him frustrated.

The trip to Georgia in the fall of 1921 was the single most important factor that led to the emergence of Jean Toomer the artist. Although he noted that he had curiosities about the South, he had never discussed them in detail. Pinchback had no relatives in the South with whom he appears to have remained in contact after he left in the 1890s. Nathan Toomer had come from Georgia, but, after his disappearance in 1895, all contact with him ceased. Jean Toomer identified the man whose place he filled for two months in Sparta only as a friend of his grandfather's, and he did not elaborate on the relationship with the friends in South Carolina whom he and Waldo Frank visited in the fall of 1922. Contrary to much that has been written about the genesis of his trip to Georgia, it actually occurred without any planning on his part, and he went there not in search of his roots but in quest of temporary release from the drudgery of the domestic activities of the previous months.

However, the impact of this venture on Toomer's life was such that its reverberations were never completely silenced for the rest of his life. In *Cane* he later wrote: "I felt that things unseen to men were tangibly immediate. . . . When one is on the soil of one's ancestors, most anything can come to one."[2] He was moved by the folk spirit and the folk as by nothing else before, and he felt that he had found the missing element that he needed to harness his creative talents: a self-confirming sense of wholeness.

It was during the period between the fall of 1921 and the spring of 1923 that Toomer most closely identified with the Afro-American experience, and the zenith of his creativity occurred within this brief period of his life. A careful scrutiny of the "Autobiography" reveals that his self-confidence increased through his newfound identification, and he was better able to define his place in the world. When he returned home from the Georgia trip, he gave himself, without reservations, to the task of interpreting his perceptions of the Afro-American experience through the artistic medium.

While Toomer had been in the South, "living in a cabin whose floorboards permitted the soil to come up between them when it rained, listening to the old folk melodies that Negro women sang at sundown,"[3] the effects on him had been enormous. These were the songs that some eighteen years earlier, in *The Souls of Black Folk*, W. E. B. Du Bois had identified as the "Songs of Sorrow," the "music of trouble and exile, of strife and hiding, [that] . . . grope toward some unseen power and sigh for rest in the End."[4] In December 1922, Toomer wrote to Sherwood Anderson: "My seed was planted in the cane-and-cotton fields and in the souls of black and white people in the small southern town. My seed was planted in myself down there."[5]

The experience in the South, in spite of its brevity, had brought his "scattered parts" together and had given him new and significant insights. The frustrations caused by his inability to organize his thinking vanished as he set himself to "put down in his own words his own thoughts and his own life experiences."[6] In a letter to Waldo Frank, he outlined his feelings this way:

> Within the last two or three years, . . . my growing need for artistic expression has pulled me deeper and deeper into the Negro group. And as my powers of receptivity increased, I found

myself loving [it] in a way I could never love the other. It has stimulated and fertilized whatever creative talent I may contain within me. The visit to Georgia last fall was the starting point of almost everything of worth I have done. I heard folksongs come from the lips of Negro peasants. I saw the rich dusk beauty that I heard many false accounts about, and of which, till then, I was somewhat skeptical. And a deep part of my nature, a part that I had repressed, sprang suddenly into life and responded to them.[7]

These words place Toomer's creative will and imagination squarely within the framework of the Afro-American experience.

The impact and potency of the Georgia experience on Toomer has been fittingly described by Eugene Holmes: "He found down there a hereditary link with forgotten and unknown ancestors. Slavery, once a shame and a stigma, became for him a spiritual process of growth and transfiguration and the tortuous underground groping of one generation, the maturing and high blossoming of the next. He found in the life of those Georgians and their forebears a sense of mystical recognition."[8] *Balo*, *Natalie Mann*, and *Cane* survive as testaments to Toomer's early creative energy and artistic trial and accomplishment. *Balo* was written between the end of 1921 and the beginning of 1922, and *Natalie Mann* was completed in early 1922. *Cane* was written in three phases. The first took place between November and December 1921, the second was early in 1922 in New York, and the third occurred at Harpers Ferry during the time between the late spring and the early fall of that year. That fall, Toomer took a second trip to the South in company with Waldo Frank.[9]

Jean Toomer's life was in its ascendancy. He had returned to New York, and the circle of his acquaintances among the city's literati enlarged. Among those whom he now met were Kenneth Burke, Hart Crane, Van Wyck Brooks, and Paul Rosenfeld, men who were in the vanguard of American letters. A new American literature was in the making by this younger generation of writers. Mencken's *Prejudices* (1921), Anderson's *Winesburg, Ohio* (1921), and Lewis's *Main Street* (1920) were the heralds of the time. *Broom*, the *Dial* (considered the best literary journal of the day), and the *Nation* expounded on the ugliness, emptiness, and duality of American life. Toomer shared in the spirit and vitality of the intellectual and artistic energies of these artists. He was one of them.

Toomer now wrote with enthusiasm, and the reward of seeing his work appear often in several of the literary magazines provided added incentive; publishers were anxious to receive his work, and the criticism was favorable. He was sought out by Sherwood Anderson for high praise, and both men corresponded for a while. In addition, he enjoyed an especially warm and close friendship with Waldo Frank, and he was in love with a young woman named Mae Wright. After years of abortive attempts to find his place in the world, he was coming into his own.

The early works of Jean Toomer to appear in print in 1922 were reviews, short stories, and poems that were published in *Broom,* the *Crisis, Double Dealer,* and the *Little Review.* In June, he received a letter from John McClure of *Double Dealer,* a New Orleans-based journal established in 1921 by a small group that had much in common with Toomer's New York friends. McClure was enthusiastic about Toomer's work, but in spite of the group he represented, he was concerned about the feasibility of printing some of his pieces in the southern journal. He wrote that he predicted a brilliant future for the new writer whose early work was "not only full of rich promise but of rich fulfillment."[10] He made special reference to Toomer's ancestry, which he said had been known to "produce remarkable literature in the past [and] will do so in the future." He complimented him on his "accurate conception of literature [and] . . . [his] firm grasp on the aesthetics of language," and he pointed out that Toomer's work had "the elemental, universal human reach."[11] He liked both "Fern" and "Karintha" a great deal and would have been glad to print them if he were not "afraid" of the bigotry and prejudice of some southern readers. He noted that while some of those directly involved with the journal were in favor of publishing such material, there were "guarantors" on whom they depended for support and whom they could not risk offending.[12]

However, the *Double Dealer* published "Calling Jesus" under the title of "Nora" in its September issue. Sherwood Anderson read it and wrote a highly complimentary letter to Toomer. Before Toomer responded to Anderson's first letter, he received a second from him. Anderson had liked the piece because it "lyrically, impressionistically [fused] concrete details of setting with suggestive, symbolic images."[13] He liked "Avey" even better although it was less impressionistic, and he felt it was the "real stuff but molded by something outside yourself."[14] In his article, "An Intersection of

Paths," Darwin Turner examines the relationship that developed between the writers from 1922 to 1924.

Toomer was grateful for Anderson's attention. He wrote Anderson that he had read his books shortly before going to Georgia and had found them essential to his thinking on literature as art. In another letter, he told Anderson that his [Anderson's] art came from "a creative elevation of experience," which had enabled it to make an important connection between art and religion in the "spiritualization of the immediate."[15]

Anderson's response to Toomer's generous praise was to inform him that he thought Toomer was the first Negro whose work was "really negro." He thought that most blacks were too preoccupied with racial matters to be creative artists. For his part, he had wanted to write not "of the negro" but "out of him," but he had found that impossible because he was not a Negro. He praised Toomer's art, offered to secure a publisher for his pending book, and volunteered to write the introduction for it. Although Toomer did not need this assistance from him, he continued to praise Anderson's work, pointing out that it evoked an emotion and a sense of beauty that was typical of Negro culture and that it had been a powerful influence on the shaping of his own work.[16] He tried to explain the psychological motivations of many blacks, who, because of their curious position in Western civilization, are forced to one of two extreme positions: either they deny their blackness and seek as close as possible an approximation to white ideals, or they overemphasize the importance of their blackness. He claimed that these responses are a result of feelings of inferiority and of denying such feelings. He was confident that his art would "aid in giving the Negro to himself."[17] He told Anderson about his desire to start a little magazine that would concentrate on contributions of the Negro to the Western world, a magazine that would contribute to "the building of Negro consciousness." Toomer saw a great need for such an organ, which could enlighten Negro youth among whom "talent dissipates itself for want of creative channels of expression and encouragement."[18] He made an implicit appeal for financial backing for his project.

As Darwin Turner points out, this was an astounding move on Toomer's part.[19] He was championing the cause of blackness and being critical of blacks who imitate whites without knowing what Anderson's response would be. In a typical white-insensitive attitude toward black America, Anderson dismissed the idea of the magazine out of hand, emphasizing that such a venture was out-side of the field of the artist's prerogative. He was supportive of Toomer as an individual artist, but he saw no need to promote black art in general. He advised Toomer to spend his energies in the perfecting of his craft.

What Anderson did not know or suspect in this exchange was that in spite of Toomer's enthusiasm for, and his defense of, an art directly expressive of the black experience, even at this time Toomer felt the dangers of creative suffocation if he committed himself wholly to a narrow artistic perspective. Sometime before *Cane* was published, Toomer wrote to Waldo Frank, expressing disaffection with Anderson's attitude toward his work. He sus-pected Anderson of seeing him only in a one-dimensional perspec-tive and of wanting him to confine his work to the perimeters of his Negro identity. He resented this and wrote Frank that he sus-pected his relationship with Anderson would be short-lived—"to try to tie me to any one of my parts is surely to lose me."[20] He believed Anderson lacked sensitivity and did not understand what he called "the circle of expression" that transcends race and color. In contrast, he saw Waldo Frank differently, and he was convinced that Frank saw him as a human being of many parts unlimited by racial stereotypes.

The Toomer-Frank relationship yielded mutual benefits. Toomer was pleased to have the regard and friendship of an established writer, especially one whose work he respected. Frank's *Our America* (1919), *City Block* (1922), and *Rahab* (1922) all influenced Toomer's literary thought. The older writer's bent toward mysti-cism and his quest for higher consciousness were concepts with which Toomer identified. In *Our America*, Frank had argued the case for a richer, fuller life in which the individual could embrace all of experience and be aware of his link with the cosmos. He argued that in order to develop the creative energy for love of life what modern man needed was to regain the mystical, spiritual awareness that had been destroyed by materialism. In this work, Frank examined various aspects of American culture, but the book lacked one important element, according to Toomer. "I missed your not including the Negro," he wrote to his friend. "No picture of a southern person is complete without its bit of Negro-deter-mined psychology."[21] The absence of black culture in the analysis, he said, left the work incomplete.

*City Block*, a set of stories that make up a structural whole but differs from *Winesburg, Ohio* because it has no central character, helped Toomer to see how his own stories could be similarly used. In *City Block*, Frank's characters are lonely, bewildered, and battered by the impersonal blows of life, yet they dramatize a kind of spiritual triumph. Toomer saw this same response to experience in the lives of the characters he portrayed. "Fern," "Esther," and "Blood Burning Moon" were added to the first section of *Cane* after he read Frank's book.

Toomer claimed to have liked *Rahab* for its literary forms. In this novel, Frank uses flashbacks interrupted by scenes from the present to tell the story of a woman's struggle to find meaning in her life—she is in search of mystical growth, and a birth-in-life motif signals her eventual triumph. It is easy to understand why Toomer found these works helpful to his own writing. The flashbacks, the use of women characters to illuminate broad human concerns, and the search for the meaning of life through the exploration of the mystical were some of the avenues he wanted to pursue in his own work.

Toomer helped Frank work on *Holiday*, an impressionistic study that explores the tragedy too common in a world where racial conflicts undermine humanity. Toomer assisted his friend with the southern black dialect in particular. Thus the relationship between the men was one in which each found opportunities to help the other.

**I I**

While he was writing in 1922, Toomer was pleased with his progress. In another letter to Frank in April, he stated:

> . . . Kabnis sprang up almost in a day, it now seems to me.
> It is the direct result of a trip I made into Georgia this past
> fall. . . . There, for the first time I really saw the Negro, not a
> pseudo-urbanized and vulgarized, a semi-Americanized product, but the Negro peasant, strong with the tang of fields and
> soil. It was there that I first heard the folk-songs rolling up the
> valley at twilight, heard them as spontaneous and narrative utterances. They filled me with gold, and tints of an eternal purple. Love? Man, they gave birth to a whole new life. . . . I am
> certain that I would get more inner satisfaction from a free

narrative form. . . . When I say, "Kabnis," nothing inside me says, "complete, finished." By this I know that I shall go over it. . . . Those Ancients have a peculiar attraction for me. I am very apt to let them say too much.[22]

There is no question of his excitement about "Kabnis," and the tone of this letter bears no trace of personal reservations toward his subject. Here he conveys his spiritual connections with the folk culture and pays tribute to his artistic indebtedness to it. In May he wrote:

. . . I am writing. Twelve pages are almost done. About eight more, I should judge, to finish. The skeleton is knit by the dry cartilage of the two races. But what are bones! The flesh and blood and spirit are my own. It is struggling, of course, to an impartial birth. My recompense is its creation. It is a leaf that will unfold, fade, die, fall, decay, and nourish me. For the outside world, I shall be happy, if, on opening its eyes, someone sees there a promise of power, or because of it, feels that it is in some small measure beautiful.[23]

There is even more exuberance here. The book was taking the desired shape, and he was happy.

Toomer's commitment to an in-depth artistic analysis of the Afro-American experience was a priority during this year. In July, he wrote to Frank from Harpers Ferry and discussed life in that section of the country. He had been to Harpers Ferry many times before, beginning in his boyhood, when he visited in the summers with his grandparents. This time his interests were honed by the previous fall's experience in Georgia. He observed the details of life in Harpers Ferry. On one hand, racial attitudes appeared less harsh, more tolerant, and even more friendly than in Georgia, but, on the other, the folk songs were missing and the Negro church, although essentially the same, was less dramatic. However, he saw in this situation the possibility for intercourse between the races that was neither difficult nor hazardous. But the black community paid a price for these reduced tensions and for the overt absence of "ugly emotions."[24]

In another letter from Harpers Ferry, Toomer talked of the "Negro in solution." He pointed out that the culture of the Afro-American was becoming diluted within the larger American culture and that the whole was approaching "a common soul." It was his belief that the "common soul" meant the eventual complete loss of black culture, and the artist in him was anxious to capture what still remained of it. "A hundred years from now," he wrote, "these Negroes, if they exist at all, will live in art. . . . Let us grab hold of them while there is still time."[25] He also notes that this racial dissolution is not altogether a negative situation, for he is by now convinced of the emergence of the "American" as a race with a multiracial and multicultural heritage.

In another letter written to Frank that summer, Toomer addressed the role of the Negro church in the community and paid tribute to the power of the feelings it evokes and to the music that had touched him more deeply than anything else he knew. "[T]heology is a farce (Christ is so immediate), . . . religious emotion [is] elemental, and for that reason, very near the sublime," he wrote.[26] Over and over we are brought back to an awareness of how much the Georgia trip affected him. The black church, with its music and drama, impressed him as the heart of the folk culture, and he was unstinting in his credit to it.

Perhaps the most important letter in the Toomer-Frank canon is the one in which Toomer makes a very personal evaluation of his work. Although undated, it was probably written toward the end of the summer of 1922:

> . . . In my own stuff, in those pieces that come nearest to the old Negro, to the spirit saturate in folk-song; Karintha and Fern, the dominant emotion is a sadness derived from a sense of fading, from a knowledge of my futility to check solution. There is nothing about these pieces of the buoyant expression of a new race. The deepest of them: "I ain't got long to stay here." Religiously: "I (am going) to cross over into camp ground." Socially: "My position here is transient. I'm going to die, or be absorbed."
>
> When I come up to "7th Street" and "Theatre," a wholly new life confronts me. A life, I am afraid, that Sherwood Anderson would not get his beauty from. For it is jazzed, strident, modern. "Seventh Street" is the song of crude new life. Of a new people. Negro? Only in the *boldness* of its expression. In its healthy freedom. American. For the shows that please Seventh Street make their fortunes on Broadway. And both "Theatre" and "Box Seat," of course spring from a complex civilization and are directed to it.
>
> And "Kabnis" is *Me*.[27]

This is the most complete personal statement we have by Toomer in regard to his relationship to *Cane*; it is a statement in which he unequivocally places himself in the work and within the tradition of Afro-American culture. Later, he refers to the book as a swan song, and it is evident that he began to see it that way when he refocused his vision. But in 1922, this letter represented the artist's critical evaluation of his work; it was written at the time of *Cane*'s creation, and it reveals his close personal involvement to the central elements of his composition.

That fall Toomer invited Frank to take a trip to the South with him. Frank welcomed the opportunity to observe and participate in Negro life as an insider. Toomer, on the other hand, was anxious for Frank to meet some of the older generation of blacks, and he himself wanted to verify some of his earlier impressions of black southern life. Earlier, he had written to his friend: "The older families that rose to prominence after the Civil War are passing. Others, commercialized and socially climbing, are taking their places."[28] Frank arrived in Washington in September 1922 and met several members of Toomer's family, including his grandmother. The two men traveled to Richmond, Virginia, and from there were forced to travel by Jim Crow car to Spartanburg, South Carolina. From the long summer in Harpers Ferry, Toomer's skin had become quite dark, and because they stayed with friends of his, it was agreed beforehand that both would "pass" as Negro professors.

In South Carolina, they saw the full application of racial segregation. There were drugstores in which they could purchase medicines but not soft drinks, restaurants in which they would not be served, and theaters in which they could sit only in the balcony.[29] Years later, in recalling these aspects of the trip, Frank noted that their impact had left him with a sense that his "place on earth had frighteningly shifted" but that he had also come to understand that blacks were a "potent people" whom white oppression had failed to crush.[30] The trip strengthened the bonds of understanding between the friends.

None of Toomer's literary relationships with white men was as important to him as his relationship with Mae Wright. During the course of his life, before his marriage, he appears to have had a number of romantic affairs. No matter what his internal struggles, there was a side of Toomer that was vivacious, charming, witty, and attractive, especially to women. Mae Wright was a young black woman with whom he had a serious relationship in the year immediately after his first visit to the South, and this relationship is significant to a critical evaluation of Toomer.

He met Mae Wright at Harpers Ferry in the summer of 1922 and was instantly attracted to her. She was sixteen years old, he was twenty-seven, and it appears that he exercised the roles of intellectual and romantic mentor to her and shared his philosophies toward life and writing with her. In July, he wrote a poem in her tribute:

> There is no transience of twilight in
> The beauty of your soft dusk-dimpled face,
> No flicker of a slender flame in space,
> In crucibles, fragilely crystalline.
> There is no fragrance of the jasmine
> About you, no pathos of some old place
> At dusk, that crumbles like moth-eaten lace
> Beneath the touch. Nor has there ever been.
> Your love is like the folk-songs flaming rise
> In cane-lipped southern people, like their soul
> Which bursts its bondage in a bold travail;
> Your voice is like them singing soft and wise,
> Your face, sweetly effulgent of the whole,
> Inviolate to ways that would defile.[31]

In a letter to Frank, he had noted that he was "falling in love with a wonderfully emotional, rich dark-skinned, large-eyed girl."[32]

To Mae Wright he expressed the idea that American creativity was hampered by ties to an outmoded tradition, to the "tyranny of the Anglo-Saxon Ideal." Americans believed that the ideals of the Puritan fathers represented the proper attitudes to life. These ideals held that "white skin is the most beautiful and desirable in the world; the minds of the white races are the chosen of God."[33] It was Toomer's belief that such ideals were concerned only with surfaces, with material rather than spiritual goals. For the early Puritans, art was of questionable value; they were concerned with survival, but subsequent generations of Americans had continued to accept their values uncritically. In one of his letters to Mae, he noted that as "paradoxical" as it sounded, often black people, the group most culturally and emotionally removed from the Puritan heritage, were the most bound to it. He wanted to see black reaction against the Anglo-Saxon Ideal, and he pointed out that blacks needed to be aware of the significance of their own lives and the sensitivity of their beauty.[34] He saw no reason to deny white beauty, but for the other, "their faces must open to the charm of soft full lines. Of dusk faces. Of crisp curly hair. Their ears must learn to love the color and warmth of mellowed cadences, of round Southern speech. . . . Their souls must feel (and glory in the feeling) the abundance and power of Negro derived emotions."[35]

Toomer's sense of mission and his role as a teacher comes through clearly. Black people must be made to use their minds and emotions to create a new ideal for everyone—an ideal not based on skin coloring. He believed that he had been called to communicate this message, and he thought it his "privilege and duty . . . to crystallize this ideal."[36] He wished to be an involved individual, taking pride in those things that were unique to the individual—"not the cheap pride of peacocks, but the deep thing that has its source in the very soul of being."[37] The black artist was important; he had access to great material but was inhibited in using it. Black artists had to be made aware of their creative vitality, reminded of their ancestors, shocked, and thus forced to realize their emotional energy.

These were the ideals he discussed with Mae Wright in 1922. His correspondence with her and with her mother were his frankest discussions of himself as an Afro-American. In late November, Mae visited Toomer and afterward he wrote to Frank lamenting the reception she had received from his friends. He had taken her to the Howard-Lincoln football game. "Her loveliness didn't have a chance to show. Only her skin. She really seemed insignificant—and black. . . . My friends . . . [saw her only] in terms of her color."[38] Instead of repudiating his friends' behavior, Toomer was saddened by it. His reaction raises new doubts about his unconscious feelings toward blackness. On one hand, he was promoting black cultural ideals; on the other, he was advocating a universal humanity that disregarded racial separations. Yet he seemed unable to apply either of these positions to this case. At best, his sentiments in the letter to Frank are another example of Toomer's racial ambivalence even at a time when he was deeply involved with the black experience.

The Toomer-Wright relationship came to an end before *Cane* was published in 1923, and there is nothing left behind to indicate the cause of its termination. However, while it lasted, Toomer's feelings for Mae were strong and stamped by the intensity he brought to other aspects of his life. What is clear is that the relationship followed the now-familiar pattern in his behavior: a propitious rising and a subsequent falling away of interest, the hallmark of unfathomable ambivalence toward his goals and his self-worth, behavior that kept him from bringing his many ventures to a successful ending. But the association with Mae was a valuable experience for him, especially at this time. It gave him an opportunity to express his ideas to someone whom he trusted and who was not part of his largely white, intellectual, artistic world.

In that world, Jean Toomer's closest friends and associates were largely found among the disillusioned men and women of the Lost Generation, who had put their energies to the task of making themselves the new heroes of American culture. White and middle class, very few had interest in or concern for black people as an important group in American society. In spite of this, Toomer made no secret of his relationship to P. B. S. Pinchback, and he discussed his racial makeup with several of them. In March 1922, he wrote to Waldo Frank that he had inherited seven bloodlines: French, Dutch, Welsh, Negro, German, Jewish, and Indian. He claimed that the culture, history, and traditions of six of them were fairly well-known and discussed with an "approximation of the truth" but that the "Negro" line had been subject to perversion for "purposes of propaganda." He was determined, he wrote, that in his life and work he would symbolize "a synthesis in the matters of the mind and spirit analogous, perhaps, to the actual fact . . . of the racial minglings."[39]

The contradiction in all of this is that while Toomer did not deny black heritage to these friends in these years when he was achieving literary success through the exploration of black life and culture, he did not identify with the incipient Harlem Renaissance, associate with its young writers as literary colleagues, or acknowledge a tradition of black letters. However, we know that he was cognizant of the new developments in black art and literature. In April 1922, "Song of the Son," one of his earliest poems to be published, appeared in the *Crisis*. Jessie Fauset, literary editor of that journal from 1919 to 1926, was responsible for "discovering" every single significant black writer of that period, and most were published first in the *Crisis*. Although Toomer had published an earlier poem in *Broom*, in January of that year, he was in contact with Fauset for some time. In her biography of Fauset, Carolyn Sylvander makes references to a glowing letter the editor wrote to Jean Toomer, in which she expressed pleasure and praise for the poetry, play, and short folk tale that he had sent to her. Advising him to read and travel to enlarge his life experiences, she offered abundant encouragement for his budding career.[40] Both Langston Hughes and Countee Cullen had their first poems published in the *Crisis* in 1921.

In addition to knowing about new black writings and writers, Toomer also knew of at least one exciting development in black music as well. In a letter to Frank, undated, but certainly written in 1922, he gives his friend his impressions of the young musician, Will Marion Cooke, whom he had met and heard perform in Washington. He was impressed with Cooke, who was "putting negroid thrusts and rhythms in the orchestration of Hungarian dance music," he said, and he called Cooke a creative man with "a tragic, pathetic, wistful beauty about him."[41] This was worthy praise for the talented Cooke, but it seems almost unbelievable that Toomer should add that he [Cooke] was the only black person in America whose work qualified as art.[42] Was this a manifestation of Toomer's racial ambivalence, racial chauvinism, or ignorance of the scope of the Harlem Renaissance?

On the other hand, the black literati received Jean Toomer's work with enthusiastic praise. Both the young writers, hoping to make careers for themselves in the field, and the older, established nurturers of the young praised him. Publicly and privately, W. E. B. Du Bois, Alain Locke, James Weldon Johnson, Claude McKay, and Countee Cullen, among others, lauded his publications. Many of the themes and ideas he used in his early works were similar to those used by many of the other black writers—Toomer simply used them more effectively.

That Toomer did not develop strong personal and professional ties with the Harlem writers must be seen as a matter of his choice, and most likely he was hindered from developing these relationships because of his racial ambivalence. But at the end of 1922, he was in great spirits and confident of a bright future in art and letters. He had published, his work was respected, *Balo* and *Natalie Mann* were done, and *Cane* was on its way to completion. He was more excited and happier than he had ever been. He was an artist in the making.

# First Fruits: *Balo* and *Natalie Mann*

## I

In the early 1920s, in addition to his engagement with poetry and fiction, Jean Toomer was also a pioneer among writers who had ambitions to see their works on the American stage. Unlike several of his contemporaries, he sensed the possibilities of both folk and expressionist theater before they did. In "The Failure of a Playwright," Darwin Turner points out that "he was . . . ahead of his time . . . [and] success would have assured him an important place in the annals of American drama."[1] Two extant plays from that period are important to such an assessment. In its rightful place, *Balo* was an antecedent to such works as Paul Green's *In Abraham's Bosom* (1926), which became a Broadway Pulitzer Prize winner, and DuBose Heyward's *Porgy* (1927), a classic in our time. And only Eugene O'Neill's *The Emperor Jones* (1920) and *The Hairy Ape* (1922) supersede Toomer's *Natalie Mann* in the use of expressionist techniques among stage writings of the period.

In fact, in *Natalie Mann*, Toomer was working with a form that was still new to much of the theatrical world. It had taken hold of the European stage after World War I, but it did not come into its own until the years between 1919 and 1925. Because of his wide interest in the effects of style and form in language, as well as his sense of artistic adventure, Toomer went beyond a wish to imitate European writers. He wanted to demonstrate that, in the hands of a skillful artist, language was sufficiently flexible to "objectify mankind's spiritual struggle[,] and . . . [to] ridicule the society which chains man with false moral standards and false values."[2]

Many of the best American expressionist plays, such as *The Adding Machine* by Elmer Rice and *Roger Bloomer* by John Howard Larson, were not produced until after Toomer's early plays had been written. But success did not come to him through public recognition of his dramatic daring or acumen. *Balo* made a brief appearance at the Howard Theatre in 1923–24, but *Natalie Mann* remained locked in the author's unpublished manuscripts until 1980, when it became part of a new anthology of his works.

*Balo* and *Natalie Mann* are products of the brief time during which Toomer had the desire to add the unique richness of the Afro-American experience to American literature. American literature had always had its black characters. In the early days, these blacks became stereotypes in the hands of white writers, even of such well-meaning people as Harriet Beecher Stowe, who was sympathetic to the plight of the slaves. As a consequence of the constraints of slavery, it was not until the second half of the nineteenth century that black Americans began to produce a significant body of writing, and, unfortunately but not surprisingly, much of their early literature addressed only the outrageous discriminatory attitudes and practices that blacks faced in white America. Many black writers succeeded only in creating other stereotypes of blacks, even if they were different from those negative images that were popular in most white romantic novels of the Old South. The positive aspects of Afro-American culture were almost completely neglected. The writers of the Harlem Renaissance were the first of their race to attempt to explore the intrinsic nature of black life and its traditions and to express the strength, beauty, and vitality of the black experience in the face of racial oppression.

Although Toomer did not identify with the new movement, he did explore some of the same aspects of black culture in *Balo*. An important expression of the range of Toomer's artistic development in the early 1920s, *Balo* represents an appreciation of the unique, positive characteristics of black folk culture and is thus history-making black drama. ("Kabnis," which he wrote during this period, will not be discussed here because it contains many similarities to the dramatic section of *Cane*, where it appears by the same name and in which context I discuss it at length. It is important to note, however, that Toomer tried unsuccessfully to have the original version of "Kabnis" staged for a number of years.)

Toomer's middle-class upbringing, his wide reading in Western philosophy, his ambivalence toward racial categories, and his unfamiliarity with the black folk culture all played a role in his emotional reactions to Georgia in 1921. He believed he was present at a historical intersection of American cultures, observing the waning of one and the merging of the others, and this belief made claims on his imagination. Fortunately, for him and for us, he flexed his artistic muscles and set out to preserve his responses to the experience, not only in *Cane,* but also in these early plays. Among the black people whom he knew in Washington, the mores of black folk life were almost extinct, and deliberately so, and it was with fresh eyes that he saw certain qualities in the more primordial black culture. Beyond preserving artistically the cultural mainsprings that were lost as more black people moved from rural to urban environments and became enmeshed in the modern technological world, Toomer laments and warns of the self-destruction of the black "soul" in what he observes is its indiscriminate haste to take on white middle-class values and ways.

*Balo* and *Natalie Mann* are two very different plays, and in them Toomer explores two distinctly separate forms of dramatic techniques. The first is a one-act folk play, the second, a full-length experiment in expressionist theater. In *Balo,* the southern setting, the single-day action, and the poor, rural, close-to-the-earth and very religious characters contrast sharply with the living rooms of the Washington, D.C., middle class, the cabarets of the counterculture, the year-long action, and the affluent, urbane, and upwardly mobile characters who make "refined" culture their religion, who engage in endless conversations about the definition of art and whom we meet in *Natalie Mann.* In these plays, the differences in basic values between these two groups of people—a result of the development of class differences among black people between the end of the Civil War and 1920—becomes clear as Toomer describes folk culture and regionalism in one and the black need for erudition and cosmopolitanism in the other.

*Balo,* a documentary account of one day in the life of Will Lee, a black peasant farmer, and his family, begins in the early morning and ends late at night. The historical past is everywhere, beginning with the original slave cook room (where the action occurs) that the black family owns and lives in, having added three rooms to it. Memories as well as more tangible relics of former times surround them—the old-fashioned fireplace with hooks for pots and kettles; the "ghost" of an old frame mansion on the same property, once the "big house," which a poor white family owns and lives in; hand-me-down furniture, cumbersome and awkwardly large for the space it occupies, which the black family inherited; and the reticent social interactions between black and white people, to name a few. A number of symbols serve as magnifying glasses through which we observe both negative and positive influences on the lives of the characters. For the most part, Toomer is exploring themes of positive cultural identity and cultural wholeness within black folkways, against the background of white American racial attitudes.

In the faint light of dawn, in the glow of the fire he lights, we see Will first and note his ill-fitting gray garb, his "pleasing" American-African-Indian profile, and the neatness of a room that the stage directions tell us is used for sleeping, living, and social occasions. The action centers around his family—a small family that reaches out to join an extended family which disregards the differences between actual and fictive kindred ties. A strong religious faith in fundamental Christian theology is the guiding moral principle in Will's family.

Will and his wife, Susan, a yellow-complexioned woman with large, deep-set eyes that are sad and weary, a cracked voice, and a frail body, have four children. Two of their sons are grown, but they still live at home and apparently feel no resentment toward parental authority. The family works, plays, and prays together, each contributing to the welfare of the whole. The serious economic problems of the community are felt in the low price at which it must sell cane syrup, for this is a year when bountiful harvests have forced demands below the levels of production, and the cotton crop has been lost to the boll weevils. In the lives of peasant farmers, profit, loss, or breaking even depends on the whims of nature and the crude self-interest of the dominant capitalistic culture. As a result of segregation, the black community enjoys an unconscious group security because its contact with the white world is circumscribed and self-conscious. The dramatic effects of these differences can be seen in a meeting between Will and his white neighbor, which Toomer places at a strategic point in the play, midway between the separate actions within the small black family and the extended black family.

Prayers and breakfast are the important morning rituals in the home of the Lees, the former led by Will, the latter prepared by his wife. These completed, the couple settle before the fire to talk. Their grown sons, having been up all night boiling cane, sleep on the floor, also in front of the fire. The voices of the younger children at play reach in from outdoors. It is a tableau of harmonious domesticity.

The conversation between Will and Susan is not a new one. He complains of the economic difficulties and the other hardships that small farmers are facing. We learn that, despite Susan's disapproval because it steals time from farming, he is studying to become a preacher. But this is important to him. He believes that the hard times they are experiencing represent divine retribution for the sins of the community, and he envisions himself called to lead wayward sinners back to the narrow paths of the righteous. Although he has a strong aversion to frivolity, he consents to his wife's wish to have a party at home that evening, because it will give him an opportunity to proselytize.

The first scene of the play establishes the major themes in the life of this black rural family. It is important to note that the black folk are not black—Susan is yellow-complexioned and has other characteristics that betray her mixed-blood heritage, and Will is the incarnation/representation of Toomer's American race through his apparent mixture of European, African, and Native American bloods. Will's drab clothes symbolize a black man's entrapment and impotence in a society that ignores or abuses his sensibilities and in which he has been taught to cope with circumstances on a utilitarian level. In the combination sleeping/family/living room, the presence of the old, heavy furniture conveys the same sense of defeat as do Will's poorly tailored garments.

The black people whom Toomer saw in the South in 1921 were more than half a century removed from chattel slavery, but they were still surrounded by many elements of that past. The setting of the play—the old cook room with its peculiar fireplace—is a constant reminder of earlier times. The older folks in the play recall experiences from those days and tell stories of their dead grandmother, who, by performing miracles it seemed, contrived to cook meals in this place and then to carry them, steaming hot, to the "big house" dining room, a hundred yards away.

As poignant as the symbols of oppression, which are like a brooding presence, are the manifestations of the will of the black folk spirit, which has not been destroyed either by slavery or by segregation and discrimination. Neatness, order, structure, purpose, and wise management of their affairs are qualities that are evident among these folk and attest to how they perceive themselves. Toomer notes, for instance, that at the very early hour at which the play begins, this room of multiple functions is neat and orderly, the bed is fully made, the fire is crackling, and the breakfast is ready to be served. There is no evidence of tardiness or lack of self-worth here; instead, the environment is one of industry and productive activity.

The role of religion is a constantly repeating motif throughout this short play. The activities of the day are preceded by Will's prayer at breakfast—a simple prayer that thanks the unseen Giver for his protection through the night and for the food they are about to eat and ends in a plea for divine help and guidance through the day. Later in the morning, he enjoins his older sons, who have just returned from a night's work of boiling cane, to read their Bible before going to sleep. As a result of this Bible reading, Balo, the younger son, has a transcending religious experience. This family's belief gives meaning to the hardships of their existence, guides their actions, and promises rewards for fortitude and endurance.

Routine activity and conversation occupy the Lees during the morning until they are interrupted by a visit from Jennings, their white neighbor. At dawn, fog had obscured the view between their houses. This ethereal separation is an unmistakable comment on black/white relations, particularly since Toomer points out that the land belonging to both families has no fence or other divisive mechanism and that the boundaries of their properties are designated only by a single oak stake.

Will and Jennings are alike in dress, philosophical ideas, and daily concerns; only the difference of race, which determines social interaction, separates them. There is no trace of hostility in their exchanges. The times are just as hard for both; they agree about mutual problems and congratulate themselves on having made some prudent financial decisions the previous year. Without ceremony, they share resources. When Jennings offers an axe handle, he receives a barrel of cane syrup in return. But the spectator observes that both men stand during the entire visit and that, in spite of the closeness of their homes and their longtime acquaintanceship, there is an awkwardness in their mannerisms toward each other, expressed through cautious reserve rather than congeniality. Susan never speaks, except when spoken to, as long as Jennings's visit lasts.

In his stage directions, Toomer comments that the lives of black and white people in the rural South are so intertwined that in the interests of peace and survival there has to be a facade of amicable coexistence. To achieve this, the two groups have accepted a code of behavior that contributes to "an understanding and bond between them little known or suspected by northern people."[3] Harmony generally prevails—and even kindness and concern are mutual—but neither black nor white attempts the pretentions of social friendship.

The final scene of the play takes place during the evening. Guests arrive for Susan's party—a gathering of friends and relatives, children and adults. These are "country" people, and some of the women bring covered baskets of food. They talk and laugh heartily, and there is an atmosphere of genial well-being. Soon the food is brought out, and all sit close to the fire, most of them on the floor, to share the fellowship of a communal meal. One man is very old, and blind. He resembles a biblical patriarch. They all call him Uncle Ned. He treats them like children, and they reciprocate by treating him with deep respect for his hoary head.

On one hand, it is an evening of secular enjoyment, as some of the group play cards after the remnants of the meal are cleared away; on the other, it is one of religious confirmation, as Balo, who seems to respond readily to emotional stimulation, has a full mystical experience after some hymns are sung. Although by the end of the evening the cardplayers are embarrassed into feeling like sinners, the play ends on a note of community wholeness shared by all. The playwright demonstrates that bloodlines and age are unimportant to effective communication and that it is the quality of the emotional and spiritual strength that holds the folk culture together.

Toomer does not suggest that this life is a workable ideal, or that the people in the play are content, or that modern civilization should return to the conditions of premodern-age folk culture. On the contrary, it is a play that illustrates his personal dilemma of cultural ambivalence. This rustic existence was economically more precarious and more unstable than the industrial/technological world; it demanded physically hard, back-breaking work, and was emotionally fraught with uncertainties. However, what he saw, admired, and thought were positive in it were its earthy values, its intrinsic art, and the spirituality that enveloped it. Realizing that it could not survive much longer in the modern world, he felt sharp sadness for the meaning of its imminent demise. This does not make *Balo* a romantic or sentimental rendition of a passing era. It is Toomer's attempt at a serious dramatic study of Afro-

American folk culture. It represents his wish to extract from its simplicity and complexity, from its strengths and weaknesses, the essence of a people's soul for the edification of all human culture.

The strengths of the black folk culture, as Toomer portrays them, had their roots in the community's respect for the order of the natural universe. In work, play, and worship, the values these people espoused kept them in close contact with the rhythms of the earth and the natural world around them. In the transition from slavery to freedom, and beyond, in a rigid system of racial segregation that cut them off from the American mainstream for a long time, they exhibited cohesion, continuity, and stability within their own culture. These they preserved and perpetuated through secular and religious beliefs that placed emphasis on man as part of a larger but hidden scheme in nature, on the temporality of suffering and pain, on respect for old age and kinship, on blood ties, and on the belief in ultimate divine justice. Theirs is a supportive community, where people have come to terms with the difficulties of their existence, and within which they respond creatively, imaginatively, and with integrity to their experiences.

Within this community, thought and action, as well as perceptions of the natural world, are unconsciously infused with art and spirituality. Toomer recognized this in the demeanor of the people he saw: in the "black faces that in repose are sad and weary, but when they break into smiles become light-hearted and gay";[4] in the unself-consciousness of the gathering when Balo becomes mystical; and in the songs the women sing at the end of the workday, "the supper-getting-ready" songs that filled the air at sunset. These people were of the land, and the land was in them—the earth and the sky—and, unconsciously, they carried out the functions of their daily lives as a natural part of the unity between man and his environment.

On the practical level, religion was a significant element in shaping the psychology of the community, and music was its most powerful artistic manifestation. Toomer's letters to Waldo Frank in 1922 repeatedly mentioned folk music and the Negro church. He was also aware that the black church is exciting drama. But music was not confined to worship, and Toomer noted that in the South the tradition of song and music touched everything in the lives of the people. "They worked and sang as part of living," he wrote.[5] He heard this music for the first time, he said, while he was becoming initiated into the lives of the folk and when its impact was greatest on him. He wove song and worship into the folk play.

At the same time that Toomer identified strengths and positive qualities in the black folk culture, he also noted its weaknesses. It was a difficult way of life, and it was neither suited nor adaptable to modernism. That made it vulnerable both internally and externally. On the inside, currents of restlessness and dissatisfaction with the available options to improve the quality of their lives were taking a toll from many people. Although their economic situation was different from what it had been during slavery, because now they farmed in their own interest and were concerned with the yield and market, life on the land remained hard, and its rewards too unpredictable for relaxation from constant anxieties. Its harshness is visible on Susan, for instance, who is worn and tired beyond her years. Yet, in earlier times, the entire family would have lived in one room; now there are three rooms. There is more comfort and privacy. But this is not sufficient to offset the daily stress and strain, and Susan articulates this frustration.

Early in the play the audience learns that during the previous year, when these farmers had done well financially, both Will and Jennings had saved their money and had not succumbed to purchasing luxuries—a car or a player piano, for example. Some of their friends had done this, and this year they are destitute. Jennings and Will had acted out of practical wisdom, and their commendable action shows their full grasp of their economic realities but also highlights the starkness of those realities. They can expect little more from life than bare necessities, and they are always aware of impending indigence.

In the play, Susan is the voice of the growing number of those who want more from life. She knows there are things other than what she has, and while she is unable to define them concretely, she wants to have some of them. Perhaps in the North, she surmises, she might have some of these yet intangible benefits.

Jean Toomer knew that dissatisfactions would increase and that the young adults especially would leave for the towns and cities in search of more immediate gratifications. They would leave behind much of what was good in their past and had held their forebears together for generations. They would adopt new ways and be absorbed into the larger culture. Their own culture, rich in values that were close to the spirit of nature, was in its death throes. But no one could stop the march of progress. What grieved him was the sterility of modern American culture, which in its growth and development seemed inevitably to choke out the most positive characteristics of its subparts. The black folk culture, he knew, could not survive the advances of modernism. As an artist, he also knew it was important to preserve the memory of it through his pen.

*Natalie Mann*, a play that examines the negative aspects of black middle-class life, focuses on one black woman's search for liberation from the stultifying values of people in her social group. Through imitation, these people have acquired white middle-class values but are unaware of the emotional and spiritual cost. In the play, Natalie, with the help of her ally, Nathan Merilh, struggles for the independence to choose a more human value system for herself. The group she rejects suffers from alienation and has lost the qualities that engender a harmonious community such as we saw in *Balo*. Hypocrisy and an unhealthy preoccupation with social status and materialism are highlights in the lives of these characters, while honesty, creativity, and a greater sense of well-being, in spite of bitter struggle, define the opposing clan. The stilted and mechanical dialogue, and the exaggerated, distorted characterizations that produce an abundance of caricatures and stereotypes emphasize the ironic quality of this play.

Mary Carson, middle-aged, with an "exaggerated high-strung poise," Nora Hart, with an "appearance of futility," Mrs. Mann (Natalie's mother), whose "gestures are brief and determined," and John Kemp, who wears an "appearance of futility" have denied their identity with the black heritage. By contrast, Natalie Mann is in search of personal freedom from all constraints to her creative impulses, and with Nathan and Etty Beal, a dancer, represents the individual's need to be judged on ability and experience. Mertis Newboldt, a young schoolteacher who "tries to evade the prime urges of life by fatiguing herself with less fundamental issues" and who pays dearly for this in the end, is an ambivalent character.

At the beginning of the play, most of the characters are in Mary Carson's living room, where they have assembled for an evening of discussion on "race betterment," that is, how to "uplift" the larger numbers of black people to a social position that is respected. Their ideas focus on definitions of acceptable public behavior and visible accoutrements of cultural refinement. Having compressed themselves within a mold of fixed social conventions, they are anxious for others to conform in a similar way.

The setting is symbolic of middle-class white values. Mrs. Carson's living room is neat and scrupulously clean—"almost to a fault"—even if comfortable and "lived in." The walls are papered and hung with old-fashioned, nondescript pictures; a hearth at the center of the room, a bay window, and a piano are part of a deliberately studied effect. During the course of the play the action moves to the living rooms of other characters; all are duplications of each other. A sameness, without indication of racial or cultural identity, is stamped on each, and a noticeable tension between control and the fear of loss of control is apparent among the residents.

Against this display of "correctness," with its elements of repressed individuality, Nathan's study is a striking contrast: walls of bookcases, portraits that announce individual taste and preference, and the careless arrangement of dissimilar objects. The pictures are especially revealing: a lithograph of Tolstoy; an etching of the breast and face of a powerful black man with massive forehead, full lips, no beard, and daring eyes; and a third—an idealization that is a composite of the other two. African figures decorate a lampshade, and a reproduction of the African Guardian of the Souls rests on a slim pedestal. Nathan Merilh, a thinly disguised Jean Toomer, also a literary artist, assumes the role of mouthpiece for his creator.

The composite portrait on the wall of the study reminds us of Toomer's preoccupation with the idea of the American as a combination of different races and cultures. Tolstoy's life exemplified a concern for matters that were very important to Toomer: religion, ethics, and moral aesthetics. Since Tolstoy was also a man of letters, it is easy to see why he represented the best in Western culture to the young writer. For Toomer, he accepted the artist's responsibility of perpetuating the tradition of humanistic values. Tolstoy had proved his moral courage when he renounced title and status, wore the clothes of a peasant, and braved the wrath of family, state, and church to live by his convictions concerning the nobility of the common man. By combining Tolstoy's moral strength with the physical strength and dignity apparent in the portrait of the black man, Toomer implied something deeper than the superficial aspects of the mixture of bloods and cultures.

This composite portrait, an expressionist work, represents the positive interlocking of Western civilization's most outstanding opposite parts. Nor is it accidental that the painting is done in this style, which, although largely attributed first to the German postimpressionists of the first decade of this century, doubtless received much of its inspiration from the strength and vitality of earlier African art. In Merilh's room, the books, the African Guardian of the Souls, another artifact from Gabon in Equatorial Africa, and a guitar standing in a corner make European and Afro-American cultures equal partners in defining his American identity.

A third place in which some of the action of the play occurs is the Black Bear Cabaret, a "commonplace" room, painted a cheap (now dirty) yellow, and without windows. Chairs and tables surround the dance floor, and the atmosphere is earthy and unpretentious. Etty Beal finds this to be a suitable setting in which to express the freedom of her inner self through dance. Toomer considered dance an important form of artistic expression, and Beal dances from her soul. Her performance is living art.

Stage directions inform the audience that Natalie Mann is not very beautiful, but she has a sparkle and animation in her personality that is sufficiently contagious to be reflected in the faces of the others in her company. Her spontaneity manifests itself through such seemingly unimportant events as the manner in which she responds to another guest's request that she play the piano. She complies, Toomer says, without the "silly modesty of . . . parlor artists."[6]

All of the major characters, excluding Natalie and Etty Beal, distrust Nathan Merilh. His values remind them of things they want to forget. His use of folk-song materials in his writings is only one of his many unapproved-of actions. A group anxious to escape the distinctive elements of its past finds little of worth in those elements and does not wish to "have them served up on a silver or any other kind of platter by the name of art,"[7] he points out. When Merilh responds with unabashed emotions to Natalie's rendition of the "Love Death" of *Tristan and Isolde* by attempting to embrace her, the assembled highbrows make it known that such a public display of intimate feelings is uncouth and unacceptable in polite company. This incident leads to one of the points of conflict within the play.

The play develops around the evolution of Natalie Mann, who at its beginning is a "girl at the crossroads," Merilh tells us. In time she rejects the social conventions of the world in which she has grown up and achieves her freedom from them. Among the ideas she refutes is one that maintains that the middle-class black woman's life choices are either marriage at any cost or prostitution. Natalie not only leaves home to find her own way to support herself, but she also supports her man as he pursues his career in art. In a break with convention, she does not resort to teaching or any of the other professions that are considered acceptable for poor, respectable women.

The role and place of the black woman was an important issue for the black middle class in the 1920s. During slavery, black men and women were commodities in the labor market. Free nineteenth-century black men, before and after emancipation, acknowledged the importance of these women in the various aspects of the struggle for complete freedom. Several, including Frederick Douglass and Martin DeLany, were outspoken in their support of women's rights.

However, with the emergence of the black middle class in the twentieth century, a small group of black women with social advantages faced pressures to limit their career ambitions and make wifehood and motherhood their sole endeavors. Toomer was aware of this. He must have thought of what such ideas meant for his mother. Nina Pinchback, gifted and full of exuberance for life, had been given a gentle lady's education that did not prepare her for either financial or psychological independence from men, and this may have been indirectly responsible for her early death.

From what Toomer has written, it appears that she had married Nathan Toomer because she had fallen genuinely in love with him, but the motives for her second marriage are highly suspect. When Nathan Toomer deserted her, she was forced to return to her father's house. All indications are that she remarried as a matter of convenience. It was the only way in which she could escape paternal dominance without the penalty of destitution. Later, her timid husband delayed the surgery she needed until he could obtain Pinchback's consent, and although the procedures were reported to be successful, she died. Certainly, neither of these men wanted Nina Pinchback dead, but one can indict a system in which the issues of responsibility, authority, and power over her person were never in Nina Pinchback's hands. For most of her adult life, she was an object of controversy between her father and the men she married. Her dependence on male financial and social protection and her frustrations at not having fulfilled her potential were major reasons for the tragedy of Nina Pinchback Toomer's life.

Jean Toomer's attitudes toward this problem in women's lives were ahead of his time. Although there were grave limits and flaws to his vision, he saw the oppression of women as a microcosm of a larger oppression—that of the entire social system. What many men did not perceive, he thought, was that in restricting women's options to fulfill themselves, they too were oppressed. For men to be free, women had to have similar opportunities to develop creatively. Although he does not permit Natalie to be free on her own, he releases her from some of the stereotypes of middle-class women in the 1920s.

The women in the play respond to their oppression in a number of ways. Mrs. Carson, Mrs. Mann, and the other matrons internalize it and see their situation as one of privilege. They are educated and married to men who are able to support them economically. They read leather-bound books, are pretentious in matters of art and music, observe all of the proper social conventions, and maintain their homes in a way that shows they are knowledgeable about Western culture and good breeding. These women, Toomer believed, make up a group that symbolizes much of the condition of the larger society. They are on the desert island of modern Western civilization, cut off from the mainland of imagination and creative self-expression by pretenses that are rooted in repressive social conventions. Mrs. Carson advises Natalie:

> "You should be married. It is the only thing. You are too fine to become a prostitute. You are too fine to become a white man's concubine. What else is there open? You couldn't be an old maid if you tried. All this talk about talent is aimed in the air. Don't you suppose that other girls of this group have had talent? . . . The white people of this country won't let you develop it. . . . Oh yes, you have talent. . . . I have known it all along. I have wanted to spare you the suffering. . . . There is a fineness about you. You don't want to have to touch the ugly sordid things of life. You were cut out for polish and courtesy. . . . Get married. Any man will do. Surround yourself with a home. And live there."[8]

Here she encourages Natalie to reject her true self in favor of the emptiness of appearance, to deny her inner needs for spiritual regeneration and growth. As Merilh points out, "the call to love, the call to create, is castrated by the servile toleration of custom, of ingrained modes of thought, of man's frantic desire to fit his nature to them at whatever cost."[9]

As Toomer sees it, living conventionally diminishes the essential part of a human being, and the alienation evident in the relationships between the wives and husbands in the play is one result. Partners appear together only infrequently. For several, this occurs only in the final act of the drama at the Black Bear Cabaret, where they are attending a benefit performance. In this scene, the women are nervous and manifest this anxiety through constant chatter, while the men are bored and ill at ease. They are uncomfortable with both the unconventional atmosphere of the place and with each other. Wife-husband relationships have not grown close with time, and harmony and understanding have not developed in the course of years of domestic separateness.

Toomer felt that men and women suffer because of repressive social conventions, but it is clear that he recognized that women were particularly victimized by them. The wives in the play lead stagnant lives. They spend most of their time alone or in the company of other women like themselves, devoting their energies to the trivialities associated with their prescribed roles. On the other hand, the men have their work in the daytime and their clubs for relaxation. The clubs are formidable social bastions where the exclusion of women reenforces the privileges of men. In work and play, these men and women, physically and emotionally separated from their past and from one another, are trapped and spiritually strangled by their efforts to conform to the ways of the culture into which they seek unquestioned assimilation. Nora Hart, one of the more aware of the women, complains of the lack of understanding and companionship between herself and her husband. Not only does he go off every evening to his club, but he objects if she has company of her own. "Even marriage cannot teach men what it is a woman wants," she tells a disinterested male companion. "I mean they never seem to consider her at all," to which her friend replies: "You can't blame individual men and women for the failure of the home; . . . it is a larger thing, more general forces that thwart and defeat us."[10] The dearth of shared experiences—intellectual, recreational, and otherwise—is one of the main causes of the failure they experience in developing sympathetic marital relationships.

In addition to the stress between wives and husbands in this world, the effects of alienation manifest themselves in the problems caused by the generation gap. Natalie is estranged from the older women, including her mother, whom she tells:

"... my life has whirled and eddied past like a river which you glance at now and then from the remote security of a steelspan bridge. Whenever the river has risen higher than its accustomed mark, people on the shore have shouted, and you ... have called down, don't flow too fast, don't rise so high, don't whirl and eddy so. You are not a mother; you have

never been. . . . I have never expected that you understand me;
. . . but a daughter's starvation rations should include at least a
bare crust of love. . . . it has nearly crushed my soul to feel not
even a spark of blind faith and sympathy."[11]

Nathan Merilh has a similar problem with his father. During the
years in which he was busy making his fortune, the elder Merilh
had no time for his son. The result is a wide chasm of misunder-
standing between the two, which neither is capable of crossing.
The son is bitter:

> "'Father' implies attachment. Of what sort? Really, that in
> exchange for bread and butter he demands obedience. What a
> farce. Most men denied suitable expression in the world, come
> home at night and try to bully their families. He bulldozed the
> world, developed that attitude towards everything, and seemed
> to have no desire to consider his family as anything more than
> a convenient segment of it. He killed my mother, and then be-
> came sentimental over it. I lost respect for him. I tried to grow
> close to him on the proposition of financing a little theatre.
> He thought only of money and profits; I, only of art. I saw we
> couldn't make it. After that, he might just as well have died
> for all he meant to me. How far we drifted apart, how little
> understanding there was between us."[12]

The final blow to the relationship comes over the disagreement
that Merilh has with Tome Mangrow, a minor character, at the
Black Bear Cabaret. The father sees in this a compromise of his
social position—his son engaged in a barroom brawl—and re-
nounces him publicly, making their separation absolute.

As the emerging black middle class assumes values that deny
those qualities that the larger society associated with black sponta-
neity and closeness, the emotional separation between wives and
husbands, and between children and parents, becomes wider and
more destructive to the welfare of the individual and the entire
community. Some of the tension in Toomer's relationship with his
grandfather had roots in this kind of generational clash of values.

Another type of woman in the play, different from the ones
just examined, is the newly-arrived-from-the-South young woman
whom Merilh and a friend, Therman Law, observe at the cabaret.
Transplanted from the more spontaneous culture of rural black
America, she is anxious that she not appear conspicuous in her
new environment. Her voice is beautiful, and Merilh notes that

she has a "singing laugh." He wishes he could hear her when she is "off-guard" and laments:

> ". . . her walk is conscious and stiff, God it's criminal. . . . a perfect symbol of what happens to the physical charm, the emotional possibilities of that type of girl after she has been respectably familied, pressed, rolled, straightened, powdered by the goody-goody sheep dust of the Negro's rational increase. . . . I don't know what she's fit for—but whatever it is she's fundamentally capable of doing it creatively."[13]

It is inevitable that in her new surroundings she will sacrifice her imagination to the requirements of conformity.

Mertis Newboldt also fits into a separate category. A single woman of the middle class but without financial independence, she is the respectable schoolteacher. Aware of the social restrictions on her place in the world, she resents them but tries to conform and repudiates her inner urgings for a fuller life. Eventually she finds her denials intolerable and rebels against the system. But she has delayed too long, and her later actions lead directly to her death. The dream has been too long deferred.

Etty Beal is the woman who has completely rescued herself from the oppressive conventions of Western culture. She had not always been emancipated. First, there was her father's rigid moral code to shed, one imposed on large numbers of black women by parents intent on reversing the stereotype of the promiscuous, morally loose black woman, a stereotype that originated in slavery. Then she had to overcome the actualities of white male lust. A need for respectability led her to take her talent to churches and community centers. She gave them up, too, and explains: "I quit dancing for churches and community centers because I couldn't stand the hypocrisy of the people. I quit the stage; there you've got to be vulgar but you can't be sincere."[14] Now she is free to choose her place in the world and express her artistic soul without regard for public opinion. She helps Natalie achieve her own limited liberation.

Finally, there is Natalie Mann whose evolution into a free woman—as Toomer understood "free"—is the raison d'être of the play. Her achievement, in Toomer's terms, is significant, for it embodies the concept of an individual's struggle and victory over repressive social customs. Toomer had no illusions of how difficult it was for someone to shift from a position of social conformity to one of considered creative nonconformity. He was well aware that it was even more difficult for black people concerned with educational, financial, and social advantages to challenge the assumptions of mainstream American life. To demonstrate the dimensions of both the struggle and the rewards in the achievement of freedom, he uses his definition of the plight and success of a black middle class woman.

At the beginning of the play, Natalie, having completed the gentlewoman's education, is ready to marry and take her place in the company of young accomplished matrons. She had been brought up to look forward to male dependency in a certain kind of marriage, in a home in which there are external manifestations of comfort, and to see that her place in the social register of her group was the primary aim of her life. Rejecting this goal makes her an outcast from her class and her former identity. She has drastically altered her concepts of who she is and wants to be by the end of the play. Her first step in this direction occurs when she refuses to take Mrs. Carson's advice to marry in order to escape the world's difficulties. "I would rather die outright, be burned or lynched, than to build myself such a sepulchre, to cheat death by calling it home," is her adamant declaration.[15] In quest of freedom she gives up her home, her family, and their values to live with Merilh in New York, not in a world of comfort, such as she had been accustomed to, but under difficult financial and emotional circumstances, for both young people are cut off from support by their families. This is the beginning of her journey to liberation. Unfortunately, Toomer is incapable of enabling her to become an autonomous human being.

As the result, the portrayal of Natalie Mann falls short of the ideal of woman's self-affirmation; she never achieves freedom in terms of a feminist consciousness. What freedom she gains comes through Nathan Merilh on whom she depends throughout for emotional support. More than that, it is through Merilh's dance at the conclusion of the play, the execution of which leaves him prostrate, that Natalie is expected to achieve her liberation. Merilh, in this scene, exhibits his willingness to sacrifice himself for her so that she can experience her freedom. Thus Toomer remains locked into believing in woman's dependence on man and in man's making the ultimate sacrifice for woman, even when he moves beyond the boundaries of sterile, repressive social conventions in general. It is an unfortunate limitation of vision on his part, and it overshadows the effectiveness of what might have been a revolutionary attitude toward women's freedom.

Jean Toomer's concerns in this play focus on the lack of spiritual wholeness he thinks he perceives in the black middle class in Washington, D.C., where he lived for most of his life prior to the publication of *Cane.* In the process of their Americanization, upwardly mobile black people were unable to admit that some aspects of what they sought were empty and superficial, for to do so was to question the values they were anxious to assimilate. In his search for internal harmony, Toomer was disenchanted by many things he observed in conventional middle-class life for a long time before he went to Georgia in 1921. His search for a fuller life began before he met Waldo Frank and his friends, who were then taking issue with the increasing mechanization of modern American life. In 1921, during his first trip to the South, Toomer saw that much of the richness in the black American subculture was lost when it became integrated into the middle-class American mainstream. Since he felt that middle-class white values weighed heavily on the side of sterility and antihumanism (as he and his friends defined that term), he believed that people who subscribed to those values were on a course of spiritual self-destruction. Black people who imitated white middle-class America were losing their "souls." Through an examination of black relationships—between wives and husbands and between generations—and by showing ways in which black women were denied the opportunity to pursue personal freedom and satisfactions in their work outside of home and family, Toomer revealed how these values affected the community.

Toomer also knew from personal experience that black parents were eager for their children to achieve conventional success, so that black Americans could lessen the educational, economic, and social gaps between themselves and white America. The goal of the American dream was to become educated, wealthy, and socially acceptable, and black Americans were not in a position to be critical of it. His own years of searching for a life's work were marked by bitter struggles with Pinchback. The older man, for most of his life politically astute and practical in matters of money, could not understand the younger man's ambivalences. All of his sons were professional men, and his grandson's seeming inability to follow a similar course was an enormous disappointment to him.

Toomer's concern for the dilemma of the middle-class black woman was echoed in other writers of the 1920s who followed him, especially black women writers. Several outstanding black women emerged in the arts during the decade, but they found it difficult to escape the traditional role expectations that were socially approved for them. Nella Larsen and Jessie Fauset, in particular, are cases in point. The characters in their novels evoke the realities of middle-class black women's lives in the 1920s, realities of frustration in and assault by the world of male dominance. Black women's search for self remained painfully unresolved until the heroine in the fiction of Zora Neale Hurston's *Their Eyes Were Watching God* emerged in the 1930s.

As a lyrical dramatization, *Natalie Mann* is an artistic achievement that depicts the conflicts between the values of materialism, hypocrisy, and antihumanism and the values of the intellect, the spirit, and creativity. The play proceeds from the idea that the life-giving spiritual heritage of mankind is in jeopardy of strangulation by the antilife forces of the modern world, which separate people from an awareness of their spiritual connections with the universe. This concept was central to the thinking of Waldo Frank, Van Wyck Brooks, and others who made up Toomer's closest friends in 1922, and they were attempting to bring it into the American consciousness. Natalie Mann and Nathan Merilh represent "creative revolution." They make demands on themselves and on life, want honest friendships, and seek to love freely and be loved in return. They renounce all that stifles freedom and creativity.

The ideas of Frank, Toomer, and their friends were radical in their time. These writers wanted to strip away the pretense that made people wrongfully see their lives as full when in fact they were empty. To do this they experimented with new forms in language and technique in an effort to expand literature so that it would accommodate and convey the subjectivism of their views. For Jean Toomer the playwright, realism, the most commonly used dramatic medium of the day, was not sufficiently flexible to meet the intellectual challenges that he hoped his works would provide. He turned to expressionist techniques to satirize American business and materialistic ideals. In *Natalie Mann*, Toomer uses dialogue, action, and stage props to highlight intensity of emotion and give language greater impact than it otherwise would have. Unlike many plays in this genre, which use only expressionist staging, this one uses many modernist techniques at once.

I I

The differences between *Balo* and *Natalie Mann* make it clear that although Toomer was critical of some of the realities of black folk life, its good qualities made a positive impression on his imagination, whereas there was little he could recommend in the culture of middle-class America, the negative aspects of which he wanted to expose. From an emotional and philosophical standpoint, Toomer looked back to the African/American folk culture, identified himself with what he found spiritually uplifting in it, and made it a source of artistic inspiration.

The style and technique of the two plays are experiments in language and form. The use of realistic techniques for the folk play was appropriate to the material. Unfortunately, Toomer's knowledge of dialect was weak, and he was not able to capture the tone of the folk rhythms. This is not surprising; rather it would have been astonishing had Toomer, after only two months in the South, been able to produce a work that realistically captured the mood, feeling, and complex nuances of the folk group. Thus the effort has merit, not because it is effective drama, but because it reveals Toomer's intellectual sharpness and his sensitivities to certain values in black American folk culture.

What he identifies most positively comes through in *Balo* in the strength of the community, within and without the family. Within the family, Toomer seems to be saying, wife and husband should be partners in the division of labor, in their concerns—financial and otherwise—and in time shared in work and play. Children are a logical extension of this sharing. Outside of the family there should be strong ties between relatives and friends, which are continually and naturally reenforced by expressions of caring, sharing, and understanding, and by close contact. The generational gap, so prominent in other strata of society, is bridged in black folk culture by a mutual acceptance that wisdom is the province of age and that youth is expected to respect the venerable aged. The gaiety inherent in the ripple of children's laughter, the nurturing qualities of the women, the communal breaking of bread, the folk songs and the folk religion are symbols of ongoing life and renewal; they ironically represent the vitality of the dying culture. *Balo* not only preserves the moment in time but pays tribute to those qualities that served well in their time, and still could, if they were given a chance.

In *Balo*, Toomer imitates great writers like Tolstoy and Turgenev by using the lives of common folk as the subject of legitimate art. In so doing, he foreshadows the works of such black writers as Langston Hughes, Zora Neale Hurston, and Sterling Brown. They, too, would find the folk culture a source of rich artistic inspiration.

In *Natalie Mann*, the positive qualities of *Balo* are missing, and their negative counterparts are prominent. Community, within and without the family, is weak as a result of hypocrisy, separateness, material values, and the need to conform to repressive social conventions. There is no intensity of joy or sorrow here from which spontaneity and creativity could emanate. There is no laughter in *Natalie Mann* and there is no song. The characters live like actors on a stage delivering studied lines, always fearful of missing their cues. There is no celebration of life in them.

The repression and sterility of this world are reflected in the stilted, artificial language that masquerades as conversation between the characters; in the inconsequential nature of talk that is often full of malicious gossip; in the deficiency of loving-kindness between the husbands and wives; and in the absence of children. In the nascent culture of the up-and-coming middle class, the women do not nurture. Instead, their actions and words are a conscious denial of all that is natural to the human spirit. It is as though having denied the past they are forced to sublimate the loving-kindness in themselves. The group seeks a "respectability," Merilh says, "which is never so vigorous as when it denies the true art of the race's past. They are ashamed of the past made permanent by the spirituals."[16] Toomer repudiates this denial of life and past, this crushing of the human spirit, and indicts the values that are sterile and repressive.

It is interesting to note that for all of Jean Toomer's negative reactions to the black middle class, in creating the characters of Natalie Mann and Nathan Merilh he demonstrated confidence that the social forces he opposed could be reversed. Man's creative will was dormant, not destroyed, only suppressed, awaiting renewal. Natalie Mann remarks to Merilh, several months after the beginning of the story, and after they have moved to New York:

> ". . . what really struck me about the case . . . wasn't the fuss and the racket or the episode of the detectives. . . . It's the tale that grew up around your going to the cabaret that night. Not the gossip or its consequences, but the fact that underlies the gossip. This: suppose they should take some simple and beautiful fact of life and apply the same processes. What would you

have? An epic tale, a folk tale, or a folk song. In the twinkling of an eye, and all for nothing, you became the bold leader of a desperate band of outlaws. You might just as easily have been invested with legendary powers and become an heroic center."[17]

Like many other critics of his time, Toomer was convinced that society needed to slow down the advances of automation and mechanization that were beginning to encroach on all areas of modern life. This was a cause that appealed to his artistic sensibilities and to his idea of himself as a leader. Essentially a poet, his ambition was to invest poetic language with the capability of conveying the awful truth about the erosion of the human condition. He was eager, too, to show that happiness is to be found in the attainment of higher consciousness. He was not so naive as to think that Americans could return to a life-style reflected in the black folk culture, nor would he have wished that to occur, but he felt strongly that there was a middle ground between the obsolescence of the past and the philistinism of the present, and he offers these philosophic opposites in these two early plays.

But Toomer was also genuinely interested in the drama as an art form, and these two separate ways of life gave him an opportunity to experiment with dramatic techniques. The realistic techniques of *Balo* differ from the modernist techniques of *Natalie Mann*, but each is appropriate to the content and each is effective dramatically.

Although Jean Toomer's early plays met with only slight interest, he pursued the genre sporadically until the end of the decade. *Balo* was performed in 1923, but *Natalie Mann* was rejected mainly because producers felt it was unsuitable for the American theater. Both works are immensely valuable because they offer previews to the themes, problems, and ideas that the author explored in the years that followed. Toomer had learned his craft; he had completed his apprenticeship; he was now an artist, and his first fruits foretold a bountiful harvest.

# Search and Recovery: *Cane* (1)

**I**

On the train from Georgia to Washington, D.C., in No-
vember 1921, Jean Toomer began to write the sketches
that became the first section of *Cane*. He had been un-
prepared for what he saw and heard in the South, and
he was incapable of holding back his creative responses to the
experience. By Christmas of that year the first draft of those first
sketches and of "Kabnis" were done. Through most of 1922 he
worked at his writing with zest. His friend, Waldo Frank, suggested
that he put the pieces together for a book, and so, in order to form
a book-length manuscript, he added to his southern narratives se-
lections based on the black urban experience. Frank wrote an in-
troduction to the completed manuscript and recommended it to
Boni and Liveright, who accepted it for publication in 1923.

When he was done he wrote, in wonder, "My words had become
a book.... I had actually finished something."[1] It was the mo-
ment for which he had waited a very long time. Now he felt he
had arrived and that, in the company of his literary friends, he was
in the "upswing of natural culture" with a "function in the regen-
erative life that transcended national boundaries and quickened
people."[2] He saw himself as part of a living world of promise. He
and such men as Waldo Frank, Hart Crane, and Gorham Munson
were "men of mission, pioneering up a new slope of conscious-
ness."[3] He was ecstatic. The feeling gave him a sense of experienc-
ing new life. He felt the mystery in being. He wrote: "I gave with
abandon the flow of myself. And as I gave I was given to myself.
My soul was resurrected and we were joined. . . . There was holy

union. And I, united in myself, found myself thereby joined to people and the whole of life, in love. . . . In my soul I found new life. There I discovered what I had sought elsewhere, without finding."[4]

Toomer took great pains in *Cane* to make sure that the structure of the book reflected the relationship of the individual parts to the whole. The design is a circle, he said. Aesthetically, *Cane* builds from simple to complex forms; regionally, it moves from the South to the North and then back to the South; and spiritually, it begins with "Bona and Paul," grows through the Georgia narratives, and ends in "Harvest Song."[5] The first section is about the life of the southern folk culture; the second section is about the urban life of Washington, D.C.; and the third section is about the racial conflicts experienced by a northern black person in the South.

In the original edition of *Cane*, there was a set of arcs on the blank pages before each section, symbols of the book's internal unity. For unexplained reasons, either oversight or intent, the arc preceding the first section has been left off all subsequent editions. On the dust jacket of the original edition, Toomer tells us that the work is a "vaudeville out of the South," with its acts made up of sketches, poems, and a single drama. He notes that although no consistent movement or central plot is present, the sensitive reader can find a beginning, a progression, a complication, and an end.[6]

When the first euphoria over its completion had passed, even before it was published, Jean Toomer saw *Cane* as less of a splendid beginning to his writing career than he had hoped to make. "The book is done," he wrote, but "when I look for the power and beauty I thought I'd caught, they thin out and elude me."[7] In particular, he thought the Georgia sketches lacked complexity and described them as "too damn simple for me." Of "Fern," he wrote in a letter to Sherwood Anderson, the "story-teller style had too much waste and made too many appeals to the reader." He noted that he could rework it, only he did not think it sufficiently important to spend more time on it.[8]

He liked Section 2 better. These narratives had the unrestrained energy that black people brought with them from the South to the North, an energy that was the source of their spiritual strength. He saw possibilities for greater development of this energy, which he thought he had especially demonstrated in "Theater" and "Box Seat." Of John and Dorris in "Theater," he noted that the barrier of class separated them—"stage folk are not respectable, audiences are."[9] Dorris attempts to break through the arbitrary social division by using her art—the dance—to try to win John. But he, a slave to conventions, is unable to respond to the challenge she raises, and she perceives his inadequacy as willful rejection of her, and it humiliates her.[10]

In "Box Seat" the raw energy belongs to Dan Moore. Toomer describes it as "ragged, dynamic, perhaps vicious." Dan attempts to save the woman he loves from the suffocation of oppressive social conventions. But like Dorris of "Theater" he does not succeed—in this case because the woman is already trapped and unable to break from her world. Toomer had doubts about the plausibility of the ending of this sketch. He questioned Waldo Frank on whether Dan's energy would allow him to walk away from the fight he initiated: "Would the ego and consciousness of the new Dan permit such an ending?"[11]

Toomer placed himself at the center of "Kabnis." He completed this section after he had made a second trip to the South, and he said that it stood as his immediate response to the dilemma of Afro-America as he saw it when he discovered the folk culture. In a letter to Frank, he points out that he is the source of both Lewis and Kabnis, Lewis with "the sense of direction and intelligent grip on things that Kabnis lacks, Kabnis with the sensitivity and emotion Lewis does not have."[12]

When the manuscript was completed, Jean Toomer appeared happy to his friends. In a letter to Waldo Frank, he intimated that he was in full agreement with Frank's introduction. In February 1923, in response to a letter from Horace Liveright he noted that nothing short of being hit by a "street car" would keep him from having more manuscripts for publication in the near future. He had two pieces in mind, each about the length of "Kabnis," and another long story; these were to be the three pieces for his second book. "[T]he mileau [sic] is ... Washington ... the characters dynamic, lyric, complex."[13] His autobiographical writings suggest that *Natalie Mann* was one of the works intended for this book. In his letter to Liveright, he mentioned that he did not feel confident to tackle writing a novel yet but nevertheless had one in mind. "At any rate, the horizon for the next three years seems packed and crowded," he concluded.[14] During that time he joined the Poetry Society of South Carolina because he believed the South was in an upswing and ready to provide the material for a new literature.[15] He was full of enthusiasm and confidence in his ability to become an important writer.

*Cane* was published in September 1923 and immediately took on a life of its own. His family welcomed his achievement. His grandmother was overjoyed and regretted only that his grandfather had not lived to see it happen. His uncle, Bismarck Pinchback, had many good things to say about it. He found the stories and sketches familiar to him, but he was especially pleased with the "beauty and interest in [Toomer's] wonderful descriptions, and in the strength and vigor of [his] language generally."[16]

Among Toomer's friends who praised the book were Hart Crane, Alfred Stieglitz, Georgia O'Keeffe, and Allen Tate. Tate pointed out that one of its strengths was the absence of the "pathos of Harris and others of the southern school of sentimental humor."[17] Black writers and critics immediately gave it high praise. W. E. B. Du Bois and Alain Locke, Countee Cullen and Claude McKay were among those who wrote Toomer their personal feelings. Du Bois called him the "writer who first dared to emancipate the colored world from the conventions of sex."[18] Locke praised his writing and thought process;[19] Cullen called it "a real contribution, a classical portrayal of things as they are";[20] and McKay was equally generous in his compliments. Aside from the personal responses, the book was widely reviewed in newspapers, magazines, and journals. Although it received some negative comments, most of those who read it found it praiseworthy. A large number of people saw it as the dawn of a new day for Afro-American literature and writing. Many people called Jean Toomer a new Negro writer of great promise.

*Cane* and Jean Toomer have now been talked about and written about for close to six decades, yet they remain among the most intriguing and tantalizing American literary topics of this century. As a work of art, the book has been subject to numerous critical interpretations and doubtless will continue to stimulate interest among new generations of scholars for a long time to come. Toomer's disappearance—by free will or force, by caprice or from feelings of compulsion—from the world of letters shortly after the book was published and at the moment when his success in literature seemed almost assured, has piqued the curiosity of a great many people and has led to various speculations on its causes and meaning.

In addition, for more than a decade, critics and scholars, captivated by *Cane*, have explored Toomer's subsequent writings for further glimpses of the genius who wrote that book. All agree that his most important, most powerful, and best writing is in *Cane*, which differs significantly even from those things he wrote during the same period. Why then did he turn his back on the possibilities that art in literature held for him, especially after all of those years of searching for his own voice? Why was *Cane* a swan song, not only, as he believed, for the folk culture but also for Jean Toomer's writing career, which he never understood or accepted?

These are questions that have not been definitively resolved in the minds of many who admire *Cane* and Toomer's art in this book. While the issues of race and society are undoubtedly of the utmost significance to his decision, the "facts" do not constitute the whole answer. Those who continue to pursue Toomer studies are themselves in search of the meaning in his motivation, a meaning that he consciously sought to understand for most of his life. In the discussion to follow, my aim is to discover a nexus between some of the tangled threads of conscious and unconscious thought that propelled him away from the people and ideas that culminated in *Cane* and to demystify his actions by attempting to understand the complicated emotions from which they originated. Toomer's relationship to *Cane*—and how that differs in observable ways from his relationship to some of his other works of that period—is what this particular inquiry seeks to clarify.

*Balo, Natalie Mann,* and *Cane* were projects that engaged Toomer in 1922. In my examination of the plays, I noted that Toomer wrote them in the process of experimenting with dramatic forms in an attempt to analyze particular aspects of the American experience. What is most important about them in terms of the relationship between the author and his work is Toomer's conscious use of artifice—of forms then still very new to American literature—to gain his ends. In other words, Toomer's relationship to the plays has to do with the way in which he uses language and form, just as the relationship between a sculptor and his work has to do with the way he uses clay or wood or marble. He molds and carves them to fit the particular contours of his imagination.

On the other hand, *Cane* comes from a separate frame of reference. From its multiplicity of literary forms that have been a source of confusion, frustration, and/or admiration for many readers to the realistic details that can be understood even through its maze of impressionism, there is an intricate and intimate relationship between Toomer and *Cane*, which differs from that between him and his other works. In this connection, the book claims close ties of lineage with the stream of consciousness writing that first gained wide attention in James Joyce's *Ulysses* (1922), a year before

*Cane* was published, and that William Faulkner would make popular in American literature later in that decade. If we believe Toomer's account of the inception of the work, and we have no reason to doubt it, in writing *Cane* he gave expression to feelings that overwhelmed him concerning the southern experience. He created in art, from those feelings, his own consciousness and reality as he confronted the history of black and white America—the pain, oppression, and strength of the past, the complications he saw in the present, and the ambivalences they all raised in him. Recalling his feelings while he was in Georgia, he wrote that "at times I identified with the whole scene so intensely that I lost my own identity."[21] Indeed, *Cane* is the outcome of the process of writing *out* of himself, out of the identity he discovered and recovered in the experiences he had in the South in the fall of 1921.

The epigraph on the title page of the book establishes the relationship of black Americans to its subject:

> Redolent of fermenting syrup,
> Purple of the dusk,
> Deep-rooted cane.

It is the metaphor for the experience of a people's connection to the land and soil that made them what they are. The symbol appears repeatedly in Sections 1 and 3 of the book, which are set in the South, but only rarely in Section 2, which represents aspects of the urban world.

Karintha's purple-dusk beauty opens the Georgia narratives, which, in part, take place against a background of the grinding of cane and the boiling and stirring of the sweet syrup. At the end of the day, black men gather around David Georgia's stove with its hot mellow glow that rose and "spread fan-wise into the low-hanging heavens" (p. 29) at the edge of the forest, and they are drenched in the heavy fragrance that exudes from the copper cauldron. In the final section, Kabnis's nightmare in the canebrake culminates in the sun's rising on the treetops of the forest. The tenacity to survive the harshness of black American reality is mirrored in the hard and grinding work from which the sweet cane syrup comes.

The most immediately striking feature of *Cane* is its language, which Toomer uses masterfully to create tones and atmospheres. Section 1, the Georgia stories, embodies a good deal of nature imagery, which makes it the most vivid, mystical, and sensuous part of the book. At the same time, as the section develops, the lyricism gives way to dissonance, sarcasm, and irony, all of which lead up to a bloody finale. The imagery in Section 2, set in Washington, D.C., and Chicago, reflects the industrialization and mechanization of the urban environment. The dominant themes are concerned with man's alienation in a repressive society. There is no canebrake in Section 2, no lyric or mystical language, but there is energy that comes from the tension between free will and arbitrary restraints. In Section 3, the action moves back to Georgia but the language does not incorporate all of the lyric qualities of the first section. However, the nature imagery restores a sense of contact with the earth. The predominant themes of Section 3 are ambivalence and fear, and the sensuousness and elusiveness of the women of Section 1 are replaced by the impotence and uncertainty that Kabnis experiences in the land of his forefathers. Only at the end is there a sign of hope for healing, and it comes from expectations that the voice and the pen of the artist will help to make it possible.

Toomer uses two modes of presentation for the sketches in Section 1 and Section 2 of *Cane;* in one, the narrator is the detached observer, and in the other, he is a character in his own story. In both sections, the narrator's mood ranges from disengaged pathos to subjective involvement. The narrator as persona also goes through stages of development. An important difference between Sections 1 and 2, aside from those of language and tone, is the fact that although the narrator has a degree of identification with the people and the region in Section 1, he never fully becomes integrated into either the richness or the pain of Georgia. In Section 2, however, one instinctively feels that he belongs to this world of the city and shares intimately in its shortcomings and its failings. In both sections, Toomer explores positive and negative aspects of each culture and shows how they reflect meaning in the lives and experiences of the people.

Section 3, a single dramatic piece, is less a presentation of experience than an opportunity for the reader to share the experiences of the artist—to observe his intentions and note the sources of his despair and his hopes. Neither an observer nor merely a character in the drama, he is the central figure around whom the action revolves. Ralph Kabnis is in search of his identity. He is a northerner, but he is also a southerner. He despises his southern history, which he cannot disregard, and he despises himself because he finds that history so painful. It challenges his weakness, and he is afraid to claim his heritage. He moves from painful resistance to painful acknowledgment of his history, and readers share his expectations for full, positive self-acceptance in the future.

## I I

"Song of the Son," which holds a position halfway through Section 1 of *Cane*, is the most widely anthologized of the individual selections of the book. There are good reasons for its popularity. It is a poem that appeals to the sense of cultural heritage, and it articulates responsibility to that heritage. There is also nothing elusive or oblique about the poem. The unambiguous intent of the poet is to convey his personal commitment, through his song, to the restoration of the glory of his history. In the evocation of heritage and past, he hopes to save the cultural remnants from oblivion and make them immortal:

> O land and soil, . . .
> Thy son, in time, I have returned to thee,
>
> .   .   .   .   .   .   .   .   .   .   .
>
> To catch thy plaintive soul . . .
> . . . one seed becomes
>
> An everlasting song, a singing tree,
> Caroling softly souls of slavery,
> What they were, and what they are to me,
> Caroling softly souls of slavery.                    (p. 12)

In brief, the poet, calling himself a son of the soil, but separated from it for a long time, returns to pay homage to his heritage: the swiftly passing culture of the slave past. He is enthusiastic, and he has a sense of urgency, for the soul of the culture is in danger of being lost. He takes the responsibility to create "an everlasting song, a singing tree," an indestructible monument to the past.

In the opening stanza, he notes that he is called to "the sawdust glow of night, / Into the velvet pine-smoke air" to capture the "parting soul in song . . . [so that] the valley [may] carry it along" (p. 12). Encroaching civilization, an ever-present theme in *Cane*, threatens the life of the folk culture. Time is of the essence.

Addressing the "land and soil" in the second stanza, the poet recognizes its previous exploitation and present decline. No longer lush and fertile, the "red soil [is] scant of grass . . . profligate of pines," and now "an epoch's sun declines" (p. 12). This is not just an unusual season, but the swift waning of an era. However, the tone of sadness is relieved by the announcement that the long-absent son is returned and acknowledges his kinship with this land:

> Thy son, in time, I have returned to thee,
> Thy son, I have in time returned to thee.

The use of "time" is important here: the son for all time has returned in time to catch the parting soul.

The remainder of the poem reiterates both the state of decline of the culture and the poet's intent to restore it in art. He addresses the "song-lit race of slaves." Because of long oppression they are "dark purple ripened plums, / Squeezed, and bursting," no longer ripening but swiftly disintegrating. Fortunately, "one plum" is saved for him, and from its seed he will produce the "singing tree" that will carol the "souls of slavery" for the rest of time.

"Song of the Son" is the emotional outpouring of a poet who recognizes his place in time and in the history of Afro-America. He accepts this identity and vows to save the "parting soul" of the folk heritage in the way in which it can be done most effectively— through art. This may be the moment of decline, but it is also one of hope and renewal for both the poet and the black American heritage.

For black readers and critics this poem has been especially important in identifying the ambivalent Jean Toomer as a foremost figure among the bards who come from the "song-lit race of slaves." From this point of reference, he records his impressions of the "parting soul" in songs that imprint their messages on the minds of those who hear them. His impressions are not new to Americans, for the stories of black southern life have been told many times, but readers are entranced by his vision and through his eyes perceive an inextricable tangle of pain and suffering, rich humanity, and the will to survive. Much of the first section of the book is completely sensory, and readers share the poet's response to a new and powerful experience. This is a journey that they also take with him.

From "Karintha" to "Blood-Burning Moon," through the six narratives and twelve poems of Section 1 of *Cane*, the narrator focuses on many of the conflicts, insecurities, and pressures, internal and external, that led to the eventual demise of the black southern folk culture. Black women, as symbols of the culture, are identified with nature. In varying degrees, they are beautiful, innocent, sensuous, and strong, yet they are also vulnerable, misunderstood, and unpossessable. Nature is rich, beautiful, lush, benevolent, and always helpless against the onslaughts of industrialization and the ravages of the modern age. The industrial age destroys the pastoral environment, just as racial and sexual oppression are responsible for the alienation, madness, and death of the women in this part of the book. Through them, the artist shows how the black folk culture succumbed to defeat in the face of forces more powerful than itself. Jean Toomer's women are of the earth in their sensuousness and fecundity, but they are not earth mothers. Like the despoiled earth, they are not able to nurture, and the children who survive perpetuate the destiny of the oppressed. To Toomer, this was the sad fate of a people who were once rich in their closeness to the natural world but were by 1921 losing their culture even as they resisted dehumanization.

"Karintha" incorporates symbolic and realistic details of one humiliating aspect of the lives of southern black women: sexual oppression. It is not surprising that Toomer begins his portrait of the southern experience by exploring this form of oppression, but it is interesting that he turns the spotlight on an intraracial treatment of it. Karintha is abused, not by white, but by black men. He demonstrates how a community horrendously oppressed from the outside further oppresses itself by destroying its most valuable asset—the psychological and emotional health of the young women who later become the bearers of its sons and daughters. Karintha is also a larger symbol. She is a manifestation of the powerlessness of women in a society where men dominate, but beyond that, she reflects the fate of black people in a world in which blacks are victims of the politics of race, class, and economics.

> Her skin is like dusk on the eastern horizon
> O cant you see it, O cant you see it,
> Her skin is like dusk on the eastern horizon
> . . . When the sun goes down.                    (p. 1)

These lines place Karintha in nature as a natural being, "carrying beauty" as effortlessly as does the physical landscape. She is a dusky-skinned beauty, glowing and sensuous. But if the opening lines seduce readers into expecting positive things to follow, that prospect is quickly shattered, for Karintha's beauty is the source of her victimization. "Men had always wanted her . . . even as a child" (p. 1), the narrator informs us. Lest we might consider this attraction affirming and complimentary to her, he dispels such ideas by further telling us that it meant "no good to her." Unable to protect or defend herself against this "want" of men, "the soul of her became a growing thing ripened too soon" (p. 2). Old men, as they "rode her hobby-horse upon their knees," secretly prayed not to get older; young men cavorted with her when they should have been dancing with grown-up women. And both groups "counted time to pass" so that they might mate with her. This unseasonable sexual attraction foreshadowed only doom for her.

Through the poetic introduction and the first prose paragraph of this narrative, Toomer interweaves images of beauty, innocence, and majesty with others of distortion, corruption, and sordidness. Karintha, allied with nature, is unspoiled and initially shares in its positive aspects, while the thoughts of the men are lustful and destructive to her. The values are in conflict, and having come together, they collide. Eventually one overcomes the other.

At age twelve Karintha is an example of "what it was to live." The narrator approves of her energy and her mischievousness. She "was a bit of vivid color" who "stoned the cows, and beat her dog, and fought the other children" (p. 1). But she was also out of place; her ingenuousness combined with her energy and beauty made her "as innocently lovely as a November cotton flower" (p. 1), an unseasonable phenomenon associated with impending misfortune.

There are other negative environmental factors in her development. In rural Georgia, where a lot of people are very poor, many houses have only two rooms: one for living and cooking, the other for sleeping. In this situation, children, very early in their lives, become aware of adult sexual activity. Karintha was such a one, and like a "good child," imitated her parents. She played "home with a small boy who was not afraid to do her bidding" (p. 1), then she was no longer innocently lovely, and the men counted time faster.

At twenty, Karintha reaches full womanhood, and the impact of her childhood reveals its tragic consequences. Her life is unfulfilled and empty because she cannot love, although she continues to carry "beauty, perfect as dusk when the sun goes down" (p. 2). She has had many men, but they feel only bewilderment in the face of her depleted passion, in her lack of warmth and tenderness. She, in turn, has only contempt for them. She even had a child, but she is incapable of mothering. The passage describing the birth of the child is full of contradictory images that highlight the subversion of the miracle and awe of the process of human perpetua-

tion: "the child fell out of her womb onto a bed of pine-needles
. . . elastic to the feet of rabbits" (p. 2). The "falling" child and the
reference to rabbits mingle fertility and birth and life and regenera-
tion with death and bestiality and reduce the scene to an anti-
human life drama. Readers never learn the explicit fate of the baby,
but "weeks after Karintha returned home the smoke was so heavy
you tasted it in water" (p. 2). Suggestions of lifelessness pervade
the entire description, including the destructive tension between
the world of nature with which Karintha continues to be identi-
fied, and the man-made world in which she must live. "Pine-
needles are smooth and sweet," but the smoke from the sawmill,
a symbol of industrialization, signals its triumph as its "odd
wraiths" spread pollution over the valley.

Karintha's life is a tragedy—a double tragedy—because she is an
unresolvable puzzle to those who have helped to make her the way
she is. Toomer notes that men do not understand her—old men
remind her of the times she used to sit on their knees, and young
men "run stills," or "go to the big cities and run on the road" (p. 2)
to bring her money, like offerings to a shrine. Once they thought
that all they needed to do was count time; now they are baffled.
More important is the fact that they cannot replenish what they
have destroyed, and they will continue to destroy other Karinthas,
because they do not comprehend that they are the source of her
withered soul. She is a victim because of her defenselessness
against a social malignancy; they are victims of ignorance. "They
will die without having found . . . out" that her soul was "a grow-
ing thing, ripened too soon" (p. 2).

One of the short poems that follows "Karintha" and precedes
"Becky," the second narrative in *Cane*, is "November Cotton
Flower," which serves as an extension of the first narrative. Images
of scarcity, drought, and death in the natural world of the poem
parallel the oppression of race, sex, class, and economics that com-
prise the reality of Karintha:

> And cotton, scarce as any southern snow,
> Was vanishing; the branch, so pinched and slow,
> Failed in its function as the autumn rake;
> Drouth fighting soil had caused the soil to take
> All water from the streams; dead birds were found
> In wells a hundred feet below the ground—                    (p. 4)

It is a dismal landscape into which the flower blooms. The old
people are startled by this omen of false spring that they know can

only be a sign of greater misfortune for them all. In their superstition, they perceive in it the human dimensions of "Brown eyes that loved without a trace of fear, / Beauty so sudden for that time of year" (p. 4). This is as Karintha was before exploitation eventually ruins her beauty, natural urges, zest for living, and innocence.

In "Karintha," Toomer examines three strands of oppression in black southern life: the oppression of black women by black men, the communal self-destructiveness of intraracial oppression, and the oppression of the weaker black community by the stronger white community. The first serves as a metaphor for the internal breakdown of moral responsibility, which leads to the second, and together they have an impact that makes the third even more devastating than it would be alone.

Toomer examines the first strand of oppression by describing the behavior of the black male community toward the sexuality of black women. It is a damning revelation that exposes the failure of the men to exercise restraint, appreciation, love, and respect for black womanhood. In the only world in which black women can expect safety from racial oppression, they are victims of sexual abuse by those who should otherwise protect them. The message is clear. The intraracial exploitation of women is a symptom of internal problems that can only weaken the community's fabric and make it more vulnerable to the external hostile forces that constantly assault it.

Toomer suggests that the second strand of oppression is a result of the first and has far-reaching consequences for the entire community. Karintha the woman is personally diminished because she is unable to carry out, in a normal way, the functions that would insure her a rich, full life. But the community shares in this diminution because it prevents her from contributing to its ongoing emotional health and strength. Unable to give or receive love, or to nurture, she in turn contributes to the community's internal erosion of positive values. Her inability to bear and raise sons and daughters who will themselves be new sources of vitality and renewal is an indication of her powerlessness. In short, Karintha is not able to participate in building a future in the community in which she will be able to resist those elements that seek to destroy her. What seems at first to be the oppression of one woman comes to be seen as a reflection of the moral and psychological deprivation that the community generates against itself.

Even though Toomer does not directly refer to the third strand of oppression, he draws our attention to the relationship between the black and white communities, to the relationship between the powerless and the powerful. Although internal sexual oppression is the most obvious factor in the abuse of Karintha, race, class, and economics are the factors that perpetuate the cycle of poverty in which she—and those who follow her—live. In a world in which men manipulate the souls of women, Karintha is a paradigm for the black community's powerlessness over the control of its own class and economic status in a white, capitalistic society. "Karintha" incorporates many of the best elements of Jean Toomer's artistry as he explores the effects of race, class, and sex throughout his book.

"Karintha" is much like a photograph in words. From this point of view, it is a photograph that captivates the eye at an initial glance; its rich details, however, cannot be fully comprehended until the eye has grown accustomed to the total composition. Then there is no end to what one can see in it. The depictions of beauty, innocence, and art are as bold as those of perversion, ignorance, and poverty. Toomer describes natural beauty as well as the pressures that undermine that beauty. Because the narrator remains separate from his material, although the scene filters through the lens of his perceptions, there are no distractions caused by his interrupting presence. Readers are responsible for discovering the details.

The power of "Karintha" is in Toomer's manipulation of language. His visual images evoke feelings of both pleasure and pain, and readers experience a tension between what pleases them and what outrages them. In short, "Karintha" bears the mark of a poet creating a language in conflict with itself, a language that forces others to respond to it intellectually and emotionally because of its intensity.

For example, Karintha's beauty is at the center of the narrative and everything else flows toward it. It never diminishes, even as she changes from innocent child to cynical woman. Her beauty remains dynamic, a background against which the strong, bold colors of the realistic details occur. It provides the introduction and the coda to the piece. Yet the voice of the Furies is never silent, and the beauty and ugliness in the human condition are inseparable throughout the whole.

Color is an important component of the portrait, and the ones that Toomer uses are bold. Karintha's skin is the color of "dusk on the eastern horizon . . . when the sun goes down." At other times she is "a bit of vivid color," or like "a black bird that flashes in light" (p. 1). In this yoking of color, beauty, the perfection of nature, and Karintha, Toomer breaks with the usual tradition of female beauty—even in much of Afro-American literature—and establishes the dusky-skinned woman as naturally beautiful. Color also denotes creativity, and there is a quality of wholeness in the linking of sunsets and the "supper-getting-ready-songs" the women concoct at the end of the day's work. Finally, Karintha's energy is colorful: her "running is a whir" and like "a wild flash"; she is no static beauty.

The tension between the positive and the negative aspects of the narrative rests in the conflict between what nature generates and what human beings subvert. Men respond to the natural beauty of Karintha by spoiling it, just as the pine smoke from the sawmill "hugged the earth" and made it impossible to see more than a short distance ahead. The men's desire for Karintha is like the smoldering sawdust—polluting in its effects, it destroys the beauty it touches.

Other aspects of Toomer's style are repetition, the use of poetic refrain, and references to the deity. The narrative begins and ends with the same serenade to Karintha's beauty. These poetic lines also appear at the division between the account of Karintha, the innocent child, and Karintha, the alienated woman. Other lines, at the end of the childbirth account, take cognizance of the negative force that clouds, shrouds, and contaminates the world around it:

> Smoke is on the hills. Rise up.
> Smoke is on the hills, O rise
> And take my soul to Jesus. (p. 2)

But the smoke rises only to hang like ghosts from the trees.

The repetition of words and phrases also occurs within the prose portions of the narrative, and together with the references to God and Christ, it adds a haunting, otherworldly quality to the work. By building evidence through images, Toomer makes us aware that a part of Karintha died partway through the narrative, and when the last sun goes down, readers are ready to accept it as a symbol of death.

"Karintha" is a fitting beginning to *Cane*. A detached Jean Toomer, in his first contact with the folk people, responds with deference and some awe to what he perceives, but he does not fail to comprehend and convey the complexity of beauty and tragedy in the situation.

The second short poem that follows "Karintha" is "Reapers,"

which like "November Cotton Flower" has a direct relationship to the narrative. Here the prognosis for the future is even harsher than in the earlier poem. It is a short work of eight lines that divides evenly to project two separate views of reality. The narrator of "Karintha" continues in his detachment, and the piece is dispassionate:

> Black reapers with the sound of steel on stones
> Are sharpening scythes. I see them place the hones
> In their hip-pockets as a thing that's done,
> And start their silent swinging, one by one.
> Black horses drive a mower through the weeds,
> And there, a field rat, startled, squealing bleeds,
> His belly close to ground, I see the blade,
> Blood-stained, continue cutting weeds and shade.     (p. 3)

In this poem, the dichotomy between the wholesomeness of Karintha's beauty and the evil, destructive lust of the men takes the form of the differences between the worlds of human and nonhuman actions. Black reapers—men—prepare for the harvest by sharpening their scythes, but a mower, driven by black horses, cuts through the weeds with indifference, unknowingly destroying a field rat with its blades. Toomer creates a contrast between the knowledge and purpose of responsible human beings and the automated disinterestedness of machines. The reapers are deliberate in their preparations, and they have an objective and expectations of rewards. But no human awareness governs the actions of machines, which cannot comprehend the devastation they cause.

In establishing this division, Toomer indicts those who carry out acts of oppression against others and asserts that they act out of elements in themselves that are less than human. Such actions violate the human reason for being, and the doer becomes like the machine, without the ability to nourish human life.

The experience of women, as a microcosm of southern life, takes on a different shape in "Becky," another narrative of female victimization. Toomer opens the sketch thus: "Becky was the white woman who had two Negro sons. She's dead; they've gone away. The pines whisper to Jesus. The Bible flaps its leaves with an aimless rustle on her mound" (p. 5).

This moving introduction describes a situation unlike that which is experienced by most people. The first two sentences have a rising dramatic impact; the others provide a falling action. They remind the reader of the southern racial codes that openly forbade black male/white female sexual liaisons. When these relationships occurred, white male society acknowledged them only as products of black male bestiality and its desire to ravish the purity of white womanhood. Such violations of the racial codes were dealt with swiftly and effectively, with measures to extinguish the male and forever protect the woman from the beast. But Becky had two "Negro" sons, and that is no ordinary situation. But why death? Why separation? Why is the Bible portrayed as a symbol of uselessness in the religious South?

The answers are not long in coming. First, the narrator explodes the myth of the racial purity of white southern women. Becky, in maintaining the secret identity of the man, appears a willing partner to the relationship. But such a blatant violation of the social code requires drastic punishment, and Becky pays the supreme price. In its treatment of their mother, the community has made outcasts of her sons, and they have left. Only the leaves of the Bible, flapping aimlessly on her grave, provide a tangible reminder of the tragic lot of the human beneath the mound.

It all began when Becky had her first "Negro" son. At that time, the people of the community—white and black—joined together to reject her. Resorting to various subterfuges so that each would pretend noninvolvement, they nevertheless built her a house away from the town—"a single room held down to the earth . . . by a leaning chimney" (p. 5). They brought food and left it by her door. "Poor Catholic poor-white crazy woman," the black people said; "God-forsaken, insane white shameless wench," the white people said (p. 5).

Five years later Becky had a second "Negro" son. This time the town told itself that she was dead. The people stopped leaving food at her door. They rationalized that, with the boys there, there could be no room in the diminutive cabin for her. Maybe they had killed her and buried her in it, some people thought. But no one was bold enough to approach her door in search of truth. The boys grew up in the manner of Ishmaels. They talked with neither black nor white people, drifted from job to job, and eventually left town after retaliating in violence against those who had made them feel unwelcomed and unwanted. "'Godam the white folks; godam the niggers,' they shouted as they left town" (p. 6). For a brief period packages of food were once again left outside of Becky's door, but then abruptly the packages stopped coming. If Becky were dead, the town did not want to feed a ghost.

One Sunday afternoon, as the good people—including the narra-

tor and Barlo, one of the few black characters who plays a significant role in several of the sketches in the first section of *Cane*—
were returning home from church, Becky's house fell in beneath
the leaning chimney with a "thud . . . like a hollow report" (p. 6).
No one went to investigate, to verify if she were there, alive or
dead. On the fallen house that becomes her tomb, "Barlo, mumbling something, threw his Bible on the pile. (No one has ever
touched it). . . . The pines whisper to Jesus. The Bible flaps its
leaves with an aimless rustle on the mound" (p. 7).

"Becky" is one of two narratives in *Cane* in which the white and
black communities act in concert, and in each case a common
threat to the status quo causes this solidarity of action. The community casts Becky out, but yet it builds her a house and feeds her.
Such behavior highlights problems of communal hypocrisy and
self-righteousness in a society that practices racial and sexual victimization. In her fallen state, she is important to the community,
for, through her, it is able to assert its false concepts of religious
and moral superiority.

Becky's predicament and fate has roots in the racism that permitted white men, from the days of slavery, to make black women
the objects of their sexual lusts, and at the same time made it
impossible for black men to have open relationships with "respectable" white women. Becky's behavior makes her a nonconformist,
a rebel against the mores of her society, and for this, she is punished. She is physically isolated, suffers from social alienation, and
consequently dies from malignant neglect.

In this community, the intersecting paths of religion and superstition play an important part in what happens to Becky. Religion
is a strong component in folk life. Self-assured in the rightness of
their actions, white and black people "prayed secretly to God
who'd put His cross upon her" (p. 5). They considered it a measure
of their "charity" that they built her a house and for a time did not
permit her to starve.

At the same time, religion is deeply tinged with superstition and
a fear of the supernatural. The whispering pines, heard throughout
the narrative, give it a mystical and mysterious aura. Because the
townspeople already believe that Becky is dead after her sons leave
town, "a creepy feeling came over all who saw the thin wraith of
smoke" rising from the chimney of the cabin (p. 6). They also note
the shaking of the ground around the house when the trains are
passing. This too is sinister. Most people are not brave enough
even to talk to her.

According to the narrator, on the fateful Sunday afternoon when the chimney topples the cabin, there is a sense of foreboding in the air. The church people on their way home from visiting a congregation in another town must pass Becky's house. Some distance from it, the horses, sensing something weird, "stopped stock-still, pushed back their ears, and nervously whinnied." Someone noticed smoke curling up from the leaning chimney: "Goose-flesh came on my skin though there still was neither chill nor wind. . . . Ears burned and throbbed. Uncanny eclipse! Fear closed my mind. We were just about to pass . . . Pines shout to Jesus! The ground trembled as a ghost train rumbled by" (p. 6). Becky, alive or dead, is a supernatural phenomenon to them.

Becky's death—swiftly, from the impact of the fallen house, or slowly, from the suffocation of being buried alive by its rubble— was the direct result of the racist, religious, and superstitious beliefs and actions of the people of her town. She suffered because she violated the most sacred taboo on which white southern society depends for its sense of superiority over other groups. In a society in which women depend on men for protection, the nature of her misconduct left her unprotected, defenseless, and powerless against the drastic reprisals she confronted. It is not innocence that is her downfall—as it was Karintha's—but the exercise of individual human will in conflict with the restrictive social codes of her society.

In both "Becky" and "Karintha," the narrator sees and conveys a communal moral blindness. But in "Karintha," he emphasizes colors, light, and beauty in positive ways. In "Becky," he emphasizes the absence of seeing and of insight in the community despite the many functions of eyes in the narrative. In "Becky," the connection between the absence of humane actions and religious and political blindness is more sharply drawn than it is in "Karintha."

The narrator never sees Becky, and neither does anyone else. The description he receives of her is negatively vivid: "eyes . . . sunken . . . neck stringy . . . breasts fallen." Her house is built on an "eye-shaped piece of land," but although six trains go by each day, "no one ever sees her." Because she is unseen, it is easy for everyone to dismiss her existence. It was easy to think that she was dead, even when she was not. At the end, as the house crumbled in front of those passing at the time, "eyes left their sockets for the cabin," and at the scene the narrator notes "we saw the bricks in a mound upon the floor" (p. 6). Still no one had seen Becky. She had only been a presence.

Images of death also contribute to the absence of seeing in this story. Becky suffered psychological and social death as soon as she was turned out of the community, and it followed that long before anyone could be reasonably sure of her physical death, she was spoken of as a ghost. The house that was the instrument of her banishment from human contact served the function of a grave while she was still alive and, appropriately, became her tomb when she could be presumed dead.

Jean Toomer noted a number of times that the lives of black and white people in the South were bound together in ways that made it impossible to separate the groups in any comprehensive survey of southern experience. The portrayal of Becky, a white woman, as a victim of racist oppression, is one of his attempts to demonstrate this point. It is ironical that the code that gave license to those who treated her cruelly was one that was intended to protect her. Racism and sexism join to deprive white women of any autonomy they might have. The pervasiveness of both isms produces devastating effects, not only on the lives of black people but also on the lives of those who supposedly benefit from racial oppression. In "Becky," Toomer shows that racism corrupts even the positive elements within its periphery, as it corrupts religion in this narrative. At its worst, it creates the moral blindness that engulfs an entire community and justifies wanton acts of human tragedy.

In "Karintha," the narrator was an objective observer who did not participate in the action. In "Becky," although the narrator has never seen Becky and has presumably arrived in town a long time after the early events of her story, all of which he only hears about, he is a participating figure in the final scenes of the drama. For one thing, he bears some of the responsibility for never speaking out against the isolation of Becky and the accompanying alienation of her sons. Recognizing his and the community's culpability, he asks: "We, who had cast out their mother because of them, could we take them in?" (p. 6). In the final scene, he is among the returning church people who witness the falling of the house and is one of those who approach the rubble: "I thought I heard a groan. . . . Somehow we got away. My buggy was still on the road. The last thing I remember was whipping old Dan like fury; I remember nothing after that—that is, until I reached town and folks crowded round to get the true word of it" (p. 7).

When the narrator changes from passive observer to participant observer, his identity with the community begins to develop. First, he tells us that he was one of the group returning from Ebenezer

Church on the Sunday afternoon when Becky's tragedy occurred. He was also closely associated with Barlo, who is the only person he mentions by name in the group. The two must have been traveling together, for he notes that they "were pulled out of their seats" in the buggy by fear and curiosity and "dragged to the door that had swung open" (p. 6). Before they found the courage to mobilize their limbs into flight from the helpless woman trapped beneath the ruins, Barlo threw his Bible on the heap, where it remains, flapping its leaves in useless motion.

The actions of the narrator in this episode and in his silence about the unjust treatment of Becky conflict with the values of his northern background and education. As a character in the story, he emerges as a cowardly, immoral conformist. At the same time, his situation is complicated by the reality that a nonwhite, erudite, northern male in the South faces enormous difficulties from both the white and black communities, who view him with suspicion, anxiety, and mistrust. The irony is that because he was unwilling to risk the disapproval of the black community and the hostility of the white community in his need to identify with the former, he illuminates some of the tragic aspects of what it was to be black and male in the South. Thus, "Becky" extends beyond "Karintha" to illustrate the moral impoverishment caused by fear, ignorance, racial oppression, and religious hypocrisy.

"Face," the poem that follows "Becky," provides a vision of women and oppression different from that in the narrative. The poet traces the contours of the face of an old black woman—"purple in the evening sun / nearly ripe for worms"—and projects onto her an image of strength. While Becky's defiance of her society's sexual codes of behavior led her to a miserable and inhuman end, this black woman's face shows that she has withstood the pressures of her life and has emerged heroic in the struggle. Using water imagery to make his point, the poet associates her with its perpetual flow. Unlike Becky, who is "held down to earth" within her cabin and from whom there is never a sign of autonomous movement, this woman's strength and independence are expressed in her silver-gray hair, which is "like streams of stars." Her brows, like canoes turned upside down, show ripples of pain; her eyes reflect the morning mist of tears; and the sorrow of the years is prominent in the muscles of her face, which are like the purple grapes at sunset. Here Toomer establishes a contrast between the old woman and Karintha, who, though also associated with sunsets and purple, does not transcend the oppression of her environment with the strength that characterizes the face of the old woman. "Face" is a poem that speaks to the possibilities of endurance that rises above the fates of Karintha and Becky.

"Karintha" and "Becky" end on notes of fatalism and defeat, which are reenforced by "Reapers" and "November Cotton Flower"; "Face" intensifies the mood of acceptance in the face of oppression. Nothing in these pieces offers resistance to the negative forces in the environment. As aspects of southern rural life, they reveal only the strength of some of the agents that undermine the positive elements in the cultural structure. This attitude of quiescence changes abruptly in "Cotton Song," the poem that immediately precedes the next narrative, "Carma."

In "Cotton Song" (p. 9), Toomer moves from abstraction and reliance on metaphor for meaning to concrete portrayal. A five-stanza poem, "Cotton Song" is in the tradition of the slave work songs and makes its address directly and explicitly to a special audience. It is also a personal appeal that brings the poet closer in his identification with the plight of oppressed workers:

> Come, brother, come. Lets lift it;
> Come now, hewit! roll away!
> Shackles fall upon the Judgment Day
> But lets not wait for it.

The poem brings to mind the spirituals that speak to the time when blacks would achieve freedom from the forced labor of slavery. It is now known that the references to Judgment Day and a heaven beyond earth were not always intended literally by the slaves but served more as a subterfuge for secret messages connected to more immediate escape. The poet heeds the secret messages here, and he calls for action without delay.

From the opening call to blacks to take responsibility for their own freedom, the imperative becomes more militant:

> Cotton bales are the fleecy way
> Weary sinner's bare feet trod,
> Softly, softly to the throne of God,
> "We aint agwine t wait until th Judgment Day!"

The poet appeals to the listener to liberate himself or be held responsible for his bondage:

> Cant blame God if we dont roll,
> Come, brother, roll, roll!

The poem moves from invocation to affirmation, from acknowledging the arduousness of the lot of the black worker to asserting the assurance that freedom is within his power. It also advances the internal consciousness of the book by demonstrating an active rather than a passive stance to the conditions of life. In addition, it brings the narrator into even more of a sympathetic identity with the Afro-American experience and prepares him and his readers for "Carma," "Song of the Son," and "Georgia Dusk," which follow.

Dissonance and cacophony dominate the introduction to "Carma."

> Wind is in the cane. Come along.
> Cane leaves swaying, rusty with talk,
> Scratching choruses above the guinea's squawk
> Wind is in the cane. Come along. (p. 10)

Disturbing noises from the swaying cane leaves "rusty with talk" make even harsher sounds than the "guinea's squawk" and unsettle the equilibrium of nature. The discordant human sounds of the leaves, and the narrator's imperative to "come along," combine to heighten the feelings of foreboding. Readers prepare for the worst.

Then, in seeming contradiction, "Carma" bursts upon our consciousness in brilliant color and power. Here is no distant beauty of dusk on the eastern horizon, nor unseen victim such as Becky. This is a different woman, whose presence explodes the concept of female frailty and dependence—here is a woman who is as strong as any man.

This is the narrator's vision. He sees Carma, a black woman, dressed in overalls, behind an old brown mule, driving a wagon home at the end of the day's work. He is mesmerized by her force and vitality, and as his eyes follow her down the Dixie Pike, his imagination swells. Although he associates her with nature, and the lyric quality of "Karintha" permeates his descriptions, she is not "innocently lovely" like the protagonist of the earlier sketch. Carma is portrayed in bold and assertive tones, and with monumental force. His eyes are drawn to her as by a magnet, and the wagon, which she rides easily, although it "bumps, and groans, and shakes as it crosses the railroad track" (p. 10) rolling down the dusty road, takes on the splendor of a chariot for him.

The visual perspective is the controlling element in the narrator's impressions of Carma, but from this a spiritual power claims his imagination. He does not leave his place around the stove, where the men congregate at the end of the day, but his eyes follow her down the road until long after she is gone. Before she disappears from sight, she turns, and he thinks she looks at him because, he imagines, she feels his gaze. He thinks that even nature joins him in recognizing her unusual qualities—"the sun is hammered to a band of gold" and "slanting over her shoulder, shoots primitive rockets into her mangrove-gloomed, yellow flower face," while "pine-needles, like mazda, are brilliantly aglow" (p. 10).

Carma's presence, the aura of her, makes a profound impact on the narrator and precipitates for him a consciousness of heritage that does not occur in the earlier narratives. Drawing on the black American tradition, which very early identified its own enslavement with the Israelites in Egypt, he deems Carma's power a sign of the special favors the once-Jewish God now bestows on his newly chosen group of black people. For the first time in *Cane*, too, he links the Afro-American to his African heritage, and in his mind the girl "in the yard of a whitewashed shack" assumes the mysterious qualities of a primitive goddess. She sings; the echoes of her voice, "like rain, sweep the valley. . . . She does not sing, her body is a song. She is the forest, dancing. Torches flare. . . . The Dixie Pike has grown from a goat path in Africa" (p. 10). As Carma "disappears in a cloudy rumble," his imagination transforms the pastoral Georgia scene into an eclogue. Carma represents the remnant of Africa.

But there are discordant notes in the paean. Symbols of industrialization intrude on the primal world: the sawdust pile and the smoke that curls upward and spreads above the trees are unpleasant reminders of Karintha's life, and the "chug-chug of a gas engine" is not in harmony with nature. In addition, "no rain has come to take the rustle from the falling sweetgum leaves" (p. 10), suggesting a season of drought. These images may not diminish the brilliance of the vision of Carma, but they are disturbing elements that cannot be wholly ignored.

Then comes a drastic change in the mood and language of the narrative. The narrator's vision of the strong black woman, symbol of ancient glory, collides with the townspeople's image of her: to them, she is a defeated woman. The narrator's celebration of Carma gives way to a "tale of crudest melodrama," and in its preface, "Foxie, the bitch, slicks back her ears and barks at the rising moon" (p. 10). The change of tone is explicit.

Carma's husband, Bane, is on the chain gang, and the people say that she is responsible for that. Bane, an industrious man, had been away from home working with a contractor. When he returned, he heard that in his absence Carma had been an unfaithful wife. She denied the accusations, but he persisted in his charges. Reacting in desperation because of his harangue, she grabbed a gun and rushed into the canebrake. Sometime later, Bane heard a shot and imagined she had hurt or killed herself.

In the early night, he and some friends search for Carma. When they find her, her posture leads them to believe that she has indeed killed herself, and they feel they are returning home with "dead weight." Later, they discover the hoax: she was playing dead. Then Bane's anger gets the better of him; he thinks he has been "twice deceived, and one deception proved the other" (p. 11). He slashes the man who had found her. Now Bane is on the chain gang, and the townspeople wonder what will become of Carma.

In this version of the tale, Bane brings woe to Carma, woe that is reenforced by the images of night and darkness associated with it. These images contribute to the dominating theme of the action. In the blindness of moral indignation, Bane cannot see "that as a result of his accusations she was becoming hysterical" or that his strong words, "like corkscrews, wormed to her strength, which fizzled out" (p. 11).

A "crescent moon" in a "quarter heaven," which is all the natural light available for the canebrake search for Carma, offers only faint illumination. The men take lamps to lighten the darkness. Moths, attracted to the flames, flicker the lights and put them out, and much of the search proceeds in darkness. They find her, not by seeing her, but by stumbling over her. Bane's conviction that Carma had really deceived him comes "like a flash of light," which, when past, makes it even harder for him to see and drives him into a "blind" rage. It is this blindness that propels him toward the action, the end of which is the chain gang.

The men who tell the narrator the story of Carma do not blame her, and they see her only as a victim. As such, she was another casualty of the intersection between racial and sexual oppression. The politics of race and economics forced Bane to leave home in search of work. However, while social conventions demand sexual fidelity from women under such circumstances, men are free to be unfaithful. This double standard led to Bane's unbridled anger at his wife at the suggestion from others that she had violated that code. They were powerless to change the economic and sexual politics and were taught not to question. Thus, Carma is left to bear the stigma.

On the other hand, the narrator's perception of Carma comes from an image that is unencumbered by the details of her life with Bane, and he accepts the woman for herself. In contrast to the townspeople's story, the narrator's experience occurs in the golden light of sunset, in brilliant colors, and it becomes the source of creative inspiration. Thus, two images of Carma emerge from the narrative, that of the townspeople and that of the narrator. The people feel sorry for Carma and see that now her eyes are "weak and pitiable for so strong a woman," but the narrator finds in her the essence of the primitive past, a figure of the dimensions of an ancient goddess. It is significant that up to this point he has accepted, uncritically, the events and incidents he describes. Now, for the first time, he is cynical. This change is a manifestation of his growing consciousness, which also serves to illustrate the development of black group consciousness as it moves from acceptance and fatalism to challenge and rebellion.

Carma both symbolizes and represents the elements of the story. She is the "Purple of the dusk, / Deep-rooted cane" and also the "Wind . . . in the cane . . . / Cane leaves swaying, rusty with talk, / Scratching choruses." The brilliance of the narrative lies in the deftness with which the narrator combines these two images in the persona of Carma. His heightened awareness of the complex nature of the folk experience is reflected in his words of bitter sarcasm at the end—"Should she not take others, this Carma, strong as a man, whose tale as I have told it is the crudest melodrama?"—and they represent a turning point in his relationship to the material of *Cane*. His artistic aloofness from "Karintha" and his immoral ambivalence to "Becky" have become creative involvement in "Carma."

If "Song of the Son" represents a starting place from which to begin to understand Jean Toomer's organic relationship to *Cane*, then "Georgia Dusk" affirms the promise of that relationship. Its array of natural images, its evocation of ancestry, as well as its symbols of growing industrialization in rural Georgia, bring together a number of elements that make an impact on black southern life and that have been explored in the previous poems and narratives. The mood, as in "Song of the Son," is one of sadness because of loss, the recall of past epochs, and the poet's urgency to immortalize the experiences of history.

In "Georgia Dusk," the sunset is brilliant but passes quickly because the sky is "too indolent to hold / A lengthened tournament for flashing gold" (p. 13). With no effort on its part, night will come. But although the poet chides the sky for so willingly losing day, night is a welcome time in the black community—it brings rest from back-breaking work and facilitates "A feast of moon and men and barking hounds" (p. 13). He hails this as the time in which "some genius of the South" finds the best and richest materials for "making folk-songs from soul sounds" (p. 13).

The perspective shifts to the sounds of encroaching modernization—sawmill whistles and hushed buzz saws. The eye has time to take in the landscape of "plowed lands that fulfill / Their early promise of a bumper crop." Here, too,

> Smoke from the pyramidal sawdust pile
> Curls up, blue ghosts of trees, tarrying low
> Where only chips and stumps are left to show
> The solid proof of former domicile. (p. 13)

The focus shifts again as the poet evokes the African past. Although separated from their ancestral home, black Americans retain cultural elements of that heritage. In memories, they recall "vestiges of pomp . . . king and caravan / High-priests, an ostrich and a ju-ju man," as they go singing through the swamp. The new-world people raise their voices in song, and their songs raise "the chorus of the cane / . . . caroling a vesper to the stars" (p. 13).

The black folk culture, which evolved out of the oppression of slavery and the discrimination and segregation of the post-Civil War years before the migration to the North in the twentieth century, embodied internal resources that enabled it to survive horrendous oppression and permitted black people to demonstrate, as oppressed peoples throughout history have done, the strength of the human will to survive. However, the external pressures that created the black folk culture also prevented it from comprehending its own historical and cultural significance. That was the responsibility of those who came later, those sufficiently removed from its influence to temper vision with objectivity and who were yet close enough to feel racial and/or emotional kinship with it.

As a "son of the soil" but long separated from it by time and social conditions, the narrator in *Cane* has both the distance from and the strong ties to black folk culture that enable him to understand, appreciate, and express its soul through his gift of art. He arrives at the eventide of the culture, as "Georgia Dusk" begins at sunset, and he chooses to celebrate the richest elements of its beauty and strength. Objectively, he notes the harshness of the new landscape, compares it to the landscape of the older culture, and expresses both a sense of loss and an awareness of his artistic responsibilities.

"Carma," "Song of the Son," and "Georgia Dusk" together are a high point in Section 1 of *Cane*. In an upward swing from the incidents of racial and sexual oppression in "Karintha" and "Becky," and reenforced by the themes in the poems that are associated with them, these three pieces expand the canvas of the composite black experience and celebrate as well as mourn that experience. In addition, they cast the narrator in a new and sharper light in relationship to the materials out of which he is fashioning this work of art.

"Song of the Son" is the central piece in this trilogy. As noted earlier, this poem is an acknowledgment of kinship between poet and materials that permits him the subjectivity and emotional involvement that otherwise would be difficult to justify in the work. Placed just before "Song," "Carma" represents the narrator's breaking away from the passivity of the documentary form to an active incorporation of his subjective point of view, which is both critical of and in conflict with the community's view. With "Carma," the narrator abdicates his background position and becomes a critic of the experience he has accepted as part of his own. Black American folk culture and its ties and relationships to its past history and cultural adoptions are first expressed in "Carma." Placed just after "Song," "Georgia Dusk" locates the very heart of the folk. Its lyrical strains describe the breadth and depth of a history that is painful, but they also celebrate elements of pride. "Georgia Dusk" continues to identify the narrator with both the culture and his mission.

In "Fern," the narrator further explores his relationship to the folk culture. Here he examines his inability to achieve full access to the source of his creative inspiration. Because of his peculiar blindness, he never discovers that he sets up the same sexual barriers to understanding Fern as do other men who are attracted to her, men whom he disparages: he sees her only as a woman in a dependent relationship to men.

Fernie May Rosen has neither the dusky beauty of Karintha nor the physical strength of Carma. Instead, she is a "creamy-colored solitary girl" with an "aquiline" nose, which the narrator calls "Semitic." Her beauty and power are in her eyes, which give the "suggestion of down slightly darkened." These eyes capture the creative interest of the narrator: "Face flowed into her eyes. Flowed in soft cream foam and plaintive ripples, in such a way that wherever your glance may momentarily have rested, it immediately thereafter wavered in the direction of her eyes" (p. 14). Men looked into Fern's eyes and "fooled themselves," thinking that in them they saw the fulfillment of all their sexual fantasies. "When she was very young, a few men took her," but as in the case of Karintha, they "got no joy from it." Their frustrations generated feelings of obligations to her; "they felt bound to her," and yet they did not know how or what to do to assure themselves they were paying their debt to her. Baffled and ashamed in their failures, they vowed to do "some fine thing for her," send her money, buy her expensive presents, or rescue her from an unworthy husband. Then, because "men are apt to idolize or fear that which they cannot understand," they worshiped her instead, and "she became a virgin" (p. 14). They were completely incapable of perceiving her in any way other than as a sexual object.

The narrator insists that he had a different reaction to her. When he looked into her eyes, he "felt he heard a Jewish cantor sing. As if his singing rose above the unheard chorus of a folk-song" (p. 15). While other men saw their sexual needs mirrored in her eyes, he saw that her eyes "desired nothing that . . . [the men] could give her; there was no reason why they should withhold" (p. 14). From his angle of vision, Fern's eyes have mystical depths he would have liked to fathom in art. Sitting with her by a small stream one evening at dusk, he notes that her eyes grew even more mystical than he had seen them previously. They "held me. Held God. He flowed in as I've seen the countryside flow in" (p. 14). In a strange confusion of emotion, he held her without noticing what he was doing until she disengaged herself from him, and on her knees, she sang brokenly, in an uncertain voice, like a Jewish cantor; then she fainted.

Vision is the governing motif in "Fern." Everyone sees her and she is always visible. Almost everyday she could be seen sitting on her porch. But her eyes do not seem to take in the world around her, and they are as indifferent to the Georgia sunsets as they are to the dull gray cabins. Most often her gaze settled on "a vague spot above the horizon, though hardly a trace of wistfulness would come to them." But while she seemed not to see it, the whole countryside flowed into those eyes, "flowed into them with the soft listless cadence of Georgia's South" (p. 15).

Although the narrator claims he has no sexual interest in Fern, he too sees her only as a woman. His concerns for her reflect the dependence men project onto women. "I too had my dreams," he notes. He is solicitous of her future and wonders if she would be better off away from the South. Rather, he finally decides, it is "better that she listen to folk-songs at dusk in Georgia" than be in Harlem with its "indifferent throngs," or marry someone with a lot of money who would expect from her what she cannot give, or become a "white man's concubine." He wonders: "Something I must do for her. There was myself. What could I do for her? Talk of course. Push back the fringe of pines upon new horizons" (p. 16).

But when he goes to talk with her, he finds he does not know what to say. Instead of controlling the situation, as he had assumed he would, he discovers that in her presence he feels the full force of his southern heritage: "I felt strange, as I always do in Georgia, particularly at dusk. I felt that things unseen to me were tangibly immediate. . . . When one is on the soil of one's ancestors, most anything can come to one" (p. 17). She sings, first "convulsive sounds, mingled with calls to Jesus. And then she sang brokenly. A Jewish cantor singing with a broken voice. A child's voice, uncertain, or an old man's" (p. 17). The dusk hides her from him and he can only hear her song; it overwhelms him, although he does not understand its meaning.

Long after he leaves the South, the memory of the encounter with Fern, never satisfactorily resolved for him, remains dynamic. He is perturbed because he never found out, just as the other men did not, what he could have done for her, "the fine unnamed thing" he had hoped to do. "Nothing ever came to Fern," he laments, "not even I" (p. 17).

The narrator's involvement in the action of the Georgia sketches reaches its zenith in "Fern," and she is the only one of the women in this section of the book with whom he has direct and personal contact. There is no lack of sincerity on his part in his desire to discover her spiritual depths, but, ironically, he cannot see that his difficulties in achieving his goals are the result of his inability to see her as a person rather than only as a woman. As a metaphor for the relationship between the poet and the folk culture, the narrative points to the problems that those like Jean Toomer, removed in time and place from it, face in accurately trying to record and interpret it.

In "Fern," Jean Toomer brings together disparate elements of the black folk culture. The folk songs and the Jewish cantor's song,

Fern's surname and her Semitic nose, and the calls to Jesus unite African and Western cultures and make explicit the black American's close identification with the ancient suffering and bondage of the people of Israel. The black folk culture is rich in achievement and suffers a pain that the narrator senses deeply. His personal history separates him from it, yet binds him inextricably to it.

"Nullo" and "Evening Song" are the bridge between "Fern" and "Esther." The first is a lament for lost beauty, and the falling of pine needles at dusk in an unpeopled forest approximates the failure of the artist in "Fern" to capture the essense of the folk song and the Jewish cantor's song in the canebrake. In "Evening Song," the poet, as lover, accepts the lesser light of the moon, now that day is over, and expects to find rest and comfort with his beloved in its soft, less demanding light. Dusk, rest, and sleep identify both poems with the end of the folk culture, but while "Nullo" speaks only of loss, "Evening Song" offers the prospects of security in the appreciation of what remains.

In "Esther," the title character becomes the focus of an examination of the black-white mores in a small southern town. If Karintha, described as a "black bird," represents the epitome of pristine black beauty, then Esther is the symbol of the outcome of the white rape of black America. There is no poetic introduction to or poetic prose in this sketch. The sun does not go down and leave glowing tints on the horizon. Rather, dusk "falls," a chill wind comes up with the dark, and the impressionism and figurative language of the earlier part of the book are lost to realistic prose with grotesque and comic images. The contrast between the two subjects is striking and ironic. Contrasted with Karintha's stunning dark beauty, Esther is colorless. "[Her] hair falls in soft curls about her high-cheek-boned chalk-white face. . . . [Her] hair would be beautiful if there were more gloss to it. . . . Her cheeks are too flat and dead for a girl of nine" (p. 20). Esther, who "looks like a white child," is a most unattractive figure, while Karintha makes black beautiful.

Karintha comes from a family with limited economic resources, while Esther's father, the storekeeper, is the richest black man in town. As a child, Karintha is full of buoyancy and spirit, which she releases oftentimes to the discomfiture of those around her. On the other hand, Esther, "starched, frilled, . . . walks slowly from her home towards her father's grocery store" (p. 20). They have one thing in common: they are girls in a world in which the attentions of men have crucial impact on their lives. Karintha's soul is destroyed because at an inappropriate time of her life men shower her with inappropriate attentions; Esther's has a similar fate because they never pay her any attention.

The narrative has four parts, each focusing on Esther's thoughts and actions at a particular time of her life: at age nine, at sixteen, at twenty-two, and at twenty-seven. Barlo, who threw his Bible on Becky's mound, returns in "Esther" and, unknown to him, becomes the leading figure in the girl's fantasies. Her thoughts are always on him: "Barlo. . . . Black. Magnetically so. Best cotton picker in the county, in the state, in the whole world for that matter. Best man with his fists, best man with dice, with a razor. Promoter of church benefits. Of colored fairs. Vagrant preacher. Lover of all the women for miles and miles around" (p. 23). Although Esther goes unnoticed by him, she is mesmerized by his personal appeal and by the variety and expertise of his talents. He becomes "the starting point of the only living patterns that her mind was to know" (p. 21).

Esther becomes aware of Barlo when she is nine years old, although she has heard her father speak of him previously as King Barlo. He comes to her attention when he goes into a religious trance and kneels in the street on a spot called, for obvious reasons, the Spittoon. The white and the black men loitering on the corner do not notice him at first. They continue to squirt tobacco juice in his direction, and soon his face takes on a shine from the saffron liquid. When the loiterers become aware of his unsightly presence, a crowd gathers round to "await the prophet's voice."

There are a number of comic inversions in this scene. "King" Barlo kneels in the street in a holy state, and the idlers spit on him. The "clean-muscled, magnificent, black-skinned" man soon has his "smooth black face" shining from tobacco juice, while his "lips and nostrils quiver," more like an animal's than a man's (p. 20). The entire town comes out to witness the spectacle; people line the curbstones and sit on borrowed boxes, and even a coffin has been pressed into use for the occasion. Businesses close, and the banker, the shopkeepers, and the sheriff are all in attendance. "Soda bottles, . . . full of shine, are passed to those who want them" (p. 20). To complete the mock solemnity, a couple of stray dogs begin to fight, and a cow comes galloping up the street.

Barlo remains in a trance through the afternoon and into the evening. He begins to preach after sunset, but he has no important or new message. Nevertheless, people act as though this is a monumental event. The crowd is so quiet the boll weevils can be heard at work. People are "touched and curiously awed," and both the white and the black preachers in the gathering come together to try to devise ways to "rid themselves of the vagrant, usurping fellow." After dusk, "Barlo rises to his full height. He is immense. To the people he assumes the outlines of . . . [the] African" of whom he has been speaking. The story that Esther had heard for a long time was that at the moment that Barlo had begged the crowd to listen to his words, a host of angels and devils had descended on the town. Barlo had ridden out of town that night reportedly on a "pitch black bull that had a glowing gold ring in its nose" (p. 21). The next day, Limp Underwood, the town's rabid segregationist, woke up in the arms of a black man. How many of these things were true was unclear. What was true was that a black woman, feeling inspired, drew the portrait of a black madonna on the courthouse wall, Barlo left town, and his image was stamped indelibly on Esther's mind.

A great deal of activity takes place in this first section of "Esther," and the main character's separateness from it causes her to evolve like a shadow against a crowded background. She is scarcely perceptible. This is a study of life in a small southern town, where myth and religion intersect to relieve the boredom of day-to-day experience. Esther's outsidedness is a result of her ambiguous color, her social station as the daughter of the richest black man in town, and her decorous behavior. The men loitering on the corner ignore her, as do all the other people in town.

But the interweaving of myth and religion, and the actions of Barlo, as facilitating agent, produce a state of home-grown excitement and comic chaos. Barlo is a prophet who cannot prophesy but who awes the crowd and causes old gray mothers to weep. Yet, as he kneels in the street, splattered by tobacco juice, the sheriff mobilizes three men for a possible arrest, and the white and the black preachers conspire to drive him out of town. Exaggerated perceptions of his power and his threat to the community create the legend of King Barlo, and Esther, removed from the life of the town, finds reality in the myth.

At age sixteen, Esther has daydreams that are the stuff of sexual fantasies she can never experience in reality. In one, she thinks that the store window that she sees glowing in the light of the setting sun is in flames. From a second-story window, firemen rescue a dimpled infant whom she claims for her own. She does not know how it came to be hers, but she loves it and thinks of it as an "immaculate" child. In a later dream of the same flaming window, she finds no fire department to put out the blaze. Instead, the men on the corner form a circle and squirt gallons of tobacco juice onto it, and the air "reeks with the stench of scorched tobacco juice." In the meantime, the women scurrying for safety pull their skirts over their heads, and "fat chunky Negro women [and] lean scrawny white women . . . display the most ludicrous underclothes." She alone holds her ground and takes the baby the tobacco juice has saved: "black, singed, wooly, tobacco-juice baby— ugly as sin" (p. 23). She loves it "frantically," and the townspeople are jealous of her joy. They leave her even more alone now.

At twenty-two Esther is finished with school. She almost certainly had gone to college, but with few options for employment, she returns to work in her father's store. The black and the white men loafing on the corner still pay no attention to her. When she was younger, she had an affair with a fair-skinned boy who cruelly rejected her. Her only other opportunity for love or sex came from a traveling salesman. She turned him down. She begins to be old. "Her hair thins. It looks like the dull silk on puny corn ears. Her face pales until it is the color of gray dust that dances with dead cotton leaves" (p. 23). Only her images of Barlo give meaning to her life. She decides that she loves him and will tell him so the next time she sees him. Her resolution "becomes a sort of wedding cake for her to tuck beneath her pillow and go to sleep upon" (p. 23).

At age twenty-seven Esther's body is "lean and beaten. She rests listlessly against the counter, too weary to sit down." She does not see the faces of the customers who come into the store to buy lard and snuff and flour from her. The townspeople have long ago decided "she was always a little off, a little crazy" (pp. 23–24).

In the final episode of the narrative, Barlo returns to town, not as a vagrant preacher kneeling in the street, but driving a new car, a convertible, and displaying all of the accoutrements of affluence to a gaping, admiring audience. It is rumored that he made money on cotton during the war. Resplendent in his recently acquired wealth, he is more magnetic than ever, and Esther, more listless than before, is paler than ever. His presence close by brings her to life. "She sees him at a distance. . . . She hears the deep-bass rumble of his talk. The sun swings low. McGregor's store windows are aflame again. Pale flame" (p. 23). Esther decides to go to him, to tell him of her love for him. She notices a white girl passing and wishes that she were like her, not white, but "sharp, sporty, with get-up about her," for Barlo. She suppresses the wish. "Wishes make you restless. Emptiness is a thing that grows by being moved," she thinks. The loose women of the town will have him unless she saves him. Her passion flames, "as if her veins are full of fired sun-bleached southern shanties, a swift heat sweeps them" (pp. 23–24). She vows to save him from those women.

It is midnight when Esther slips out of her father's house to go to find Barlo. The leaves of the sweetgum have a peculiar phosphorescent glow, and their movement excites her. In her mind, McGregor's store windows are aflame in the dark night. The streets are deserted, and the chill wind that came up from the west at sunset is still blowing. She closes her eyes and holds them tightly shut as she walks along. When she opens them, she sees "iron canopies and mule-and-horse-gnawed hitching posts. . . . The house is squat and dark. . . . People's voices, muffled, come. The air is heavy with fresh tobacco smoke. It makes her sick. . . . Her head spins. She is violently dizzy. Blackness rushes to her eyes" (p. 24).

Barlo's rejection of Esther brings the narrative to its climax. Facing him, "she sees a smile, ugly and repulsive to her, working upward through thick licker fumes." She turns away, and "like a somnambulist, . . . walks stiffly to the stairs . . . as jeers and hoots pelter bluntly upon her back." All her dreams are shattered; she walks out into nothingness: "no air, no street, and the town has completely disappeared" (p. 25). Her mind closes in upon itself.

On a realistic level, in physical appearance, Esther is a painful symbol of the ignominy of bastardy in the black community. Interracial sexual relations between black women slaves and white men slaveholders were the most important factor in the birth of mixed-blood children in America before the abolition of slavery. Although these children have traditionally been accepted within the black community with impunity, Toomer, taking poetic license, uses Esther's whiteness as an extended metaphor for the powerlessness of black America in relation to white America.

Esther's existence is an example of the concrete stigma of black sexual shame. The black-white community's rejection of Esther, in contrast to its acceptance of Barlo, enables it to live with that shame in a manner that is acceptable to the black ethos. When Esther fantasizes that she is the mother of Barlo's black baby, she accentuates the hopelessness and futility of her being. By associating her throughout the narrative with images of alienation and lifelessness, the narrator further emphasizes the wish to negate her force and presence.

In a different reading, but one still connected to the cultural metaphor, the story of Esther's alienation is another exposition on the history of the racial and sexual oppression of black women. As the educated daughter of the town's richest black man, she is the victim of middle-class repressed sexuality and oppressive morality. As such, her function is to deny the stereotypes associated with the "natural" proclivities of black women. Esther's baby is an "immaculate" conception, and her sexual fantasies are "sins" she must repent and "dream no more." But it is the men in her life who define her place as woman and person within the world of the black community. Their rejection of her denies her in all areas of her life. Although men sought after Karintha and denied Esther, the life of each woman was ruined by the accepted sexual mores. However, the image of Esther, with the "chalk-white face," is contrasted importantly with the image of Karintha, who was "perfect as dusk when the sun goes down."

Once again, Toomer's vignette explores elements within the black southern community on many levels. Realism and symbolism intertwine to create a multidimensional portrait through language that probes beneath the surface of the quotidian life.

"Conversion" and "Portrait of Georgia" continue to move away from the celebratory qualities of "Carma," "Song of the Son," and "Georgia Dusk." By strategically placing the poems where he does, Toomer shows how the folk culture includes strength and the renewal of hope in heritage, on one hand, and distress, fear, and death, on the other. In "Conversion," the poet bitterly lashes out against his ancestral Guardian Spirit, who had been charged with the responsibility of protecting him:

> African Guardian of Souls,
> Drunk with rum,
> Feasting on a strange cassava,
> Yielding to new words and a weak palabra
> Of a white-faced sardonic god—
> Grins, cries
> Amen,
> Shouts of hosanna. (p. 26)

He accuses the spirit of wantonly betraying those who trusted him by accepting the religious values of another culture—of an enemy who mocks the spirit even as the spirit praises him. The cultures of the African peoples die because their gods have deserted them and become agents of the Christian God.

While "Georgia Dusk" recalled images of past glories, the concerns of "Portrait of Georgia" have to do with the oppressions of the present:

> Hair—braided chestnut,
>     coiled like a lyncher's rope,
> Eyes—fagots,
> Lips—old scars, or the first red blisters,
> Breath—the last sweet scent of cane,
> And her slim body, white as the ash
>     of black flesh after flame.          (p. 27)

This is the preface to the narrative that follows, and it highlights its tragic dimensions. The last breath of cane is consumed by the violence of which the black self becomes a symbol.

The partly impressionistic sketches of the Georgia women in Section 1 of *Cane* yield to a fully developed realistic portrait of southern life and experience in "Blood-Burning Moon." The racial and sexual oppression of the earlier sketches culminate in the physical and psychological violence of this final story. The language is figurative, but from the beginning, images of night, danger, and decay create for the reader an atmosphere of foreboding.

The opening lines set the tone and foreshadow the final gore. Dusk, with all its connotations for the folk of *Cane*, comes "up from the skeleton stone walls, . . . from the rotting floor boards and the solid hand-hewn beams of oak of the prewar cotton factory" (p. 28). A full, sanguine moon, looking like an enormous bloodshot eye, rises from the dusk. It glows like "a fired pine-knot" and "showered" the single street of the factory town where the black folks live. It is an evil omen, and before this night is over, there will be a harvest of death, madness, and despair.

The atmosphere of doom lifts briefly when Louisa appears. Young, black, and beautiful, she is the "color of oak leaves on young trees in fall." Her breasts are "firm and up-pointed like ripe acorns. And her singing had the low murmur of winds in fig trees" (p. 28). The respite is brief, for we learn that Louisa, a cook in the white folks' house, is the object of sexual admiration by young white Bob Stone and by the black field hand Tom Burwell. Tom wants to marry her, but she is not ready; Stone meets her surreptitiously in the canebrake and repays her favors with silk stockings and purple dresses.

It is a deadly game they play, and male sexual power and pride are the stakes they use. Red, the color for anger throughout, and blood, the symbol of life and death, combine to represent the explosive quality of black-white relations in the story, which is first seen in the blood-red moon that looks down and sheds an aura of impending doom on "factory town." The bloods of Tom Burwell and Bob Stone undergo changes within themselves in moments of rage against each other, and the flow of Stone's blood precipitates the final tragedy.

The full moon is the symbol of racial antagonisms. Its effects first disquiet, then wreak destruction on the black community. Louisa, on her way home to factory town, finds the rhythm of her song disturbed when she looks at the rising moon. Other women improvise songs and sing them loudly to break its spell. Tom Burwell shudders when he sees its face on his way to visit Louisa, and ultimately, when mutilation and death have left despair in their wake, the full moon is the single unabashed witness to Louisa's madness. In this sketch, black people escape the bedevilment of the moon only around the stove of boiling cane, where the forest shields them from the moon's malignant face.

Bob Stone, scion of a once slave-owning family, represents the power and pride of white male birthright. He resents the subterfuge he must employ in order to see Louisa. "His family has lost ground," he thinks. In the old days, as master, he would need only go in and take her, "direct, honest, bold," with none of the sneaking around he was now doing. But lust is stronger than vanity or decorum, and Louisa is "lovely—in her way. Nigger way. What way was that? Damned if he knew" (p. 31). Black people were so inscrutable. "Listening to them at church didnt tell you anything. Looking at them didnt tell you anything. Talking to them didnt tell you anything. . . . Nigger was something more. How much more? Something to be afraid of, more?" (p. 32) Had Bob Stone heeded the wisdom of his reverie, the tragedy would have been averted. But he wanted Louisa more; he wanted the "beautiful nigger gal."

Tom Burwell's interest in Louisa challenges Stone's power and privilege. Stone's lust for Louisa increases his sense of male competition, his racism, and his contempt for Tom. "No sir. No nigger had ever been with his girl. He'd like to see one try. Some position for him to be in. Him, Bob Stone of the old Stone family, in a scrap with a nigger over a nigger girl" (p. 32). Tom is black and hardworking, and when he takes Louisa's image into the fields with him, he can plow and pick cotton to rival Barlo. His knife is his weapon, and he has been on the chain gang three times for using it against other men. The whole town calls him Big Boy, and when Louisa thinks of him and Stone together "his black balanced, and pulled against the white of Stone" (p. 28).

In a clearing at the edge of the forest, hidden from the face of the vampire moon, a group of black men, including Tom Burwell, sit around a stove where cane is boiling. The mellow glow "spread fan-wise into the low-hanging heavens," and the heavy fragrance drenched the men "as old David Georgia stirred the thickening syrup with a long ladle . . . and told tales about the white folks, about moonshining and cotton picking, and about sweet nigger gals" (p. 29). The pastoral scene reflects the harmony of race and soil, of black men and their roots. But the fragile peace is shattered when gossip about Bob Stone and Louisa enters the conversation. "Blood ran up Tom's neck hotter than the glow that flooded from the stove," and he attacks the man who brings this news. He leaves the warmth of stove and men to find Louisa.

Tom loves Louisa. But the man of action who suffers jealous pain when Louisa's name is linked with Stone's is not very good with words. "Words is like the spots on dice," he tells her, "no matter how y fumbles em, there's times when they jes wont come" (p. 30). Nevertheless, in his own way, he assures her of his good intentions, and he hopes within a year to have the resources to secure his own farm and the means to marry her: "My bales will buy yo what y gets from white folks now," he wishes her to know. In addition, he warns her that he will cut Bob Stone in the same way as he has done to black men, if he finds Stone making advances to her.

Bob Stone's discovery that the old days have indeed ended and his right to Louisa is unacceptable to Tom Burwell leaves him little recourse. He must accept the situation or move to a confrontation with "a nigger over a nigger girl." He overhears the men in the circle around the cane-boiling stove discuss the trouble that looms ahead between the white and the black men because of Louisa. Prophetically, one announces, "Be gettin too hot f niggers round this way" (p. 32).

> Bob Stone's ears burned as though he had been holding them over the stove. Sizzling heat welled up within him. His feet felt as if they rested on red-hot coals. . . . a blindness within him veered him aside. . . . Cane leaves cut his face and lips. He tasted blood. He threw himself down and dug his fingers in

the ground. The earth was cool. Cane-roots took the fever from his hands. (p. 32)

Claims to white superiority fuel Bob Stone's bloody anger against Tom Burwell. When Louisa does not materialize at the prearranged meeting place, his rage is uncontrollable: "Veins in his forehead bulged and distended. Saliva moistened the dried blood on his lips. He tasted blood. Not his own blood; Tom Burwell's" (p. 33). But in a competition of physical strength that Stone initiates, Tom's fist "sounded as if it smashed into a precious, irreplaceable soft something. . . . Bob staggered back. He reached in his pocket and whipped out his knife." That was a fatal error. He knew Tom's incontrovertible skill with his knife. "Blue flash, a steel blade slashed across Bob Stone's throat. . . . Blood began to flow. . . . He turned and staggered towards the crest of the hill in the direction of white town" (p. 33).

The denouement dramatizes the full impact of the powerlessness of the black community to protect its rights, and the barbarity with which the white community maintains the status quo. The scenario is well known to both sides. Reprisals will come swiftly. The black people who saw the fight "slunk" into their houses and blew out the lamps. The systematic terrorism and force of the white community render the black impotent against the outrage it knows will come. The white mob comes "like ants upon a forage rushed about. . . . Shotguns, revolvers, rope, kerosene, torches. Two high-powered cars with glaring lights. . . . They come together. . . . Nothing could be heard but the flop of their feet in the thick dust. . . . The moving body of their silence preceded them. . . . It flattened the Negroes beneath it" (p. 34).

Tom Burwell is one lone defenseless black man against the might and power of the white mob with its instruments of southern justice and torture. There is no route of escape for him, no way in which to avoid the dire consequences. With the swiftness, eagerness, and efficiency of ants, the whites carry out their deadly purpose. Tom's wrists are bound, and they swarm about him, none wishing to escape a moment of the drama.

They drag him to the old factory—a fitting place for an execution. The preparations are carried out in silence, there is no need for words, the players know exactly what they have to do. The stake is sunk in the ground, kerosene is poured on the rotting boards, and blood trickles down the victim's face with its stony eyes. The human torch, the stench of burning flesh, and finally the yells of the mob combine in the ritual orgy that preserves the balance of power between the races in the South: "The mob yelled. Its yell echoed against the skeleton stone walls and sounded like a hundred yells. Like a hundred mobs yelling. Its yell thudded against the thick front wall and fell back. Ghost of a yell slipped through the flames and out the great door . . . like a dying thing [to] . . . the single street of factory town" (p. 35).

Louisa sits alone in the door of her house, completely mad. Her eyes see only the full moon beaming down its evil light on factory town. She wonders where the people are and thinks that maybe they will come to join her if she sings. Perhaps Tom Burwell will come.

In "Blood-Burning Moon," Jean Toomer presents an image of one painful aspect of the reality of the world of blacks and whites in the South, as the reality evolved through generations that knew strife, anger, hatred, fear, and oppression. For most of this time, the degradation of black men and women through the wanton abuse of the sexuality of black women by white men was one of the most poignant manifestations of the oppression of black people. White Bob Stone and black Tom Burwell, in a duel over the sexuality of Louisa, are actors in a bloody drama, the scenes of which were written out of the victimization of their shared history.

"Blood-Burning Moon" is more than an unfortunate incident or the story of southern ritual murder. It is a metaphor for the inevitable confrontation between white and black men as the latter sought to recover the human dignity they had lost through slavery, segregation, and other forms of racial oppression. For black men knew that they could regain their birthright only when they assumed the responsibility of destroying the evil power that had deprived them of it. Although it was not the only kind of struggle, the bloody encounter was the most obviously recognizable life-and-death struggle between the powerful and the powerless. By reversing the more familiar elements of the black-male–white-female often-fabricated rape accounts that end in renditions of black helplessness, Toomer is able to reduce significantly Tom Burwell's helplessness and to illustrate more clearly the interconnectedness between race, economics, and sexuality in white-black relations. Although Burwell dies at the end of a rope, he is not a passive victim.

In the post–Civil War South of "Blood-Burning Moon," the pre-war social and economic structures have already crumbled. The cotton factory where, in earlier times, black slaves worked relent-lessly without recompense now has "skeleton walls" and rotting floorboards. Now "old David Georgia tended *his* stove" (italics mine) and regaled the black men with tales of yesteryear. Under the influence of boiling cane syrup the stories recall good times for black people and the follies of white people. Bob Stone gives Lou-isa silk stockings and purple dresses for the brief moments of pleasure he receives from her in the canebrake, while his rival asserts, "And next year . . . I'll have a farm. My own," and he prom-ises Louisa that when this happens, she will no longer have to work in the white folks' kitchen to make a living. These are the words of a man confident that he can rid himself of the shackles of economic dependence and the internal feelings of inferiority that they engender. In contrast to the lust that Stone feels for Louisa, the affection that Burwell feels is too tender to be expressed in ordinary words: "Seems like th love I feels fo yo done stole m tongue. . . . Sing, honey Louisa, and while I'm listenin t y I'l be makin love" (pp. 30–31).

Economic autonomy is a vital step in black liberation from the power of white people, but full freedom depends upon integrating liberty into all human action. Tom Burwell takes a step toward that freedom when he announces his willingness to die to protect his integrity. He fights to claim his right to manhood. His choices are psychological slavery by refusing to fight or death by accepting the challenge. By killing Bob Stone with Stone's own knife, he makes it clear that he fights to be free. Physically stronger than Stone, psychologically he is also the victor even though he dies at the hands of the white mob. Even as he wrests his right to freedom and dignity in a horrible death, the rotting floorboards of the crum-bling edifice of white power are being destroyed with him.

On the other hand, Bob Stone believes that the power of the white community is on the decline. His family no longer "owns" the "niggers," and he is forced to meet Louisa in secret. Not only would his northern friends be outraged by his subversive maneu-vers to have sexual relations with a black woman, but his mother and his sister would be appalled. His worst humiliation comes from knowing that he shares that woman with a black field hand who claims her openly. He fights with Tom partly out of helpless anger at the loss of power to which he thinks he has full rights.

Louisa functions as a symbol of the black folk culture and as a black woman in a world in which men make immoral claims on women's lives. Economic dependence on the white world leaves her vulnerable to the exploitation it perpetrates on her. As a black woman in a world of black and white men, she is oppressed by both. She is the sexual object who becomes the target of the power dispute between the men of both races. Louisa finds "no unusual significance" in either man, has no conflicts in meeting Stone in the canebrake, and feels comfortable in delaying Burwell's marriage proposal. She seeks her own autonomy. However, neither of the men is concerned with her personal wishes; each wants to own her for himself as an indication of his power. In the end, as representation of the folk culture or as woman, she is the final victim. Surrounded by the chaos of racial confrontation and the brutality of abusive control, her madness is both death in life and defeat through helplessness. Toomer's portrait of Georgia, with its many contradictory elements, constitutes his search for and recovery of the meaning in the roots of black life in white America.

# Finding a Different Place:
## *Cane* (2)

**I**

After the violence and despair at the conclusion of "Blood-Burning Moon," the narrator shifts the action from the rural South to the northern urban environment, and, in Section 2, he explores a new kind of black experience. Many factors contributed to the movement of large numbers of blacks to the North in the early part of the twentieth century, but the motives were always associated with improved economic, educational, and social status and a desire to escape the ignorance and violence of southern black life. The shift brought monumental changes, both negative and positive, to the black community. It also caused the irretrievable loss of many of the qualities of beauty and art that Jean Toomer would never have encountered had he not gone to Georgia in the fall of 1921.

When Toomer began to write about his Georgia experiences, he had no overreaching plan for the book that he eventually wrote. Had he had "more" to say about the experience, the book would have been different. This not being the case, however, he was forced to include pieces about life in the North, and for these he drew on his own experiences. Many of the places and events in his own life have been woven into the fiction of Section 2 of *Cane*.

In this part of the book, the artistic tension arises from the conflict between natural human impulses and the covert violence of the man-made urban environment. In the North, blacks struggle to establish an identity out of the remnants of their past and the values and ideals of their newly acquired home. Because race is a crucial factor, they will always be a separate group within the dominant culture, but survival demands the inculcation of new modes of thought and ideas as well as practical skills suited to city life. If the black folk culture is memorable because of its connections with qualities in the natural world that could not be wholly destroyed by racial oppression, then the black urban experience is memorable because it separated the people from the basic values of the folk culture. City life initiated black people into the world of Western culture, which, in its advanced stages of industrialization and mechanization, has become sterile, limiting, and destructive to the human spirit.

The organization of Section 2 of *Cane* is different in several ways from Section 1: There are only four full-fledged narratives and five poems here, but three prose poems in the section add a new form to the book. At the same time, the narratives are longer than the earlier ones, and they include more fully developed characters. In general, a language in concert with the sounds and vibrations of the city replaces the lyricism and images of nature. Ironically, the search for a larger life, which precipitated the exodus from the South, ended in new and different constrictions for the spirit of black people.

The section begins with "Seventh Street," one of the prose poems. Compared with "Karintha," which opened Section 1, it is strikingly opposite in tone, images, and resolution. Karintha was emotionally and psychologically destroyed by an environment that could not nurture her. The individuals in this new environment have long since lost the need for a gentle nurturing. Easy money, illegal activities, material goods, and the swift movement of city life have displaced nature and perfect beauty:

> Money burns the pocket, pocket hurts,
> Bootleggers in silken shirts,
> Ballooned, zooming Cadillacs,
> Whizzing, whizzing down the street-car tracks. (p. 39)

"Seventh Street is a bastard of Prohibition and the War," proclaims the narrator (p. 39). Seventh Street, Washington, D.C., is one of the new homes of the former rural people in their flight from death and oppression. A shortage of labor in the North, because of World War I, is one incentive for the Great Migration. Untrained and unskilled for city work, the innocent, hopeful seekers soon discover that "only whites need apply" for what jobs there are. Exclusionary politics is not peculiar to the South, and most doors to economic and social advancement are just as closed to blacks in the North. The resourcefulness of generations of learning how to survive comes to the rescue. Prohibition gives them a chance to turn their moonshining expertise into an even more lucrative endeavor than it had been "down home," with the advantages that the work is not tedious, the hours are flexible, and the pay is very good.

The black presence makes an impact on the city. The folk bring a dynamic strength with them from the South, and the "crude-boned, soft-skinned wedge of nigger-life," with a pragmatic approach to the problems of strain and stress, breathes "jazz songs and love, . . . [and] unconscious rhythms . . . into the white and white-washed wood of [culturally repressed] Washington" (p. 39). The city will never be the same again. Color—literally and figuratively—has come to it, bringing new life in its wake.

This new life, new blood—strong and potent, black reddish blood, aggressive and pregnant with the will to live—forces its way into the "stale, soggy wood of Washington." It is too strong for some: "Blood suckers of the War would spin in a frenzy of dizziness if they drank [it]" (p. 39). Others would like to stop its flow: "Prohibition would put a stop to it," but it will not be deterred. Instead, it will absorb everything along the route of its flow, and the narrator, in mock wonder, and sarcastic about the "white and whitewash" that it devastates, asks where it gained the power that propels it "down the smooth asphalt of Seventh Street, . . . [from] shanties [of black people], [into] brick office buildings, theaters, drug stores, restaurants [of white people], and [back to the] cabarets [of black people]? Eddying on the corners? Swirling like a blood-red smoke up where the buzzards fly in heaven?" (p. 39). Even God does not escape its challenge or the narrator's satiric comment: "God would not dare to suck black red blood," not unless he is a "Nigger God!" "Who set you flowing?" the narrator asks.

There are no delicate sensibilities here, no sunsets and dusky colors; there is aggressive force that cannot be ignored. The flow of this life-giving blood is associated with violence, and all the imagery of "Seventh Street" reenforces that concept. From the blood and ashes of so many Tom Burwells, phoenix-like, a new people have begun to rise.

"Seventh Street" is an extended metaphor for the black life that entered the city at a particular time in history. The prose poem captures the irony and pathos of that entry. The bastard of prohibition and the war, Seventh Street is a "natural" child, denied a name, and with no legal claims upon its sire: it is an offspring of the failure of America and the West. Robbed of its rightful heritage and forced to be an abused slave in the household of its father's other children, in righteous anger it comes to claim its place in that father's house. Nor does it come meekly, beseeching charity, or love, or justice at the back door. It enters forcibly, tearing at and splitting the portals.

"Seventh Street" exudes the energy and determination of the black people who left the oppression of the South, those who did not share the fates of Karintha, or Esther, or Louisa. Beyond disillusionment and hurt, separated from the land and soil of two pasts, they know they can return to neither. Rather, they face the challenges of a different place, resistant to them, too, with the aggressiveness and resourcefulness that do not easily concede defeat, even against awesome odds. The irony of their existence and the pathos of their condition are balanced by their ability to take a practical approach to the needs of survival. They transcend insurmountable hardships through the creativity of poetry and music.

From the initial shocks of new confrontations and difficulties, the folk people make adjustments to urban life and discover new meanings for themselves in its seductions and rewards. "Rhobert," the second prose poem of the section, explores how "Seventh Street," blinded by the dazzling aspects of an improved condition of life and inexperienced in appraising its true merits, loses its soul in the mire of modern urban life. Like the Israelites in bondage in Babylon, these people too forget the songs of their fathers in this strange land.

Rhobert's sense of values, in his new life, is the issue. Material goods and social conventions have become his main concerns, and they cause a moral disfigurement in him. His present condition—entrapment by the physical and mental accoutrements of his social status—is analogous to the physical deformity of his "banty-bowed" legs, which he has as a result of having had rickets as a child. The narrator is not unsympathetic to Rhobert's plight. The experiences of deprivation in early life leave Rhobert vulnerable to a distorted sense of values.

Rhobert and his house are inseparable. He is the "stuffing" of the house—the dead thing stuffed with the living man.

> Rhobert wears a house, like a monstrous diver's helmet,
> on his head. . . . Rods of the house like antennae of a dead

thing, stuffed, prop up in the air. . . . He is sinking as a diver
would sink in mud should the water be drawn off. . . . Life is a
murky, wiggling, microscopic water that compresses him.
Compresses his helmet and would crush it the minute that
he pulled his head out. (p. 40)

Rhobert's preoccupation with his "house" causes him to lose his
perspective on what constitutes the important things in life, such
as relationships with people. Nor is he even aware of this problem.
Instead, he sinks happily into the mud of his disfigurement: "And
he cares not two straws as to whether or not he will ever see his
wife and children again. Many a time he's seen them drown in his
dreams and has kicked about joyously in the mud for days after"
(p. 40). Although he holds him up to ridicule, the narrator does not
dismiss the seriousness of Rhobert's case. The narrator exhorts the
reader not to forget Rhobert's fate after he sinks from sight and
suggests that a "monument of hewn oak, carved in nigger-heads"
be placed on the spot where he goes down and that the tragedy be
commemorated by the singing of the folk song/dirge "Deep River."

In "Seventh Street" and "Rhobert," Jean Toomer again demon-
strates his ability to manipulate language and to control stylistic
techniques. Satire, sarcasm, and ridicule are the principal literary
tools he uses to explore the violence, ambiguities, and uncertain-
ties of life in the North for southern black people. They have
escaped the more overt oppression of one region for the more
covert and psychological oppression of another.

Human disease and physiological defects enter *Cane* for the first
time in "Rhobert" and will reappear later in this section of the
book. Always, these are symbols of greater psychic damage in the
victim. The energies and possibilities of "Seventh Street" are often
subverted and perverted by the attractions and distractions of a
repressive world.

"Seventh Street" and "Rhobert" are full of violence, but in the
first sketch, the violence represents the infusion of life into some-
thing dead, the creative violence that enhances human freedom. In
the second sketch, the violence represents decay. In "Rhobert,"
Toomer also changes the meanings of images to explode their fa-
miliar significations. In "Rhobert," "microscopic" water crushes
Rhobert, and mud-dreams drown him; the house, the dead thing,
has the live man for stuffing; and Rhobert is an "upright" man
with banty-bowed rickets legs, whom people call a strong man.
The loss of human values does violence to the human being.

Rhobert's values "weigh" him down so that he cannot escape drowning. The "antennae," which should warn him of impending danger, are imminently waiting to "cave in and [cause his] stuffing [to] be strewn . . . shredded." His Adam's apple "strains" as he fights to hold on to life by breathing and fights to let go of it simultaneously.

Finally, the narrator satirically presents God as a Red Cross man. He built the house and waits on the "opposite periphery" of earth and heaven with a dredge and a respiration pump to rescue Rhobert, who obeyed him by becoming the stuffing for the house. Thus, the figure most associated with helping human beings creates the calamity rather than relieves it. Extensive use of word play and double meanings reenforces the themes that reveal Rhobert as both a grotesque and a pathetic figure. "Rhobert" warns of the tragic consequences of misplaced values.

"Calling Jesus," the third and final prose poem, extends and elaborates on the meaning of "Rhobert." It features a black woman who has lost sight of her soul. The soul, a "little thrust-tailed dog," follows her around constantly during the daytime. She ignores it except in periods when she forgets the routine of the life that occupies her most constantly. In such moods, she changes: "Her breath comes sweet as honeysuckle whose pistils bear the life of coming song" (p. 55), and the fractured parts of her merge into wholeness. At other times, at nights, she leaves the soul in the vestibule of the building in which she lives, exposed to the cold. Kindly people rescue it and often take it to her as she sleeps.

For all of this gross neglect, the soul never deserts her. Each day it follows her around, both where the streets are lined with blooming trees and where there is only dusty asphalt. It embodies the remembrances of southern cane and cotton, of shanties where the folk sang and loved, thoughts forcing life in an enervating environment. "Calling Jesus" speaks to the loss of the spiritual aspects of the soul of the folk culture in the urban environment. The images are restraining and antihuman: storm doors, iron hinges, vestibules, and dusty asphalt. But the positive values of the folk heritage are never completely extinguished and can be revived whenever the effort is made.

The religious imagery makes this piece close in tone to the Georgia narratives. The narrator pleads for the renewal of values associated with the rural culture by emphasizing their redemptive qualities in comparison with the negative influences of the urban environment. The folk spirit waits to be "cradled in dream-fluted cane" (p. 55).

The five poems of Section 2 reflect the themes of the prose poems and narratives of the section, providing further insight into the narrator's vision of black urban life. "Beehive," "Storm Ending," and "Her Lips Are Copper Wires" are closely connected to the three prose poems. They are all concerned with the initiation of black people into a new environment and with their experience with a new system of values. The final poems of Section 2 extend the narrator's sense of disillusionment that is illustrated in the narratives.

"Beehive" compares the black community with a black beehive at night, and recalls the energy of "Seventh Street." As black people break into the whiteness of Washington, so the bees, swarming and buzzing intently, pass in and out of the pale moon. This is productive energy, and the "silver honey [comes] dripping from the swarm of bees" (p. 48).

The poet, on the other hand, calls himself "a drone, / Lying on my back, / Lipping honey, / Getting drunk." He places himself in the position of an observer of the activity as one who participates in its rewards without having contributed to its making. As the narrator of *Cane*, he recognizes the richness of the culture and is satiated with it. Anticipating the frustrations and pessimism that will follow, he wishes he could return and remain in an earlier time when life was easier and more innocent.

"Storm Ending" advances the action of the previous poem through an analysis of how external violence makes inroads into a vulnerable culture. No longer hiving bees, black people become "Full-lipped flowers / Bitten by the sun / Bleeding rain." In a reversal of the positive qualities of nature, both the rain and the sun have become hostile and are the perpetrators of pain. The flowers, great, hollow, and bell-like, are offspring of the storm that "thunders" them "gorgeously" and has them "rumbling in the wind." The poem emphasizes the clash between beauty and destruction, as the life of the flowers, which had once been like honey, drips away. "Storm Ending" comments on the loss of the positive aspects of the rural culture and on the rise of urban ugliness as "the sweet earth" flies from "the thunder" (p. 49).

In the third poem, "Her Lips Are Copper Wires," the narrator as persona is more intimately involved with the culture and addresses it as an agent providing love and care. Earlier values now rejected, this poem is a companion piece to "Rhobert" and "Calling Jesus," and what is important to the speaker is what he sees. He concentrates on the mechanistic attributes of his object of affection: the gleam of yellow globes of which she whispers, the instant contact with the "power-house," and the flashy billboards. Like Rhobert, he welcomes and craves the attentions of the automaton whose lips he wants pressed to his own until they become as bright and glowing as hers. The poem satirizes the adoption of the values of the mechanized, industrial world.

These poems move from that which has been positive—if not "good"—to that which is negative. The writer maintains a tension throughout the poems that comes from his awareness that the victims of the violence of the Georgia scenes are losing the values that were the most important strengths of their earlier experience.

"Avey" is the first realistic narrative in Section 2 of the book. Here the storyteller recalls events from his childhood and young adulthood, which can also be seen metaphorically in relationship to his search for a cultural identity. Avey, as Woman, was at the center of the life and thought of his boyhood and that of his young companions from their first sexual awakenings until they became young men. They pursue her, angrily at times, always lustfully, and she mostly ignores their advances. In many ways, her behavior recalls that of Fern, the unreachable woman, for whom boys and men compete and never understand why they are motivated to do so.

On this literal level, Avey is another woman in a world in which men define women sexually. Because she does not conform to their expectations of her, they become anxious, frustrated, and even violent toward her. One way of reading the end of the story is to see her, in her rejection of a male-defined womanhood, as a woman in control of her selfhood.

On a more symbolic level, Avey represents the creative elements of the black folk culture that were brought to the North. The narrator and his friends are the urban black people who recognize the culture's values but who exploit them for self-serving purposes that do not enhance or enrich themselves or others. The four episodes of this account take place in Washington, D.C., and Harpers Ferry.

In the first, in Washington, we meet the narrator and a group of his friends holding a curbside conclave. They are at that stage in adolescence at which they realize that girls are "more . . . than . . . skirted beings whom boys at a certain age disdain to play with"

(p. 42). It is also a time in a sensitive person's life when he compares himself with inanimate things. For instance, the narrator feels a similarity between himself and the young trees lining his street, which have not yet "outgrown their boxes." He thinks their vigorous roots, in their box confinement, must feel as his own legs do when he sits on the curb for a long time and they grow cramped and stiff from the cold stone. One of the group's favorite pastimes is to hack the trees with their knives. He believes that the trees are as restless as the boys and "whinnied to be free."

The narrative begins on the night when Ned, the one of the group most superior in his "smutty wisdom" on the "emotional needs of girls," wore his first long pants. The event also marks the narrator's first awareness of his sexuality. The boys discuss Avey, who at the time is visiting with an out-of-town college man in the apartment building before which they are congregated. While the others are purely aggressive in their sexual fantasies of her and plan to "stone and beat that feller out of town," the narrator realizes he has come to "love her, timidly, and with secret blushes," and Ned's bawdy boasts cause "something like a fuse" to burn up inside him (p. 42).

The curbside session reveals the activities of a group of adolescent boys straining at the boundaries that separate childhood from adulthood. The recognition of male and female sexuality is a hallmark of this period of development. The physical violence of the knife-hacking of the young trees is a mirror image of the pent-up psychological violence that they release mainly through language. The talk of girls as "skirted beings," the boys' chagrin at Avey's attentions to the man from out-of-town, Ned's boasts of sexual conquests and his appraisal of women's needs—"they werent much different from men in that respect. . . . 'It does em good'"—and his impatience to have Avey for himself: "hell, bet I could get her too if you little niggers weren't always spying and crabbing everything," are examples of this psychological distress.

Avey's cool aloofness is in marked contrast to the anxieties and frustration of the boys. Her evening with the young man over, she leaves the building "as unconcerned as if she had been paying an old-maid aunt a visit" (p. 42). The play on sexual images continues as the narrator "turned hot as bare pavements in the summertime" when she passes by. She ignores the group, seeming not to see them, while they watch her until she enters her own door. In their newfound sexual awareness, they see her only within the confines of their sexual fantasies. They even predict that she will soon leave home to marry someone. Ironically, when the gang breaks up, it is the narrator who "went home, [and] pictured [himself] married."

The second episode, still in Washington, begins with the narrator's lament: "Nothing I did seemed able to change Avey's indifference to me" (p. 43). The adolescent boys are seriously competing against each other for her attentions. Each excels in sports—the narrator in basketball and swimming—and each hopes his accomplishments will cause her to take a special notice of him. Avey is polite and impartial toward them, but she does not give approval to their rivalry by acknowledging it.

Her attitude produces great frustration in the young men. They seem forever searching for ways to please her sufficiently to earn her attention, but they do not know how to do so. She strains their patience when their efforts to "buy" her favors by spending their money on her bring no results. The socially prescribed routes to success, especially in the world of men—perseverance, competition, sports, and the power and politics of money—are no match for Avey's indifference: "I'd meet her on the street, and there'd be no difference in the way she said hello. She never took the trouble to call me by my name. On the days for drill, I'd . . . call for a complicated maneuver when I saw her coming. She'd smile appreciation, but it was an impersonal smile, never for me" (p. 43).

When the narrator finally gets Avey alone, he is with her on the dance floor of a boat on the Potomac. A good dancer himself, he believes that this is his perfect opportunity to conquer the elusive maiden. But his hopes do not materialize: "although I held her tightly in my arms, she was way away." Then, as they sit on the deck of the boat in the moonlight, she takes him in her arms, but surprisingly in a manner that is humiliating to him:

> I could feel by the touch of it that it wasnt a man-to-woman love. . . . I felt chagrined. . . . She ran her fingers through my hair and kissed my forehead. I itched to break through her tenderness to passion. . . . I wanted her to love me passionately. . . . I gave her one burning kiss. Then she laid me on her lap as if I were a child. Helpless, I got sore when she started to hum a lullaby. (pp. 43–44)

He has pursued her unsuccessfully for years, but when she claims him, she does so on her own terms and in a way that leaves her in control. Like the male figure in "Fern," he decides to reorder the balance of power by talking: "I knew damned well that I could beat her at that." But his tactic does not succeed: "Her eyes were soft and misty, the curves of her lips were wistful, and her smile seemed indulgent of the irrelevance of my remarks. I gave up at last and let her love me, silently, in her own way" (p. 44). At the end of the second episode of "Avey," the attempts of the men to entrap Avey within their vision of her have failed, and the narrator is confused and ambivalent about himself and her.

The third episode moves the action up one year, takes it out of Washington, and places it in Harpers Ferry. Overt sexual imagery dominates the scene. The narrator and Avey are sitting on a "projecting" rock called Lover's Leap. The river is six hundred feet below, and the whistle and echo of the engines of the train in the valley sound like gasps and sobs to him. He thinks of them as "crude music from the soul of Avey." They hold hands, and he wants to make love to her. He kisses her and fondles her breasts. She sits with him on the rock for many evenings. He worries about her reputation, but she seems impervious to the possibilities for scandal. He thinks it would be easy for him to have his way with her, to "strip" her "like a tree." However, when his passion flares, Avey takes his hand and holds it until his "pulse cooled down." She never loses her control over her actions and does not allow him to dominate or manipulate her.

Avey's uncompromising behavior produces conflicts within the man's feelings for her. The narrator, even as he presses his suit, is ambivalent about her. He finds other areas of her life about which he can be negatively critical. He is particularly piqued at her lack of "ambition" for the future, which he measures against his own desires to go to college and achieve "success." Her lesser goals permit her to accept employment at a normal school. He "resented . . . her downright laziness. Sloppy indolence." He thinks she is no better than a cow and is certain she is one when later he feels an udder of a cow in a stock-judging class at the University of Wisconsin.

At the university, "among those energetic Swedes," the narrator makes up his mind to forget Avey altogether. He does not see her for two years, and they never correspond, a fact that he blames on her "laziness." Yet, at the university, he discovers that the women whom he meets, who give themselves to him "completely," do not excite the passion in him that he had experienced in just holding Avey's hands. Neither time, distance, nor physical absence lessens her attractions for him, and he remains frustrated over her. He cannot have her in the way he wants, he tries to reject her, but he cannot forget her.

The episode concludes on a discordant note. The narrator, having failed to "succeed" at the university, leaves it for "good" without accomplishing anything. He returns to Washington hoping, for his own peace of mind, that the city has "forgotten" Avey. To his discomfiture, Ned, "between curses" of outrage at his failure to "have" her, declares "she was no better than a whore." For himself, he decides that she is irremediably intractable because her mother is an "old pinch-beck, jerky-gaited creature." Only Avey is in calm control. When she loses her teaching position, she sends the narrator a note in a perfumed envelope. Years later he remarks that he has never forgotten its faint smell.

The concluding episode, which takes place five years later in Washington, comes after a period in which the narrator has experienced many unfulfilled expectations. His high hopes for himself, beginning with the promise of a university education, have ended in his admission that "the business of hunting a job or something or other had bruised . . . [his] vanity so that . . . [he] could not recognize it" (p. 45). In this condition of collapsed ego, his soul yearns for Avey desperately. Hearing that she has moved to New York, and having no money to travel there in a conventional way, he hitchhikes and works in a shipyard on the way to the city. At nights, he searches the streets for her, but without success. Feeling more defeat and failure, he returns to Washington and unexpectedly encounters her on a street there. It is an evening in June, at the "time when dusk is most lovely on the eastern horizon," and her eyes "were still sleepy-large, and beautiful" as he remembered them from years before. She was walking with a man, and her dress seemed fine and costly, but she readily left her companion to join the pining narrator.

He takes her to the park overlooking the city, holds her hand in his, and recounts his life during the period in which he has not seen her. He also tries to tell her that his earlier perceptions of her have changed:

> I traced my development from the early days up to the present time, the phase in which I could understand her. I described her own nature and temperament. Told how they needed a larger life for their expression. . . . I pointed out that in lieu of proper channels, her emotions had overflowed into paths that

dissipated them. I talked . . . about an art that would be born, an art that would open the way for women the likes of her. . . . I recited some of my own things. . . . I sang a promise-song. (p. 46)

At this point the narrator believes that he has achieved a new level of awareness in relationship to Avey, a spiritual instead of a physical union. He is so pleased with himself that he fails to note, until hours later, that she does not respond to him, not even to the "strange quiver" in his voice: "her hand had not once returned a single pressure." Then he discovers that she has fallen asleep. His passion dies.

Not wishing to disturb her, and unable to leave her alone in the park, he borrows a blanket from a neighbor close by, covers her, then sits with her through the night even though his body grows numb with the cold. In the faint light of morning "the Capitol dome looked like a gray ghost ship drifting in from sea. Avey's face was pale, and her eyes were heavy. She did not have the gray crimson-splashed beauty of the dawn. I hated to wake her. Orphan-woman" (p. 47). He loses his vision of Avey as a creative force.

"Avey" represents another attempt in the narrator's search for cultural identity. In this narrative, as in others, Toomer uses black women to symbolize aspects of black culture. Avey has the same sensuousness as the women in the Georgia narratives, and she is as elusive as they are. The narrator and his friends, black people removed from the land and soil of the past, find their efforts frustrated when they attempt to appropriate elements of the culture for their own self-serving ends.

Of all those proffered by the others, the narrator's attentions are the only ones that Avey encourages. From the beginning, he has feelings for her that go beyond the immediate gratification his friends are seeking at her expense. He does not try to buy her favors, and it is he with whom she dances and sits on the deck of the boat in the moonlight. She tries to nurture him. Nature enters the second section of *Cane* for the first time when he gives himself up to her ministrations in the second episode of "Avey." Then the "air was sweet like clover, and every now and then" one could sense "a salt tang, a stale drift of sea-weed" (p. 44).

For five years he tries to find a place in the world and hopes to forget his past. He attends the university and has a variety of jobs, but his efforts fail. Then he experiences a new magnetic pull toward his first love, who represents that early part of himself. Before he finds Avey, he feels alienation and a diminishing of self: "I felt old," he notes, and he knows that he wants to see her. He walks and works in search of her, and when she reveals herself to him, having been there all along, images of nature return to the narrative. The place to which he takes her recalls the nature imagery and innocence of "Karintha." In this place one can find "the simple beauty of another's soul. Robins spring about the lawn all day. They leave their footprints in the grass. . . . the grass at night smells sweet and fresh because of them. . . . Washington . . . [is] a blush against the darkened sky. . . . And when the wind is from the South, soil of my homeland falls like a fertile shower upon the lean streets of the city" (p. 46).

In the park, he perceives the beauty, simplicity, and fecundity of the pastoral in his southern heritage, while in the sterility of the city, which he associates with the North, the narrator is in the presence of the Janus-face that is his reality. In a building in the distance, a band plays in a jarring key—"like a tin spoon in one's mouth," he observes. Close to Avey, in harmony with the folk spirit, he wishes to hear instead the Howard Glee Club singing "Deep River, Deep River." Avey accepts his mood. She slips her hand into his and rests comfortably against his arm. She kisses his hand in a gesture that indicates her need for his nurturing, then like a secure child, she falls asleep.

Avey cannot participate in his exuberance as he reiterates his hopes because she is the past, her day is done, and he goes on into the future. All he can do is to sit up in the cold night while she sleeps and cover her with a blanket. The scene represents the wake he holds for her waning soul, for in the new day the gray ghost ship of the modern industrial world renders her obsolescent. In "Avey," the narrator discovers more about the truth of his identity and the past.

In "Theater," the second narrative in this section of *Cane*, Toomer uses the divisive effects of class distinctions among black people to continue to explore the negative results of unnatural social restraints. Uneven opportunities were responsible for promoting this particular problem within the black community in post–Civil War America. In "Theater," the narrator skillfully addresses the question of what happens to human closeness when it is punctured by social-class divisions.

The setting is the Howard Theater in Washington, the performing center for Howard University. Instead of projecting the image of the university as an arm of Western education for the "civilizing" of black people, the introduction to the theater emphasizes its closeness to "Seventh Street," to the cruder life of the black southern soul:

> Life of nigger alleys, of pool rooms and restaurants and near-beer saloons soaks into the walls of Howard Theater and sets them throbbing jazz songs. Black-skinned, they dance and shout above the tick and trill of white-walled buildings. At night they open doors to people who come in to stamp their feet and shout. . . . Songs soak the walls and seep out." (p.50)

Left to themselves, the walls are "sleeping singers."

At the center of the action are John, a writer and a brother of the manager of the theater, and Dorris, a woman who dances in the chorus. John is the victim of his social position, and like Rhobert, he is sinking into the mud of his respectability. Dorris, like Etty Beal, is a dancer and an artist; neither is thought respectable by the black middle class. It is afternoon and the dancers have assembled for a rehearsal. John, who comes to watch, sits at the center of the theater, where the light from the window above streams down on him, casting one side of his face in brightness and the other in shadows. The external separation of light and dark is an expression of his real self. On one hand, he embodies the living elements of his cultural heritage, because his presence has the ability to cause the walls to "start throbbing with a subtle syncopation . . . [as] the space-dark grows softly luminous"; and on the other, he is entrapped by his social status. His thoughts are the light on his face, but his actions are the shadows.

As the rehearsal gets underway, John is aware of the tension between the free artistic expression that many of the dancers possess and the efforts of the director to keep it in control. The walls awaken when the pianist begins to improvise jazz. As the girls in the chorus begin to dance, he notes that their movements are partly crude, partly individualized, yet monotonous. In his mind he urges them to break free of the director's control before they are tamed and their "sharp thrusts" made "blunt . . . in loosely suggestive movements, appropriate to Broadway" (p. 50). They laugh and shout as they "sing discordant snatches of other jazz songs," and they "whirl with loose passion." The mood of the room is hypnotic: "Girls dance and sing. Men clap. The walls sing and press inward. They press the men and girls, they press John towards a center of ecstasy" (p. 51).

One dancer, more impressive than the others, catches his attention. As John and Dorris become aware of their mutual attraction, they also become conscious that a formidable social distance separates them. Dorris takes John's measure and senses his ambivalence, but her own "glowing is too rich a thing to let her feel the slimness of his diluted passion." He takes in the potential he sees in her body: "Her hair, crisp-curled, is bobbed. Bushy, black hair bobbing about her lemon-colored face. Her lips are curiously full, and very red. Her limbs in purple stockings are lovely. John feels them. Desires her. Holds off" (p. 51). Ideas of a cheap affair with her run through his mind. He dismisses them. He could not trick her into it because "her suspicion [of his motives] would be stronger than her passion." She thinks that perhaps she should settle for an affair as a way of establishing a relationship with him. Then she would make him love her. At least, she would get a pair of silk stockings out of it. She dismisses the thought: "O will you love me? And give me kids and a home, and everything? [I'd like to make your nest, and honest, hon, I wouldn't run out on you]" (p. 52). She decides to win him with her dance.

As she begins, all attention flows to her and her sense of freedom is contagious. The stage men from the wings come out to watch the show. All around, black faces crowd in to see. The other dancers forget their set steps and make up their own, and even the director forgets his role and allows this outburst of expression. Dorris dances: "Glorious songs are the muscles of her limbs. And her singing is of canebrake loves and mangrove feastings. The walls press in, singing. Flesh of a throbbing body, they press close to John and Dorris. . . . John's heart beats tensely against her dancing body" (p. 53).

While Dorris dances, John dreams, transporting them both in his imagination beyond the concrete reality of the theater. He sees Dorris dressed in a loose-fitting black gown with lemon-colored ribbons splashed over it. Still in his reverie, he walks toward the stage door, and although there are no trees in the alley, he imagines that he is walking on often danced-upon autumn leaves and that the air smells of roasting chestnuts and burning old leaves. Dorris's face is the color of the autumn-tinted alley, and her perfume is of old flowers or a southern cane field. He walks into a room: "John knows nothing of it. Only, that the flesh and blood of Dorris are its walls. Singing walls" (p. 53). He reads from his own manuscript. When he arrives at a dancing scene, "the scene is Dorris. She dances. Dorris dances. Glorious Dorris" (p. 53).

Reality intrudes on John's dream when the pianist crashes a

bumper chord to signal the end of the dance on the stage. The live performance was magnificent, and everyone applauds. Dorris looks to John hoping to discover that she has reached him, that the passion she feels in her soul will be reciprocated. "She seeks for her dance in [his face]." What she sees is his whole face in shadow. "She finds it a dead thing in the shadow which is his dream." Overcome with disappointment, she rushes to her dressing room, and through her tears stares at the whitewashed ceiling with the "smell of dry paste, and paint, and soiled clothing."

Although John has the ability to inspire artistic expression in himself and others, his life denies it. His identity—imaginative writer, on one hand, and stage manager's brother, on the other—is one of conflict. Dorris tries to save him, but fails. The separation of these two people by artificial standards of class shows how repressive conventions of modern society stifle humanity.

With another cast of characters, and a different set of circumstances, Toomer relentlessly pursues the subject of Western civilization's restrictive codes in conflict with the natural free spirit of human beings, and he shows the enormous toll the former exacts from the latter. Black people—cultural outsiders, still bearing remnants of their past, but anxious to assimilate into the mainstream—are the latest victims. In the third narrative, "Box Seat," Toomer combines the boxes of the young trees of "Avey" with the seats in "Theater" to create a powerful narrative of victimization.

The opening image—"Houses are shy girls whose eyes shine reticently upon the dusk body of the street. Upon the gleaming limbs and asphalt torso of a dreaming nigger"—sets up the dichotomy between the woman in a condition of repression and the man as a free spirit, a dreamer, a poet. Dan Moore, unlike John, the dreamer in "Theater," has no social position to protect. Born in a cane field, he is only a poor black man out of work, but he is a natural singer. He comes to people's houses as a savior, urged by the narrator to "stir the root-life of a withered people. Call them from their houses, and teach them to dream" (p. 56). The images of the houses are analogous to those that describe Rhobert's house, and Dan Moore's mission is to set the "house-girls" free.

Dan walks down chestnut-lined Thirteenth Street, where the eyes of the houses, like "soft girl-eyes," touch him faintly as he passes and stir him. He wants to sing, to make music. However, when he tries to do so, he cannot. His voice is hoarse and it cracks. He tries to whistle, but the notes are shrill. Something in the houses keeps him from expressing himself. He concentrates on the woman he is on his way to visit: Muriel, whose "lips [are] flesh-notes of a forgotten song" he hopes he will recall.

Two images are prominent in this introduction to "Box Seat"— the flesh-and-blood remnant of the folk culture, around whom cling the vestiges of nature, and the repressed culture of the "lean, white spring," which makes the notes hurt Dan Moore when he tries to sing. Black women trapped in the "houses" of this culture look "wistfully over the dusk body." They are still beautiful in spite of their predicament, and he wants to produce a tune "in keeping with . . . [their] loveliness" (p. 56).

Images of nature recede when Dan enters a side street, and in the repressive environment of an iron gate and a doorbell he cannot find, his poetic demeanor undergoes a metamorphosis. Before this point, the houses had looked shyly but invitingly at him; he now wonders if he looks like someone trying to break in. He responds violently to this idea, his thoughts racing through an imagined attack on him and his retaliation:

> Break in. Get an axe and smash in. Smash in their faces. I'll show em. Break into an engine house, steal a thousand horse-power fire truck. Smash in with the truck. I'll show em. Grab an axe and brain em. Cut em up. Jack the Ripper. Baboon from the zoo. And then the cops come. "No, I aint a baboon. I aint Jack the Ripper. . . . Give me your fingers and I will peel them as if they were ripe bananas." (p. 56)

He knocks many times on the thick glass door before anyone comes to let him in.

Muriel lives in a house that is owned by Mrs. Pribby, who finally lets him in. Everything about Mrs. Pribby is associated with the coldness and impersonality of a mechanized world. Dan hates her. She has blue eyes: "the blue is steel," which "gimlets" him as her mouth "flaps amiable" to him. She fits into her chair with a sharp metallic click, "like the sound of a bolt being shot into place," which stings his eyes. The house, "sharp-edged, massed metallic," contracts around him. Mrs. Pribby's house is one in a row of houses bolted down, belonging to other Mrs. Pribbys. All the houses are like close-fitting boxes of steel into which people are bolted, and they, in turn, become a part of them. Dan realizes that was why he could not sing to them. He wonders why Muriel persists in living there.

Muriel is a schoolteacher, and like John in "Theater," she is concerned about the respectability of her profession. While Dan's behavior is openly passionate toward her, although she loves him, she resorts to subterfuge in her conversations with him. She wishes she could love him openly, but she knows she will not violate the social codes of her world.

Although Muriel "clicks" into her chair, there is still a "fresh fragrant something" that is "life" in her face. She is uncertain of herself and feels torn between loyalties to Dan Moore's and Mrs. Pribby's worlds. When Dan looks at her, "her animalism, still unconquered by zoo-restrictions and keeper-taboos, stirs him. Passion tilts upward, bringing with it the elements of an old desire. Muriel's lips become the flesh notes of a futile, plaintive longing" (p. 59). Dan's visit to Muriel is unrewarding to him. The environment of Mrs. Pribby's house prohibits the common meeting of their souls. Although Muriel feels passion for him, she will not let herself be influenced by her feelings. He is angry when he leaves.

The scene shifts from Mrs. Pribby's steel-like, bolted-down house to the Lincoln Theater. Dan and Muriel arrive separately to attend a performance. Here the seats are literally bolted down, and "each [person in a seat] is a bolt that shoots into a slot, and is locked there. . . . The seats are slots. The seats are bolted houses" (p. 61).

In the theater, images of disharmony reflect the public discord of a repressed world and the private conflicts in the world of Dan and Muriel. Muriel's friend, Bernice, is "a cross between a washerwoman and a blue-blood lady." Muriel herself wears an orange dress that clashes with the crimson draperies of her box, which clash with the "sweet rose smile her face is bathed in." The orange of her dress complements the deep purple that comes from her hair, but she hides the dress beneath her coat, which she presses around her to hide her bobbed hair. Teachers are not supposed to have bobbed hair. The audience seems to Muriel like a dense mass, which she would like to protect herself from. She finds the thought ridiculous—these people are her friends; she is pressed down by agitation from her earlier meeting with Dan.

In the meantime, Dan takes his seat next to a "portly" black woman and he begins to dream:

> A soil-soaked fragrance comes from her. Through the cement floor her strong roots sink down. They spread under the asphalt streets. Dreaming, the streets roll over on their bellies, and suck their glassy health from them. Her strong roots sink down and spread under the river and disappear in blood-lines

that waver south. Her roots shoot down. Dan's hands follow them. Roots throb. Dan's heart beats violently. He places his palms upon the earth to cool them. Earth throbs. (p. 62)

But things are not what they seem to Dan. He wakens from his dream to find the woman surveying him with hostile eyes, not the ones of his deep-roots inspiration. From the surrounding aisles, the bolted masses of people press in on him as Mrs. Pribby's house did—these withered people who have lost the ability to dream, to live.

Bored by the performance, Dan dreams of Muriel's intransigence and his own slavery to her. His thoughts are a jumble of fragments: of a dancer not bound by social conventions, whom he once knew; of relationships between men and women; of the slave past; of great historical figures; and of literary persons. He thinks of himself and his mission. He will reach up and "grab the girders of the building and pull them down" (p. 65). From the debris he will rise with the symbols of power in his hands: a dynamo in one and the face of a black god with a flashing light in the other. The flashing light of his fantasy is a flashing mirror held by a performing dwarf, which beams directly into Dan's face.

While Dan is dreaming, the show, an absurd boxing match between two dwarfs contending for the heavyweight championship of the world, entertains the audience. The winner sings to Muriel and offers her a white rose stained with the blood from his bleeding nose. She recoils from the gift as the applause of the crowd, "steel fingers that manacle her wrists and move them forward," forces her to accept. Muriel sees only the disfigurement of the little man, but Dan, looking into his eyes, sees "wisdom and tenderness . . . suffering and beauty." He sees eyes that plead for acceptance.

Dan Moore is out of place in this crowd and his very presence disturbs it. He shouts in language that is unintelligible when he should be silent, and he causes physical discomfort to those around him. He is an actively disruptive element in a setting in which his conduct flouts the rules of prescribed behavior. When he leaves the theater, he challenges a man, whose corns he has stepped on for the second time, to a fight. Then, out in the alley, with the audience following, and where "the alley-air is thick and moist with smells of garbage and wet trash," he walks away (p. 67).

The conflict in the narrative is between the heritage of the folk culture and the new way of life adopted by black people who have rejected the old values. Dan Moore, with his "curled wool-blossoms" and his hard dusk body, symbolizes a remnant of the former, while Muriel represents the new, urban, class-conscious black people. Muriel both loves and fears Dan, but she cannot give up her new position and status to return to him. Dan goes in search of Muriel, but the incompatibility between his world and hers makes it impossible for him to compromise. Muriel tries to get him to change his ways—to "get a job and settle down, . . . to work more and think less . . . [which is] the best way to get along." He cannot do this because he is a poet, a free spirit.

The narrative begins along a chestnut-lined street, moves through an iron gate, and ends in an alley with rotting garbage. Dan experiences only discomfort after leaving the street, and he makes everyone uncomfortable. Only in the dwarf, a misfit in the world, does he find empathy. As he leaves, the soft girl-eyes of the houses blink out, and the values of the folk heritage turn away from the treeless alley of the modern world.

Although the specter of racism is at the heart of *Cane*, overt violent racial confrontation occurs only in "Blood-Burning Moon." In the other narratives, it is the effect of generally nonviolent white racism on black people that provides the background for external as well as internalized oppression. From "Seventh Street" to "Harvest Song," Toomer's main concern has been with the black struggle to define its own identity. In "Bona and Paul," Toomer pursues this struggle from another angle—he makes use of a mulatto protagonist in a last effort at reconciliation between the races.

Paul Johnson, a very light-skinned southern black college student, goes to school in Chicago. He is the subject of racial mystery to his roommate, Art Carlstrom, and to Bona Hale, a southern white woman student, who is sexually attracted to Paul. No one knows for sure, but rumors are that Paul is black.

The first scene occurs in the school's gymnasium, where the students are drilling. They are training to be teachers, and they will go out "into the world . . . to give precision to the movements" of others who have also been drilling for all of their lives. Paul is out of step with the rest of the class. Bona, who feigns illness to avoid the drill, watches him. "The dance of his blue trousered limbs thrills her" (p. 70). She associates him with images of ripeness, an "autumn leaf" and a "harvest moon," and she wonders about his race: "He is a nigger. Bona! But dont all the dorm girls say so? And dont you, when you are sane, say so? That's why I love—Oh, nonsense" (p. 70). In a game of basketball, girls against boys, Bona plays against Paul. They collide, he catches her: "Her body . . . becomes strangely vibrant, and bursts to a swift life . . . ; a new passion flares at him and makes his stomach fall." He looks at her. Together "they seem to be human distortions spinning tensely in a fog" (p. 71).

Back in his room, Paul gazes out of his window, thinking of Bona. Outside, the "South-Side L" divides the window into two: one is Bona, the other is Paul. Through the Paul window, he sees tints of lavender, the glow of the setting sun, and his thoughts carry him beyond the Chicago stockyards, past wheat fields, to a pine-matted little hill in Georgia: "He sees the slanting roofs of gray unpainted cabins tinted lavender. A Negress chants a lullaby beneath the mate-eyes of a southern planter. Her breasts are ample for the suckling of a song. She weans it, and sends it curiously weaving, among lush melodies of cane and corn. Paul follows the sun into himself in Chicago" (p. 71). He looks through the Bona window. She is in dark shadow.

Paul, the "song," is the offspring of the union of the fecundity suggested by the image of the black woman and the seed of the white planter. Paul is nourished by the spiritual and artistic richness of black culture, which he takes into the white sterile world of Chicago schools and restaurants. Paul is distinguishable from the other people around because he is more exotic than they are. Could he be, they ask themselves, "a Spaniard, an Italian, a Mexican, a Hindu or a Japanese?" But he is more fundamentally different from them—"out of step" with the "rhythmical and syncopated" movements of their lives and thoughts. Yet, part of him comes from them.

Paul and Art are roommates—the "art" of Paul struggles to be both parts of himself. Paul loves the blond, slick-haired Art, who is a "purple fluid, carbon-charged, that effervesces beside him," this "pale purple facsimile of a red-blooded Norwegian friend of his" who plays jazz, "tearing down" the piano. Art loves Paul, too. Sometimes responsible for arranging Paul's social life, Art worries about Paul's blood, for his "dark blood" makes him "moony." Yet he is unsure of who Paul is: "Dark blood; nigger blood? Hell of a thing, that Paul's dark" (p. 72). Paul wants to make "art" a part of his whole life, not just the dark part that amuses him at night. He thinks: "I've got to get the kid to play that stuff [jazz] for me in the daytime. Might be different. More himself. More nigger. Different? . . . Curious, though" (p. 73). Paul's goal is to achieve reconciliation between the world of cane fields and the world of Art through the medium of art.

The task of creating wholeness out of the fractured relations between blacks and whites in America involves dealing with the doubts, hostilities, insecurities, and ambivalences that have separated the groups for generations. Paul Johnson must first find wholeness in the conflicted parts of himself, which make him different from the people around him; they see only that he is different. At the nightclub he visits with his friends

> a strange thing happened to Paul. Suddenly he knew that he was apart from the people around him. Apart from the pain which they had unconsciously caused. Suddenly he knew that people saw, not attractiveness in his dark skin, but difference. Their stares gave him back to himself, filled something long empty within him, and were like green blades sprouting in his consciousness. There was fullness, and strength and peace about it all. (p. 75)

From this position of creative isolation he sees and understands the meaning of his difference and can accept himself and his double identity. The reality of this identity runs through the narrative in language that combines the images and atmosphere of the Georgia sketches with those of the city sketches. Paul is "cool like the dusk, . . . his dark face . . . a floating shade in evening's shadow." Colors of purple, lavender, and crimson are contrasted with pink petals that are soft, pale, and beautiful. Paul imagines Negro shanties and the singing of the canebrake in a city of asphalt streets, stone mansions, arc-lights, limousines, and the smell of exploded gasoline.

In his relationship to Bona, he aims for a physical and spiritual fusion that will transcend their history. Her attraction to him is sexual and full of ambivalence; she is sometimes passionate, sometimes uncertain. She justifies pursuing him by assuring herself that men like Paul "can fascinate. One is not responsible for fascination." In addition, within her social group, her actions are part of an accepted convention: "not one girl had really loved Paul; he fascinated them" (p. 77). However, he understands that as a southern white woman, she can enjoy the luxury that enables her to "neither love nor hate a nigger," and thus Chicago offers her the opportunity to engage in a superficial relationship with him. Before his awakening to himself, he would have accepted these limits in their relationship, but now he insists that he wants to know her: "You matter. I'd like to know you whom I look at. Know, not love. Not that knowing is greater than pleasure; but I have found the joy of it" (p. 76). When Paul dances with Bona, he feels the beginning of the union he wishes to have with her. On the way out of the nightclub, the Crimson Gardens, "purple like a bed of roses would be at dusk," he explains this to the black doorman. While previously he had only passion and contempt for Bona, whom he did not "know," in the Gardens his thoughts have now become matches thrown into a dark window, the twin of his lighted window. "White faces are petals of roses. . . . dark faces are petals of dusk. . . . I am going out and gather petals . . . I am going out and know her" (p. 78). Before he can reach her though, Bona has disappeared. His attempt at reconciliation has failed.

## I I

In its focus on the urban black experience, Section 2 of *Cane* explores the effects of a restrictive segregationist society on the human spirit and the failure of black people, as a group, to achieve emotional and psychological wholeness in America. In "Seventh Street," the newly arrived rural people break the limits of custom and convention to establish a new life in a new environment. They were propelled into this new environment by the constraints that southern hate and oppression had imposed on them for generations. In the North, self-imposed psychological restraints, such as those seen in "Rhobert," "Theater," and "Box Seat," replaced the overt physical restraints that had been imposed on them in the South. In "Avey," securing a stable, positive black identity in the urban environment involved an understanding of the past, an understanding that could have been a useful asset in the present and for the future. Finally, in "Bona and Paul," the burdens of reactionary history frustrate the protagonist's efforts to forge a reconciliation between racial divisions in his personal relationships. "Bona and Paul" is a companion piece to "Blood-Burning Moon." Both are the only narratives in *Cane* in which white people and black people come together to confront issues of race. Toomer translates the physical violence of "Blood-Burning Moon" into psychological deprivation in "Bona and Paul."

By the end of "Bona and Paul," Jean Toomer had surveyed the

imaginative landscapes of the northern and southern black experiences separately and had written of Paul's efforts to create racial unity. Toomer had examined race and sex, city and country, erudition and unletteredness, beauty and pain as parts of the double experience of which neither stands alone in the search for a secure black identity. On one hand, the past of the folk culture was lost, but its influence was still a vital force for black people; on the other, the present is in flux, in search of direction. In "Kabnis," which is Section 3 of *Cane*, Toomer brings the past and the present together to provide a positive definition of the black American identity.

The final poems of *Cane*, "Prayer" and "Harvest Song," are epilogues to Section 2 of the book and prologues to "Kabnis." In these poems, the persona of "Her Lips Are Copper Wires" loses his desire to embrace the mechanical lover as he surveys the extent of his weakness and looks for more substantial nourishment. "Prayer" is the plea from the individual soul for assistance from the larger Spirit of the world. The poet acknowledges that his existence is formed by the body, the mind, and the soul or spirit. The soul sees both the body and the mind, although not clearly. While it is the most powerful of the entities, the soul is not always able to control the weaker parts, and the speaker is frustrated because of the soul's powerlessness. Thus the poet calls for aid from a more powerful source, for the individual soul is but a "little finger" of the Spirit and needs to be helped to the "lid of its flesh-eye." The plea is made with the assurance that the Spirit of the world does not reside in realms beyond the reach of the poet's call.

"Harvest Song," the final poem, returns to the rural environment and harvest time. But instead of offering the traditional, warm images associated with that time, the poet provides images of hunger, cold, blindness, frustration, and loneliness. The persona, at sunset, is a lonely reaper, isolated from others of his kind across the hills. Although he has completed the harvesting of his oats, he has no feeling of satisfaction in his accomplishment. He is too cold, tired, and hungry even to bind up his stalks. From long hours in the field, his throat is dry; his eyes and ears are caked with dust, leaving him blind and deaf as well as cold and fatigued. And in spite of his hunger, the grain he cracks between his teeth seems tasteless to him. His physical discomfort is too oppressive to enable him to appreciate any immediate comfort.

The lonely, disconsolate reaper looks out across the fields and hills at the other reapers. His own work, given his condition, seems futile:

> It would be good to hear their songs . . reapers of the sweet-stalk'd
> cane, cutters of the corn . . even though their throats
> cracked and the strangeness of their voices deafened me.
>
> (p. 69)

He is an isolated man, lonely with his harvest, but when he beats his palm against the "stubble of [his] harvesting," he feels a pain that keeps him from comprehending his hunger.

In "Prayer," disillusioned with the human condition and the failure of modern values, the poet looks to the superior wisdom of the Spirit of the world—the soul of time. He knows that the desires of the body and the mind can lead to inhumane conditions like the ones described in "Theater" and "Box Seat," conditions that are alien to the human spirit.

The reaper in "Harvest Song," having sown his fields with oats, finds that hunger and separation from his fellow reapers fill him with pain and anguish. Yet he clings to that pain and paucity rather than attempt to make human contact.

Both poems reenforce a sense of the failure of modern values to fill human and spiritual needs. The South has failed, but so has the North, and Section 2 of *Cane* represents the discovery by black people that it takes more than finding a different place to repair the damage that American slavery and American racial attitudes have wrought on their collective and individual souls. The hope in "Kabnis" is for the wisdom to understand the meaning of the northern and the southern experiences in an effort to transcend it.

# The Circle of Experience: *Cane* (3)

**I**

When the poet of "Song of the Son" discovered the beauty and art of the black folk culture, he also came face to face with its deep pain and anguish, results of the wounds of slavery and the poverty and ignorance that informed much of the black experience in America. Dan Moore of "Box Seat" serves as his creator's mouthpiece when he says "life bends joy and pain, beauty and ugliness, in such a way that no one may isolate them" (p. 59), and the slave heritage and folk culture are good demonstrations of that. In his exploration of the black urban experience, the narrator of *Cane* describes the new dilemmas that black people faced in the North and that replaced the old ones the folk had fled when they left the South. The rejection of the old values—former strengths of the folk culture—by the city-bred generations of black people added complications to the search for a black ethos in the early part of the twentieth century.

The third section of *Cane*, unlike the previous sections, is one consistent piece, a single drama, "Kabnis," in six scenes, in which Toomer combines realistic, symbolic, and surrealistic techniques to portray the conflicts that beset his main character. Ralph Kabnis, the protagonist, of Washington, D.C., and New York, now in Georgia to live for awhile, is a teacher with southern ancestry and northern upbringing who stands at a historical and cultural crossroads in search of a meaningful explanation of his own being in time and place. His journey toward that goal incorporates the fears, alienation, ambivalence, and the sense of oppressive control by others that are a part of the heritage of the black experience in white America. At the same time, Toomer also makes Kabnis a comic character and weaves elements of burlesque, parody, and mock epic into his persona. These elements serve to ridicule the situation, and they function as an ironic transcendence of oppression.

Kabnis has recently accepted an appointment in a southern, black educational system. His living accommodations are no more than a one-room cabin in the "quarters," a short distance from the large frame house that "squats" on stone pillars, where the southern black principal, Samuel Hanby, lives. Kabnis's physical appearance and demeanor suggest that he is out of place in this setting. He is a young man with large eyes, thinning hair, a silken moustache, and a weak chin. His brown eyes, in a lemon-colored face, look out on the unfamiliar world with fear and apprehension.

The character of Kabnis embodies a striking duality. On one hand, he is the schoolteacher, who is laughably fearful and seemingly malleable; on the other, he is a sensitive poet, painfully searching for meaning in the black identity. At the beginning of the drama, Kabnis, trembling in the southern night, tells us that the part of him that we see is only the shell that encases the Kabnis who is the "dream." He does not want us to concentrate on the Kabnis who is weak and afraid; he wishes to be seen as the poet who will become the soul of the South. Kabnis notes that "dreams are faces with large eyes and weak chins and broad brows that get smashed. . . . The body of the world is bull-necked. A dream is a soft face that fits uncertainly upon it" (p. 81). With Kabnis, Toomer joined the ranks of authors who explore the tradition of double-consciousness in the black psyche—a significant feature of black American literature.

The drama opens on a Saturday night. Kabnis is having difficulty going to sleep, mainly because he is afraid of the dangers he has heard of and imagines lurking in the southern night. Propped up in bed and aided by the light of a single oil lamp, he tries to calm his anxieties by reading. Shadows from the lamp, like phantoms, dance against the ceiling, the whitewashed hearth and chimney, and the unpainted yellow walls of his room. The book, against his will, slips down, and through the black cracks—the "lips" of the wall boards—the music of the night, the "vagrant poets," invade his domain. The song they whisper adds to his discomfiture:

> White-man's land.
> Niggers, sing.
> Burn, bear black children
> Till poor rivers bring
> Rest, and sweet glory
> In Camp Ground.                    (p. 81)

The implications of his black helplessness, in the face of a white oppression that he fancies sinister and ubiquitous, are sufficient to propel Kabnis into greater paroxysms of fear, and "moisture gathers beneath his arm-pits." His response to his dread of physical violence reveals his ambivalence toward the South: Does it really have a soul? "Soul hell. There ain't no such thing," he feels sure, and he slides beneath the "warm whiteness" of the covers in quest of safety from unseen, unknown terrors.

No comfort is forthcoming, however. Instead, from cracks in the ceiling, "powdery faded red dust," in the wake of a crawling rat, "sprays down" as he "thrusts his head out from the covers" to investigate the source of a slight noise. He wishes for a drink to steady his nerves, but that too is unavailable, for alcohol is prohibited on school property. Then from next door to his cabin, in the hen house, a bird resting on a shelf ruffles her feathers and scratches the soft wood of her perch. Kabnis unleashes all his pent-up anxieties on the unsuspecting creature.

A great deal happens to Kabnis in this first section of the scene, although there is no apparent advancement of the action. Kabnis's exaggerated fears and the historical meaning of place and time for him are the predominant themes. His fears lead him to irrational actions, and these generate comedy and pathos, the latter more so, because those fears, as outrageous as they appear, have their foundations in reality. In the one-room cabin in the quarters, next to the hen house and within view of the "big" house, Kabnis is initiated into the community of his past through the physical baptism of the red dust falling on him from the ceiling—the "dust of slave-fields, dried, scattered"—and the emotional baptism of fear. "No use to read," he tells himself. For his ancestors, barred from learning how because it would make them dangerous, the skill was unnecessary for the brute work that was required of them; for him, his erudition cannot diminish his terror of the night.

The senseless violence that was commonplace in the lives of black and white people in the South for many generations is the subject of Toomer's bitter satire in the seemingly trivial incident that features the restless hen next door to Kabnis's cabin. On the surface it is comic. Kabnis throws his slipper against the wall of the hen's coop and loudly admonishes her to cease her scratching. Frightened by the sudden disturbance, she cackles loudly and is joined by chickens all across the yard in a chorus of nervous cackling. The now-enraged young man jumps from his bed, and mouthing dire threats against her, chases the hen around the adjoining room until he catches her. Next, he "whirls the chicken by its neck, and throws the head away." He snatches up the bloody, headless body, still warm and hopping. He hides it in a clump of bushes, then wipes the blood from his hands on the coarse, scant grass. This is no comic episode but an ironic comparison to racial violence, the bloodied hands of which symbolize the moral irresponsibility of its perpetrator. With scathing wit, Toomer presents a portrait that mirrors the image of the senseless brutality that buttresses the foundations of white power and black helplessness in American society.

Standing outside his cabin in the cool night, Kabnis finds his own concrete doubleness in the quiet that surrounds him. On one hand, there is "the serene loveliness of Georgian autumn moonlight . . . [and] in the valley, a band of pinesmoke, silvered gauze, drifts steadily" (p. 82). Yet the half-moon seems like a white child asleep on the dark-shadowed treetops of the forest, and he thinks of black mothers forced to nurture white babies. He listens as the "white winds croon its sleep-song":

> rocka-by baby . .
> Black mother sways, holding a white child on
> > her bosom
> when the bough bends . .
> Her breath hums through pine-cones.
> cradle will fall . .
> Teat moon-children at your breasts,
> down will come baby
> Black mother. (p. 82)

Nature's ambiguity confuses Kabnis and does not help him to resolve his ambivalence about the South. If anything, the beauty and the ugliness together are agonizing. An all-ugly world would be a less difficult one in which to cope. The "hills and valleys [are] heaving with folk-songs," but he, so close to this "radiant night that touches" him, cannot reach it because of the contradiction in his double reality. "Whats beautiful here?" he asks himself. "Hog pens and chicken yards. Dirty red mud. Stinking outhouse. Whats beauty anyway but ugliness if it hurts you?" (p. 83)

The divided Kabnis does battle with his thoughts in the moonlight, and we are reminded of his doubleness by his constant injunctions to himself to pull himself together. The force of the powerfully divergent emotions that he feels—to curse and to adore simultaneously—seems to threaten him with disintegration. It also leaves him with a profound sense of isolation and alienation: "This loneliness, dumbness, awful, intangible oppression is enough to drive a man insane. Miles from nowhere. A speck on a Georgia hillside. . . . an atom of dust in agony on a hillside? . . . Come, Ralph, old man, pull yourself together" (p. 83).

Kabnis's situation necessitates that he experience loneliness. On the Georgia hillside, he has a feeling of awful separation from those things tangibly close but unfamiliar as well as from familiar people and places far away in New York and Washington. Isolation and "falling apart" are parts of the process of working toward a full sense of one's human integrity. Only in this state of confrontation with aloneness is the self best able to take full responsibility. Kabnis must endure this separation now; later he will bring together the disparate parts of his identity.

This is the last full night that he will spend in the cabin, a place he appropriately describes on several occasions throughout the scene as a hole and a grave; when he leaves it, he will have buried the burden of slave history there. Before he can do this, however, he must accept this history as his own, and he does so symbolically by living there. In preparation for leaving, new awarenesses come to him this night, not inside the cabin, but outside of it, in the moonlight where he feels the weight of his own and nature's duality. A part of the history and identity he accepts is in the recognition of himself as the bastard son of mother earth and "a profligate red-nosed man about town" (pp. 82–83).

Finally, chilled by the wind and sobered by his thoughts, Kabnis returns to his room that now seems to dance and sing in tune with the flames of the crackling, spurting logs in the fireplace. Still, he is unable to sleep. The silence is alarming. He thinks that dead things move in silence and that they are there to touch him. He lights a cigarette and notes the irony that smoking is also not allowed on school property, in a land "where they burn and hang men." The nature of the duality that Kabnis embodies surfaces again in the contrast between his keen insight and his next action.

When he hears a noise, he is sure it is a ghost and again goes outdoors to attack the night, this time with a poised poker. Here Kabnis is a modern-day Don Quixote fighting windmills, for the ghost is only a calf, dragging a yoke to which it is attached, and it scampers down the road as he emerges from his door. He returns to the indoors and wills himself to sleep, for Saturday night has already passed, and it is now Sunday. Thinking of the day's activities to come, he slumbers while the night winds, "like soft-voiced vagrant poets," continue with their song of terror.

The first scene establishes the double reality that Toomer will present through every aspect of Kabnis's experience. Kabnis is pragmatic as well as creative, and at the same time that he is paralyzed with fear, he appreciates the beauty that surrounds him. In the natural environment, there is beauty so breathtaking that it strikes him "dumb," but the "half-moon is a white child" in the bosom of a black nurse and will grow up and oppress her. The squalor of red mud and stinking outhouses are as sharply effective as the beauty of the landscape. All of this "touches" and "tortures" Kabnis. Does he, the educated northern black man, on a mission to "educate" the black South, also believe in the superstition of ghosts? He tells himself: "It wouldnt surprise me at all to see a ghost. People dont think there are such things. They rationalize their fear, and call their cowardice science" (p. 84). Finally, Toomer invests the actions of his character with double meanings that he builds through both comedy and satire. He gives us his simple-minded hero against a backdrop of oppressive white America.

Kabnis begins his inquiry into his identity by a symbolic exploration of the shame of the past. He learns through experience the nature of the fear and helplessness that had trapped generations of black Americans. As he pulls his history together, recording his doubts and ambivalence toward it, his words and thoughts are those that must have been used by his forefathers too in a bondage they could not understand: "Five years ago; look at me now.... How did I ever land in such a hole?" (pp. 82, 84). In a land where justice resides in a white courthouse, where there is no justice for black people, he imagines his own lynching while the rest of the town sleeps. Only in embracing this history can he ever be free of it.

The second scene of the narrative takes place that Sunday in the home of Fred Halsey, who lives in Sempter, the small town near Kabnis's school. Halsey's great-grandfather was an English settler and his great-grandmother a woman of mixed-blood heritage. Photographs displayed around the walls of Halsey's parlor reveal his lineage, and household furnishings tell the history of seven generations of middle-class shop owners. He had deep southern roots that were never transplanted in northern soil. Halsey had left home only once in his life, when he was a boy, to go to school in a distant town. But he did not stay away, and he returned home to work with his father until he was able to set up his own blacksmith's shop. Later he tells Kabnis: "An been here ever since. . . . An its always been [good]; give me a good job an sure pay an I aint far from being satisfied. . . . Prejudice is everywheres about this country. An a nigger aint in much standin anywheres" (pp. 108–9). Professor Layman, a visitor to Halsey's house, is an equally entrenched southerner. By turns teacher and preacher, he has traveled in all parts of the state and "knows more than would be good for anyone other than a silent man" (p. 86). Kabnis's pale face and mild manner are like a shadow in comparison with the strong features and composed demeanor of these men.

It is late afternoon, and Halsey, Layman, and Kabnis are grouped around the cheerily burning fire. The informality of the occasion is apparent in the array of the day's newspapers scattered carelessly on the floor, indicating recent use. The warmth and comfort of the room is in contrast to the outdoors, where the dreary autumn hills beyond look gray, with their unpainted two-room shacks and dark clumps of trees. What in the moonlight was beauty too powerful for words appears ugly in the daylight hours. Halsey's window faces a forlorn, box-like, whitewashed frame church. People are gathering for Sunday evening worship, arriving on foot, by mule, and occasionally in an old car.

The three men exchange pleasantries. Layman accuses Kabnis of being "stuck-up," remaining aloof from the community because he does not like "folks down this way." The host defends his slow-to-speak guest: "Aint a thing stuck-up about him. He likes us, you an me, maybe all—its that red mud over yonder—gets stuck in it an cant get out" (p. 86). Kabnis evades the issue and instead evokes his daytime views of southern life: "theres lots of northern exaggeration about the South. Its not half the terror they picture it. Things are not half bad, as one can easily figure out for himself without ever crossing the Mason and Dixie line: all these people wouldnt stay down here, especially the rich, the ones who could easily leave, if conditions were so mighty bad" (p. 87). His nighttime terrors have turned to daytime forbearance.

Kabnis is not the only northerner in town, and Halsey and Layman discuss Lewis, another young man who recently came South. Without any display of timidity, with no reservations and no apologies, Lewis expresses strong opinions on the life he sees around him. Halsey explains his outspokenness: "I heard him sayin somethin about a stream whats dammed has got t cut loose somewheres. An that sounds good. I know th feelin myself. He strikes me as knowin a bucketful bout most things, that feller does. . . . Damn queer feller" (p. 89). The entire town, both white and black people, are curious and wary about him. He is a potential threat to the fragile racial peace of a small southern town. Among other things, Lewis has been asking questions and taking notes about a brutal murder of a black woman and her unborn child that occurred the previous year. Layman recalls the incident for the benefit of Kabnis, while, audibly in the background, the service is beginning in the church across the way. The dramatic atmosphere is surreal.

Layman tells the tale of horror in "low and soothing tones." The voice of the church's preacher "rolls" into the room in "an insistent chanting monotone" and a woman at the service shouts, "her voice, high-pitched and hysterical." Kabnis is full of nervousness. Partway through Layman's recital, the minister stops speaking as the choir and congregation sing an old spiritual. The rhythm of the story flows uninterruptedly along. The storyteller is recounting how the men had ripped the dead woman's stomach open, let the child fall out, and then impaled it to a nearby tree, when the shouting woman in the church raises a cry that "pierces the room," and a rock, with a note attached, crashes through the window. The note reads: "You northern nigger, its time for y t leave." Kabnis is sure the message is for him. While Halsey and Layman scrutinize the missive, he "freezes" from the fear that "caves him in . . . flows inside him . . . fills him up . . . , [and he] bloats" (pp. 90–91). To save himself, he rushes from the room with all the strength he can gather in his frozen limbs.

In the meantime, a "false dusk has come early. The countryside is ashen, chill. Cabins and roads and canebrakes whisper" (p. 91). The choir sings, "My Lord, what a mourning, / When the stars begin to fall" (p. 91).

The first scene examines Kabnis in isolation, and the second places him in relationship to the community. We learn, for instance, that he has not been particularly gregarious and that he is viewed as feeling superior because he is from the North. Halsey's comment that his reticence comes from being "stuck" in the red mud over at the school carries multiple meanings: Kabnis may be entrapped in his ancestral past, in the mud of "Negro" education, which does not give him access to the reality of black southern life, or by the wiles of such forces as the unscrupulous Samuel Hanby. For one or all of these reasons, he believes that he does not "belong" and is not part of the community. His reaction to the practice of religion that he sees and hears is an indication that he lacks empathy for these people. He believes that their church is a major negative factor in their lives, that it fosters too much emotionalism, and that the preacher is too influential in their thinking. He tells Halsey that this church is different from the one he attends in the North, where people are more sedate and do not shout, and the response he receives is Halsey's derisive "Lungs weak?"

The southern education of Kabnis by Halsey and Layman begins in this scene, and what Kabnis learns from these men are not imagined fears but knowledge that comes from experience. Halsey's main point is that this is the land of cotton in which white people get the boll and blacks the stalk. Layman reenforces this point with the information that a "nigger's a nigger. . . . And only two dividins: good and bad." He points out that the categories are not permanent, that "they sometimes mixes um up when it comes t lynchin" (p. 87).

We learn about Lewis for the first time in this scene. His behavior is opposite to Kabnis's, and he has a political orientation to the problems of the South. He is estranged from the people because they perceive him to be a threat to the delicate balance of the racial peace that exists. Unlike Kabnis, with his concern for the aesthetic, Lewis makes an immediate impact on the consciousness of the black community. The two men become antagonists in the drama.

Race and religion are the two primary forces that define the lives of southern black people and upon which are predicated issues of their survival. Racial inequality and postures of religious subservience keep them from changing the conditions of poverty, ignorance, and psychological and physical violence that the white world perpetrates against them. Both Kabnis and Lewis resent these dual forces, but Lewis expresses his outrage through actions—his open questions, note-taking, and defiance of the status quo make him persona non grata even to those who stand to benefit most from what he does. Yet religion is the one area in which blacks are free to exercise control. Although Kabnis complains of the excesses of emotionalism that accompany worship, each such occasion is an outlet for the music and drama that he, the recording poet, defines as the "soul" of the culture. Scene 2 ends with Toomer having established the positions of Kabnis and Lewis in relation to their dramatic purposes. One is an artist, the other a political activist—each approaches in a different way the search for the ultimate freedom of the black community from the oppression of the white world.

The beginning of the third scene includes many elements that were introduced at the beginning of the drama, but now their meanings have been enlarged. Kabnis is in flight following the rock-hurling incident, desperate to regain the safety of his cabin. In his heightened awareness of danger, he is sure that the fears and anxieties he envisioned in the first scene have come fully to life:

> A splotchy figure drives forward along the cane- and corn-stalk hemmed-in road. A scarecrow replica of Kabnis, awkwardly animate. Fantastically plastered with red Georgia mud. It skirts the big house. . . . Its shoulder jogs against a sweet-gum tree. The figure caroms off against the cabin door, and lunges in. It slams the door as if to prevent someone entering after it. . . . "What in God's name did I run here for? A mud-hole trap. I stumbled on a rope. O God, a rope." (p. 91)

No longer a teacher-poet, Kabnis has become a visual phenomenon. The red dust that sprinkled his head the night before as it fell from the cracks in the ceiling of his cabin has changed into the red mud plaster that now covers his entire body. Halsey's earlier statement that Kabnis was stuck in mud has proved literally true. Kabnis becomes even more fearfully afraid, and his body and mind are in harmonic disarray. On the previous evening in the moonlight, the "big" house had been a "curious shadow in his mind"; tonight in the false dusk, it is an object that looms ominous and that he must "skirt" to avoid. Whereas before he had abstractly imagined his death by lynching, in this scene he actually stumbles over a rope. Escape seems impossible, for the cabin, yesterday's "hole," has become a "mud-hole trap."

Inside the cabin, Kabnis imagines himself trapped between those pursuing him on the outside with "eyes flaring, . . . hounds, [and] shouts" and those on the inside concealed beneath his bed. He grabs a broom to rout the latter from their hiding place, and "violently pokes [the space] under the bed." His frantic efforts yield only the hollow sound of the wood striking the empty washtub stored there to keep it out of sight. The noise unhinges him in the same way as the silence did the previous night. The scene is a burlesque. At the beginning of the drama, Kabnis worries that the fears he imagines in the external environment will lead to his internal disintegration. In the third scene, his fears take over the reality. In the metamorphosis he undergoes, he divests himself of all self-confidence and rationality and becomes the caricature of the "scared darkey."

Halsey and Layman soon arrive at the cabin, and they inform Kabnis that his fears are unwarranted—the message to leave town did not originate with white people, as he had thought: "These aint the days of hounds an Uncle Tom's Cabin, feller. White folks aint in fer theatrics these days. They's more direct than that. If what they wanted was t get y, theyd have just marched right in an took y where y sat" (p. 92). Later, when Lewis shows up, he assures the quivering Kabnis that he himself was the target of the untoward missive. In contrast to Kabnis, Lewis projects a demeanor of positive calm. Nor does the warning of the rock-thrown note intimidate him. He has his own plan of time for leaving the South and will follow his predetermined course. Lewis is "a tall wiry copper-colored man, thirty perhaps. His mouth and eyes suggest purpose guided by an adequate intelligence. He is what a stronger Kabnis might have been, and in an odd faint way resembles him" (p. 95). Each of these two men is acutely aware of the person of the other, and each attracts and repels the other. When they first meet, "there is a swift intuitive interchange of consciousness." They feel the urge to embrace, and they repulse each other simultaneously. When Lewis leaves, the aura of the southern black heritage seems to fuse around him: "A woman, miles down the valley, begins to sing. Her song is a spark that travels swiftly to the nearby cabins. Like purple tallow flames, songs jet up. They spread a ruddy haze over the heavens. . . . Now the whole countryside is a soft chorus" (p. 96). Kabnis hears the chorus—the call to create black art—and he responds to it with his own deep impulses.

At the same time, Halsey, with the help of Layman, undertakes to reconstruct the eviscerated Kabnis. Kabnis, as child or as scared darkey, and Halsey, as nurturing parent, dominate a large portion of the scene beginning with the physical representations of the shadows of the three men against the walls of the lamp-lighted cabin. The cowering Kabnis is like a dwarf beside the "moving shadows of the men [which] are huge against the bare wall boards" (p. 92).

Halsey assumes control of the situation. When he and Layman entered the cabin, Kabnis had confronted them menacingly, brandishing a poker in one hand. Halsey now disarms him, pushes him into a chair, orders Layman to build a fire and heat water in the kettle to give the besplattered one a bath, and finally hands him a bottle of "corn licker." "This'll straighten y out a bit," he announces to the nervous Kabnis. Furthermore, he tells him that it is "good stuff! . . . Th boys what made this stuff have got th art down like I heard you say youd like t be with words" (p. 93). Symbolically, Kabnis begins as "stuff," the scarecrow stereotype of the disemboweled black man, evolves into a child under the care and attention of Halsey, and in the end matures and makes art.

Halsey even defies the local authorities in his intention to remake Kabnis. When the black school principal, Samuel Hanby, expresses outrage at the violation of the ban against the use of alcohol on school property, Halsey, without consulting Kabnis, informs Hanby that the younger man is resigning his teaching position to join Halsey in his blacksmith's work: "I'm takin him home with me. . . . He's goin t work with me. Shapin shafts and buildin wagons'll make a man of him what nobody, y get me? what nobody can take advantage of" (p. 94). Caught between the intimidation of Hanby and the benevolent paternalism of Halsey, "Kabnis wants to rise and put both Halsey and Hanby in their places. He vaguely knows that he must do this, else the power of direction will completely slip from him to those outside" (p. 94).

Because he is emotionally fragmented, he is unable to resist this unwelcome domination. He gives himself up to Halsey who, when both Lewis and Hanby have left, arranges the washtub for the bath and fusses over Kabnis "as if he were a child." He and Layman have the last words of the scene:

> Layman: Teachin in th South aint th thing fer y. . . . You ought t be way back up North where sometimes I wish I was. . . .
> Halsey: An [for us] there'll never be no leavin time . . .

Kabnis's escape from Halsey's house because he is convinced that a white lynch mob is hunting for him again combines the elements of pathos and burlesque. These dramatic techniques enable the artist to seriously explore beneath the surface of experience in his search for an emotional and intellectual understanding of some of the pain that permeates the soul of black America. Kabnis discards the roles of education and rational thought in his behavior. He enters into the realm of how it feels to be aware of the all-encompassing fear experienced by powerless blacks in white America. It is unmitigated pain.

As the symbol of black fear in this scene, Kabnis is all that is pathetic in the black experience. He embodies its sheer terror and the humiliation of absolute helplessness. However, the debasement in this image is offset by the presence of Halsey, Layman, and Hanby, southern blacks who show that there are ways to cope and survive in a hostile environment without a complete loss of dignity. But their ways do not offer healing for the ever-present internal dread with which they live, and Toomer implies that there is need for new sources of strength to restore a spiritual wholeness to black America.

Scene 4 serves as a transition between Kabnis's life in the cabin and Halsey's industrial, small-businessman's world, and it introduces new characters who will be significant in the later part of the drama. A month has passed since the previous events occurred. Halsey's workshop, with its age-worn walls of falling plaster and exposed "gray and cob-webbed" laths on the inside and "crumbled and peppered with what looks like musket-shot" on the outside, is the physical setting for this scene. Images of decay are everywhere. Old wagon wheels and broken parts of even older wagon wheels, broken shafts, and other outworn wooden items litter the floor. One wall has a window with many broken panes, the chimney is rickety and smoke-blackened, and a pile of assorted junk is directly behind the door that leads to the cellar. Readers are reminded of Kabnis's feelings about his old cabin when we learn that this underground room is called the "Hole." The fire blazing in the hearth provides the single aspect of warmth in the environment. The Hole is the home of a very old man, and it is also the place where Halsey holds parties. In this scene, we learn that Kabnis has become an apprentice blacksmith in Halsey's shop during the past month.

In his own milieu Halsey is "wonderfully himself in his work overalls" (p. 97). Lewis notes that he "fits here. Belongs here. Is an artist in his own way." When he went to school he could not find in books "th feel t them there tools," and so he returned to his tools. His figure is solid and commanding as he stands in the doorway of his shop watching the street.

On the other hand, Kabnis is out of place in the workshop. Hard, physical labor has not produced in Kabnis the kind of toughness that Halsey had hoped it would. Halsey's superiority is made clear as Kabnis stoops beneath Halsey's arm in order to pass through the door. He looks "awkward and ludicrous, like a school-boy in his big brother's overalls" (p. 98). In addition, he is inept at his new trade and suffers the good-natured teasing of all the men.

Lewis, too, has had an unproductive month and is preparing to leave the South. The townspeople, afraid of what his actions might precipitate, have treated him with suspicion. To maintain communal peace, they blame their problems on boll weevils, God, and the war: "Weevils and war are the pests God sends against the sinful. People are too weak to correct themselves: the redeemer is coming" (p. 99). Lewis is not optimistic about change in the current social and political situation, and he is skeptical about whether Kabnis can do anything to improve it.

The new characters who now enter the drama are the old man who lives in the cellar and Halsey's adolescent sister, Carrie Kate. Few people except Carrie Kate pay any attention to the old man, who is very old and ostensibly deaf, mute, and blind. He seems to occupy a world all his own. Carrie brings him his meals and shows general interest in his welfare.

Carrie is a breath of new life in the action of the drama. Her virginal qualities are contrasted with the cynicism, disappointments, compromises with life, and skepticism of the other characters. Lewis notices that she is unaware of the struggle that she will face in her life, which will dissipate her potential: "He sees the nascent woman, her flesh already stiffening to cartilage, drying to bone. Her spirit-bloom even now touched sullen, bitter. Her rich beauty fading" (p. 101). He reaches out to her and takes her hand. There is a sunburst in her eyes and with his own he extends to her the call to life. She pales and pulls away from him, and he feels his own life "burdened with impotent pain."

Halsey continues to be the center of attention, the role he assumed in the second scene. His life represents the stable black presence in the South. Self-employed in a trade for which there is always need and which creates no conflicts within the community, he achieves a sense of personal worth through work that satisfies him and does not challenge the social system. Carrie Kate, with her uncertain future, represents the youth of the black culture; the old man is a composite of its history. Lewis disturbs the peaceful rhythm that the community struggles to maintain. His activities suggest the disruptive changes which are so threatening to the status quo that oppressed and oppressors join in an unspoken pact to stave them off. The men in Halsey's shop at lunchtime disperse silently as soon as he appears. They do not wish to be identified with political confrontation.

By the end of the scene, Kabnis has seen many aspects of black southern life. He is learning about its strengths, weaknesses, and strategies for survival. The fire he stokes in the hearth by constantly feeding it fresh logs—and to which he is so close that the heat stings him—is the physical representation of his efforts toward a more comprehensive understanding of the black experience. In the room, as the air gets heavy with the smell of pine and resin and the green logs spurt and sizzle, Kabnis imagines that his great reward will be the ability to express the black aesthetic.

The penultimate scene of "Kabnis" begins with three powerful, opposing images that represent a benevolent nature, the white oppression of black people, and the spiritual destitution of the man-made environment. In the first, "night, soft belly of a pregnant Negress, throbs evenly against the torso of the South. . . . a womb-song. . . . Cane- and cotton-fields, pine forests, cypress swamps, sawmills, and factories are fecund to her touch" (p. 103). This portrait of an enriching, bountiful nature is immediately offset by the second image. Kabnis hears, once again, the oppressive song of the night wind that sings of "white-man's land." The third image takes on the physical characteristics of the small southern town. It is late and the streets are deserted except for an occasional lone figure hurrying along:

> White paint on the wealthier houses has the chill blue glitter of distant stars. Negro cabins are a purple blur. . . . Winds stir beneath the corrugated iron canopies and dangle odd bits of rope tied to horse- and mule-gnawed hitching-posts. One store window has a light in it. . . . two men come out . . . Pause . . . say goodnight. Soon they melt in shadows thicker than they. (p. 103)

The chill, disintegration, commercialism, and thick shadows are the physical manifestations of the sterility and impersonality of industrialization. As *Cane* draws to a close, images of wholeness and decay continue to demonstrate the double nature of the human condition.

Five people enter Halsey's dark workshop. The interior space of the ground-floor level of the building reflects the bleakness of the external environment, from the dismantled wagon resting on wooden blocks, bereft of its wheels, to the "unearthly hush" over the place, which casts an instant pall over the group, and the "weirdly" whispering night winds, whose song penetrates the cracks in the ceiling. The atmosphere of decay and lifelessness makes it an incongruous place in which to anticipate an evening of fun and gaiety.

Halsey leads the way down into the Hole, where more images of decline and death are dominant. But down there, the warmth of the stone walls, clay floor, and candle-light illumination, which gives an illusion of infinite space, combines with the intimations of decay to suggest that it is both a womb and a tomb. The conflicts of the double reality are salient here. Ensconced in a high-backed chair that stands on a low platform, the old man who lives here sits like "a bust in black walnut." The shavings on the floor resemble the wood out of which he might have been carved. He is "gray-bearded. Gray-haired. Prophetic. Immobile," indifferent amidst the chaos and clutter of half-burned candles, rickety chairs, mattresses on the floor, whiskey glasses on the table, and broken wagon wheels. He is called Father, and Lewis immediately thinks he must be Father John: "a mute John the Baptist of a new religion—or a tongue-tied shadow of an old" (p. 104).

Lewis is given his most active role in this scene, both as a foil to Kabnis and as the voice of insight into the experiences around him. Still the outsider, he represents and articulates a different answer to the pain and frustrations of black life—an answer that is unacceptable to the others. In the end, he finds his isolation and his awareness too much to bear, and he disappears into the night and out of the play. As a foil to Kabnis, he is reticent, thoughtful, and withdrawn, while Kabnis is loquacious and exhibitionist in his behavior. Kabnis disparages Father John while Lewis studies him and speaks of his own relationship to the old man. At various times during the evening the two young men regard each other with surprise, "furtive hatred," and mutual disapproval.

Despite the efforts of Halsey, Kabnis, and the women at different times during the night, the party does not materialize into a light-hearted event. Instead, a strong compulsion forces each to recall some aspect of the burden of personal history. Only Lewis, however, takes Father John as a point from which to understand himself. On one hand, he sees the old man as a

> slave boy whom some Christian mistress taught to read the Bible. Black man who saw Jesus in the ricefields, and began preaching to his people. Moses- and Christ-words used for

songs. Dead blind father of a muted folk who feel their way upward to a life that crushes or absorbs them. (p. 105)

At the same time, he recognizes the old man as a way of understanding both the pain and the beauty of the South. He sees in him images of

white faces, pain-pollen [that] settle downward through a cane-sweet mist and touch the ovaries of yellow flowers. Cotton-bolls bloom, droop. Black roots twist in a parched red soil beneath a blazing sky. Magnolias, fragrant, a trifle futile, lovely, far off. (p. 106)

For Lewis, the old man is a symbol, the flesh and spirit of his past. From him, he sees that the black heritage combines "Master; slave [and] Soil," the hurt and pain as well as the stern substance that insured black survival in white America.

In this scene, Toomer "masks" and "unmasks" his characters to convey the difference between reality and pretense. Halsey, who until now has been the most stable force in the play, reveals the depths of his frustrations and disillusionment with life. His earlier rejection of education, he explains now, was a result of his awareness and resentment of the inadequacies of black education and of the limited options that educated black people have in American society. Although he knows his trade well and feels that his performance in it gives him a measure of independence and integrity, much of his success is the outcome of knowing how to "play dumb naturally t white folks." He even admits that partly he compensates for his feelings of inadequacy through his treatment of black women, particularly in his abuse of Stella, a young woman of the town.

Kabnis, on the other hand, has been the spectacle of all that is weak in the human response to the conditions of an oppressive culture. The extent to which this display has been a camouflage comes gradually uncovered after he puts on a gaudy ball costume he finds hanging on a wall in the Hole. Dressed in it, he carries out an imitation of a grand march around the room and appears both pompous and grotesque: "His eyes are watery, heavy with passion. He stoops. He is a ridiculous pathetic figure in his showy robe" (p. 109). Yet, in this disguise, for the first time in the drama, the real Kabnis unmasks himself in the presence of others and ridicules those who have called him weak. Rejecting what both Father John and Samuel Hanby represent as viable elements in his heritage—the Negro preacher and the black handpicked teacher—he claims his place in a long line of "orators," those who have used words to neutralize the insults of white oppression:

> I've been shapin words after a design that branded . . . m soul. . . . Been shapin words t fit m soul. . . . sometimes theyre beautiful an golden an have a taste that makes them fine t roll over with y tongue. . . . [Sometimes] th form thats burned int my soul is some twisted awful thing that crept in from a dream, a godam nightmare. . . . An it lives on words. . . . Misshapen, split-gut, tortured, twisted words. (pp. 109–10)

While Lewis looks back to the slave heritage for identity, Halsey concentrates on the oppression that stifles black growth and development in America, and Kabnis shapes his own and black America's image in words, Stella addresses the sexual oppression of black women at the hands of white and black men. "Boars an kids an fools—thats all I've known," she laments. But it is also Stella who, as the symbol of the abused folk, would like to take Kabnis "to some distant grove and nurse and mother him," nurture what his words imply. The female-identified attributes of the black folk culture that Toomer refers to throughout *Cane* are sharply focused in Stella.

By the end of the scene all of the actors on stage have divested themselves of the masks they usually wear to conceal their pain in living. Racial and sexual oppression have touched and blighted each one, but each has had the strength to cope. The psychological duel between Lewis and Kabnis ends when the former feels the pain "too intense" and leaves. Kabnis, on the other hand, remains and establishes himself as the poet who will "feed the soul" through his use of all their words. He knows his strength: "You little snot-nosed pups who've been making fun of me, an fakin that I'm weak. Me, Ralph Kabnis weak. Ha" (p. 110).

Throughout the first two sections of *Cane*, the narrator examines various aspects of the black experience and evaluates their merits in relation to his own identity. What "Kabnis" does is to pull these disparate parts together as the protagonist of the drama undertakes the final step in defining the meaning of his personal existence in the larger culture. The writing of this book is an artistic effort to understand the problems of personal and group identity.

The narrator of *Cane* and the protagonist of "Kabnis" are the sons of sons of southern soil, themselves removed in time and place from the full experience that shaped the culture of which they are part and from which they can never completely separate themselves. They are also artists who undertake the monumental task of portraying, in language, for themselves and for posterity, the full humanity and meaning of that culture. In the first five scenes of "Kabnis," the protagonist of the piece absorbs within himself the pain, fears, and intimidations that have been the central elements of its shaping, and in the final episode he is part of a resolution that embodies the acceptance of both the suffering of the past and the hope of the future.

It is daybreak, the morning after the night of the party that was not a party. Earlier intimations of the Hole as a womb are physically clearer, foreshadowing Kabnis's new perspectives on his life when he emerges from it. In the dawn it "swims in pale phosphorescence. The table, the chairs, the figure of the old man are amoeba-like shadows which move about and float in it" (p. 111). Halsey and his guests, emotionally exhausted, and assisted by generous draughts of corn liquor, have slept where we left them last.

Halsey is the first to awaken. In an effort to restore the balance of everyday living that the night's events disrupted, he is anxious to get to work, so he rouses the others. Amid protests, the two women comply, getting dressed and leaving the Hole for the breakfast he prepares. But although once again he assumes the parent role with Kabnis, calling himself a "kindhearted father" and Kabnis a "son," the younger man does not follow this time; instead, he remains behind, caught in the grip of a new and different kind of birth. He and the old man are alone in the Hole.

Kabnis finds himself at the opposite side of the room from Father John, just as he finds himself at the opposite end of their shared history. Without benefit of choice, he also finds himself sharing the responsibility to lay the foundations for an aesthetic appreciation of black culture. To carry out his mission, Kabnis must make the journey across the space between himself and Father John, literally and symbolically, and he must first understand the meaning of the old man and the journey. Jean Toomer makes such a journey through the writing of *Cane*—a journey that begins with the southern slave heritage and ends with the emergence of the New Negro of the Harlem Renaissance. In effect, *Cane's* most enduring contribution as a cultural representation is in its role as an instrument that seeks to destroy the shame of an undignified past and reveal the humanity that undergirds the strength and survival of black Americans.

As the light of the new day filters in through the small, high windows near the top of the stone walls of the Hole, Kabnis, still dressed in the gaudy masquerade costume of the previous night, tries to make his way across the room to Father John. Twice he begins, but the effects of the night's drinking and the clumsiness of the robe trip him, and he falls to the floor. Time passes. Then he "internally gathers himself together" and covers the intervening space without further incident. With the side of Father John's face directly in his line of vision, he now confronts the past.

It is a past that discomposes Kabnis. While the others in the room slept soundly, in spite of his near inebriation, he had heard the old man mumbling "death" throughout the night. What could he mean by that? Had not the old man (slavery) "died way back there in th 'sixties"? Kabnis is angry. He does not wish to remember or extol that part of himself. Yet he feels forced to stay in this place, now alone with the old man and the "clammy floors . . . just like th place they used t stow away th worn-out, no-count niggers in th days of slavery" (p. 113). He had thought that was long ago, but in fact it had not been.

He rants and raves in the presence of the seemingly unseeing, unspeaking, unhearing old man, searching for connections and disconnections between them. For all of his shortcomings, Kabnis has seen beauty in living, and having been touched by it, can never lose it altogether. He knows the sightless old man could not have had the same experience, not with his eyes "dull and watery, like fish eyes. . . . dead eyes" (p. 113). Buried alive, twenty feet under the ground, never again to see the light of day, even if he were not blind, how could he ever understand beauty?

His harangue breaks off as Halsey's young sister, Carrie Kate, arrives with the old man's breakfast. Lewis had seen her as a new woman, and in the morning light "she is lovely in her fresh energy . . . , in the calm untested confidence and nascent maternity which rise from the purpose of her present mission" (p. 114). In addition to food for Father John, she brings a message from Halsey for Kabnis. He is needed to help with the repairs of a broken wagon. The girl offers to help him to rise from his position on the floor so that he can heed her brother's call. But Kabnis knows that it is not his body that needs to be lifted up, rather it is his soul. The call to assist Halsey is not important in the light of what he really needs to do, for finally he acknowledges that he can only find his life "down in this scum-hole," and from the old man. "He's deaf; but he's a good listener. An I can talk t him," he tells

Carrie, to which she replies, "He's deaf an blind, but I reckon he hears, an sees too. . . . th souls of old folks have a way of seein things" (p. 114).

In this place in which Father John's place in history has been rightly acknowledged, the old man finally speaks. This is the moment for which Kabnis has been waiting a long time. Having acknowledged the importance of the past, he looks to it for guidance about how to act. But the old man has no new words to absolve Kabnis of the accountability of his future actions. Kabnis rails, but Carrie's reverence for the old man enables Kabnis to discover that the past best serves as the source from which to take strength to fashion the future. On his knees before her, his face pressed tenderly against her freshly starched dress, he is ashamed of and exhausted from the effects of his untoward behavior to the old man. This is the beginning of his wholeness.

As he prepares to leave the Hole, Carrie helps him to get up and take off the costume he has been wearing. Then she kneels before the figure of Father John. In Kabnis's last vision of them, "light streaks through the iron-barred cellar window. Within its soft circle, [he sees] the figures of Carrie and Father John" (p. 116). He ascends the stairs as the sun "rises from its cradle in the tree-tops of the forest." Unlike the half-moon, the white-child oppressor in the bosom of the forest's treetops, the sun is a "gold-glowing child, it steps into the sky and sends a birth-song slanting down gray dust streets and sleepy windows of the southern town" (p. 116).

The sun and the new day in positive harmony denote the triumph of *Cane*, which is a portrayal of the union of the past with the present, of the black folk culture with its modern counterpart, of those who stayed with those who left—all are part of a whole. Without either self-glorification or apology, the book presents an astonishing vision of the numerous conflicting elements out of which this peculiar culture developed and a sense of the positive identity that it is capable of creating.

**I I**

In the fall of 1921 when Jean Toomer went to Georgia, he was unprepared for the impact that the black folk culture would have on him. But he responded to it fully with all of his latent creative forces. It not only provided him with a muse, but in compelling him to acknowledge a more intimate subjective kinship with it, it gave him the benefit of an internal harmony that he had not known before. Whatever the tensions were between this new cultural relationship and his earlier life, he did not resist them. Instead, he combined both aspects of his being into the writing of *Cane.*

The book is the product of the "wholeness" that he began to experience shortly after his arrival in the South, which lasted until the early months of 1923. It enabled him—for the first time in his adult life—to face the racial ambivalence that had been his nemesis for a long time and to make it an instrument of his creativity. There is something akin to a mystical relationship between Toomer and *Cane,* which is one of the things that gives it the power and depth that have captivated readers for generations.

The imagist narratives and poetry of Section 1 of *Cane* tell us how Toomer perceived the folk culture, and they reveal his own relationship to it. He uses women in these portrayals, associating their beauty, nurturing capabilities, and vulnerabilities with the positive qualities he identifies in the culture, or folk-spirit, as he calls it. Although he feels a kinship between himself and the culture, a part of his painful reality is that he does not feel nor can he develop intrinsically close ties with it, for when he tries, it eludes him. For the most part, he views it almost always in awe, and most often from a distance over which he has no control. Karintha, Carma, and Fern, in particular, embody a mystical quality that the narrator cannot reach. He does not attempt to get close to Karintha and Carma, and the language and style of the sketches reflect the sense of mystery he feels about them. Karintha is connected most memorably with dusk on the eastern horizon, and Carma has all the embellishments of the seductive powers of an ancient goddess. After his distant adoration of the first two women, the narrator desires closer personal contact with Fern. However, for all of his efforts, he does not achieve a closeness with her. An ethereal atmosphere envelops her and places her beyond his physical or emotional reach. His emotional separation from these women is indicated by their lack of interior consciousness. He does not probe the workings of their minds because he cannot.

Natural beauty, strength, and the will to endure in spite of hardships were the qualities that the narrator hoped to express through these women. The diversity of affirmative elements within the culture is reflected in the differences between Karintha's dusky-skinned beauty, Carma's mangrove-gloomed, yellow-flower face, and Fern's creamy, brown-colored upper lip. All three women are beautiful and strong, but the strength of each affects the narrator in a different way. He perceives Karintha's strength in her psychological transcendence over the oppression of her environment, Carma's in the power and magnetism of her physical person, and Fern's in the aura of the folk spirit that pervades her being. All evoke poetic responses in him. But the women are also vulnerable, precisely because they are women, and they are abused. The folk culture is also vulnerable and is similarly abused. As noted earlier, the oppression of both women and the folk culture comes from internal as well as external sources, and it robs them of their abilities to carry out such fundamental functions as loving and caring for others. They spend their energies on self-preservation. The "son" of "Song of the Son," as the narrator of *Cane*, can preserve the memory of the beauty and strength of the folk culture for posterity, which is a laudable undertaking, but the folk-spirit and the women will die leaving no possibilities for their regeneration.

While Karintha, Carma, and Fern symbolize these aspects of the oppression, strength, and survival of the black folk culture, Esther and Louisa represent the negative effects of racial and sexual discrimination on the lives of women. The narrator focuses intensely and in sharp, realistic detail on Esther and Louisa as victims and provides no idealized rustic environment as background to their hard lives.

The portrayal of Esther invites readers to see correspondences between her character and experiences and those of the narrator of *Cane*, who is frustrated in his inability to develop a complementary relationship with the folk heritage. Esther takes the place of the narrator as "son" who finds himself outside of his heritage even in the land of his forefathers. It is significant that Esther is the only woman in the section to whom the narrator gives an interior consciousness. As his alter ego, she and her whiteness represent the gulf—in terms of education, social status, and economic advantages—that separates him from the folk culture. Esther's imaginary black baby, which she thinks is hers and Barlo's, symbolizes the narrator's dream of a contribution to the culture. He envisions making an offering to blackness that will expunge his "whiteness" and bring redemption to all. As Esther offers herself as a sacrifice to Barlo to save him from the wanton women who run after him, the narrator offers himself to save Fern in an effort to embrace his lost heritage. But he is unable to comprehend the full meaning of his loss, and, for all his good intentions, he reaps a harvest of frustrations. The returning black "son" is too white to be black and too black to be white. In this peculiar state of being, he stands outside of both cultures and becomes the epitome of the alienated man. Like Esther, he cannot be held responsible for his dilemma. Once again, the destructive influence of white America on the consciousness of black America—the effects of which are felt through many generations—must be blamed.

This portrait of the nature and condition of the folk culture and of the forces that impinge on the lives of those within it is tragic. Although it embodies indestructible elements, which the narrator believes will eventually be immortalized in art, he mourns because the continual attacks of racism, sexism, and economic disadvantage that the culture has sustained have made its death imminent. Toomer believed that the loss of the "beautiful spirit" constituted a crushing blow for universal humanity. In order to capture that beauty, he had to make the expression of the pain equally poignant. The "feeling" Toomer said he put into *Cane* was that of double tragedy: the death of the culture and the pain of its passing. By 1923, for all of these reasons, the black folk culture was one whose day was past, but in its time it had nurtured those qualities that had made it well deserving of the "everlasting song, a singing tree, / Caroling softly souls of slavery" (p. 12)—the narrator's tribute to both the beauty and the pain.

In surveying the black urban experience, which in 1923 was in its ascendancy, Toomer exchanges the women of the folk culture for male characters who now have the dominant roles. In the second section of the book, he uses images for the urban culture that are the reverse of those he used for the folk culture in the first section of the book. The metamorphosis from country to city changed the essential nature of black culture.

"Seventh Street" addresses the first arrival of a large number of black people in Washington, D.C., the seat of the government, the sire of the country's moral codes. They are, as it were, claiming their right of free access to the capital of a nation that they and their slave ancestors helped to build through the sweat of their labors, the reproductiveness of their women, the whips on their backs, and their economic and social strangulation. But if Toomer greets their arrival with images of strength, he does not maintain those images in what follows.

"Rhobert" and "Calling Jesus" are preludes to "Theater" and "Box Seat," all of which demonstrate the inability of the black urbanites to resist the soul-destroying entrapment of materialism and sterile social conventions. Avey, symbolizing the last breath of the folk culture, dies overlooking the Capitol dome, which, like a ghost ship, bears her soul away, and in "Bona and Paul," hopes of achieving racial reconciliation never materialize.

One of the main differences between Sections 1 and 2 of *Cane* is the attitude of the narrator to the material. The distance he seems forced to maintain in the first part completely evaporates in the second. In the first, he is a distant kin, at times even an intruder; in the second, he is an integral member of the household. In Section 2, Toomer includes a number of autobiographical references and personal experiences, and he depends more on realistic action than on the impressionistic portrayal of the first section. The aura of nature, with its concomitant lyrical language, occurs only rarely throughout Section 2.

That Washington, D.C., is the location where much of the action takes place is natural because until 1923 it was the place where Jean Toomer had spent most of his life. References to the young trees on the street, still in their boxes, to the Lincoln and the Howard theaters, the Howard Glee Club, and the Black Bear Cabaret are recollections from his childhood and later years. Toomer also attended the American College of Physical Training in Chicago, and issues relating to his racial identity occurred both at the University of Wisconsin and in Chicago in the manner in which they are related in "Bona and Paul."

Toomer believed that the passing away of the black folk culture was a tragedy. He grieved for the ultimate loss of those qualities in it that he considered enriching to the universal human spirit. The pain of the loss was not tempered by what he saw in the rising black urban culture, for its survival depended to a large extent on black people's adopting new values that destroyed in them the best qualities of the folk heritage. There is no song in Section 2 of *Cane*, and nature is no more than a dream of things now past when it is mentioned. The overt oppression and segregation of the South become more covert, more insidious, and they lead to a rich harvest of victims who suffer from psychological and emotional alienation. The urban industrial, technological environment has destructive effects on all people, but it is particularly harmful to the black survivors and emigrants from the black folk culture who seek refuge and safety in the city.

When Kabnis goes South to Sempter, Georgia, from New York and Washington, D.C., he does much more than go from one place to another. Kabnis makes a journey back to the black past in America, to the place of origin, and Toomer simulates a psychological journey that forces a confrontation between the remnants of the folk culture and the new black urban culture, disparate entities in his own black American identity. Kabnis goes because "sometime back . . . [his] family were southerners y'know," albeit "Southern blue-bloods," and he returns to be a teacher. From the North, he brings the gospel of education, the new religion that everyone estimates will be the elixir to the underclass. Condescendingly, he even disparages the old religion. "This preacher-ridden race. Pray and shout. . . . That's what it is," he says, although in its presence he feels "mingled fear, contempt and pity" (p. 88).

At the same time, he is aware of the beauty and worth of the folk culture even though it is in its waning moments, and he longs to be the "Son returned in time" to catch the parting song and to make his own songs become the voice of the soul of its spirit. The repressions and frustrations of "Theater," "Box Seat," and "Bona and Paul" in him come face to face with the beauty and strength of "Karintha," "Carma," and "Fern" as well as with the oppression they have suffered and absorbed, with the collective immorality of society expressed in "Becky," and with the brutality of "Blood-Burning Moon." All of these are part of his reality, forces at war with one another out of which he must shape an identity.

Kabnis the teacher fails because he is unable to rise above the threat of physical danger that hovers over black people in the South at all times. His northern erudition does not equip him to do so. Instead of imparting wisdom to others, he discovers that he has much to learn from those who stayed in the South and devised their own ways to survive with dignity. His ideas of an honorable mission are even more deflated when he finds out that he can survive neither by the work of his head nor his hands. In effect, he is disabused of all his pretentions to northern superiority.

As a foil to Kabnis's weakness and fright, Lewis is able to express strength of will and moral courage. He too is from the North, with a new religion: political action. What he fails to realize is that black survival in America has always been political and that the black folk culture is a manifestation of radical politics. In his northern wisdom, he wishes to change the oppressive nature of black southern life through swift and direct means. Like Kabnis, he fails. The people will not follow him.

During his southern stay, Kabnis learns many things about southern history and the nature of southern white oppression of black people. He learns from those who live with it from day to day and must find ways to cope with it. By the end of the drama, he is no longer just Kabnis the northerner whose ancestors came from the South, but a black man who is beginning to understand the meaning of himself as a northerner and as a southerner, that is, as a black American. Given a choice between education, politics, and art as a way of comprehending and fusing the various parts of the black American experience into a whole with dignity, Toomer clearly chooses art. Lewis leaves, and Kabnis gives up teaching, but the poet remains to catch the "birthsong" of a new day's sun and to create the "Song of the Son" through *Cane.*

Many critics of *Cane* focus on the elements in it that celebrate the beauty, strength, and dignity of black Americans and of their folk culture. These readers have been pointing out for decades that one of *Cane's* most important achievements is that it dissipates the shame of the slave past and establishes the intrinsic worth of black culture. That is correct, but the book is also a work about the pain and struggle wrung from the soul of a people and of Jean Toomer's confrontation with the meaning of that awful reality. In this work, nature is not always associated with beneficence, and Toomer shows that cynicism is often closely associated with survival. *Cane* is also as much a work of individual self-exploration as it is a presentation of an all-inclusive Afro-American experience.

By the time Jean Toomer had completed this book, he must have understood the dual meaning of his Afro-American heritage. His early life had precluded much of the knowledge that he uncovered in those brief months in Georgia, and, as a result of that trip, his previous experiences must have taken on new meaning. It is doubtful that he could have imagined the meaning of the intricate interweaving of beauty and pain, joy and oppression, and strength and vulnerability that he put into *Cane* until the book was done. When we recall that he never set out to write "this" book but only to record his impressions of the beauty of the passing folk-spirit, its achievement is phenomenal; besides, it gave him the spiritual and emotional wholeness for which he had been searching for more than ten years. The intersection between art and life in him had made that possible. *Cane* is a work of art, but it is also the result of a lived experience in the dualities of Afro-American identity. Viewed in this light, this book, which is informed, sympathetic, thorough, and honest, allows us to link the portrait and the artist in an effective way. As such, it represents Toomer's search for and recovery of the past, his probings of the meanings of a different place and a new time in black life and history, and his efforts to understand the whole circle of the black experience.

# The Gurdjieff Influence, 1923–1930

I

Jean Toomer completed *Cane* during the winter of 1922–23 and for a few months he enjoyed the exhilaration that comes from a sense of worthwhile accomplishment. But the feelings were short-lived. *Cane* was a "thing that was done," and the harmony he had hoped to derive from it did not materialize. He began to experience new manifestations of old discontents. In December 1922, Waldo Frank, who had convinced Boni and Liveright to publish the work, informed Toomer of what he would include in the foreword he had agreed to write for it. He thought that the most important thing to stress was that the younger writer had risen above the limits of race in writing this book, and in so doing had made a breakthrough for southern literature.[1]

Toomer agreed with Frank's assessment and claimed that he had a "good feeling" about the foreword, particularly about Frank's description of the form of the book as an "equivalent of the land" and of Toomer as "a force, personal [and] artistic."[2] Much later Toomer would say that the foreword was a "tribute and a send-off as only Waldo Frank could have written it," and he had been grateful because it "affirmed" him as a literary artist of "great promise." But he also said that it had upset him that Frank had made the racial issue "evasive" and "indefinite."[3] In yet another document of that later period, he claimed that his "heart sank" when he first read Frank's foreword to the book.[4]

Toomer's ambivalent feelings about the foreword were a result of the unsettling emotions that the book had created in him and his disappointment in Frank because of Frank's failure to accept and act upon Toomer's position on race. Toomer had invited Frank to meet his family in Washington in 1922 and had made a special effort then to discuss his views of himself as a member of the American race with his friend. Frank had seemed to agree and understand, but he did not follow through as Toomer had expected, either in what he told associates of Toomer and himself, or in his foreword to *Cane*.[5] A disgruntled Toomer had expected a full understanding of his philosophical stand on this matter from the literary world if from nowhere else.

In effect, Frank's foreword to *Cane* praised Jean Toomer as a poet who had transcended race and politics for the "fashioning of beauty." He called the book a song and a painting about the black people of Georgia and a drama about the black people of Washington. He noted that Toomer had escaped the propaganda pitfalls of most race literature and had produced a work that augured a robust literary awakening in the South. But Toomer disapproved of Frank's thinly veiled hints that the author of this wonderful book was a Negro.[6] In spite of his feelings, Toomer did not openly complain because of their close relationship and his gratitude to Frank for the part the latter had played in helping him achieve literary recognition. Early in the summer of 1923, Toomer moved from Washington to New York, where he fully entered the literary world.[7] In his inimitable way, for a time, he managed to have an exterior life of calm, order, and balance, and an internal one in which he felt dislocated. "I was a bit of chaos dressed in formal attire," he later noted.[8]

Toomer's literary work had begun to appear in print early in 1922, and the reading public took a keen interest in him after that time. One person with whom he corresponded in the spring of 1923, before *Cane* was published, was Claude A. Barnett of the Associated Negro Press. Barnett was interested in Toomer's racial background because he was sure that the emotional power in his writing indicated that he was not a white man.[9] Toomer told Barnett that he was the grandson of P. B. S. Pinchback and that his "deepest impulse to literature" was awakened when he "peeped behind the veil." Toomer then made this important statement:

> In so far as the old folk-songs, syncopated rhythms, the rich
> sweet taste of dark-skinned life, in so far as these are Negro, I
> am, body and soul, Negroid. My style, my esthetic, is nothing

more or less than my attempt to fashion my substance into works of art. For it, I am indebted to my inherent gifts, and to the entire body of contemporary literature.[10]

Toomer even suggested to Barnett that he would be pleased to write for Barnett's black readership on events concerning the nation and the world and on art and literature. His main ideas would focus on cultural expression through art and literature.

After Toomer moved to New York, he wrote reviews, mainly for *Broom*, and he worked on the outline for what he called "a large complex novel that was to essentialize [his] experience with America."[11] He may have felt ambivalence toward *Cane* and insecurity about his future, but he also found his life exciting, and he said that even more than ever he perceived writing to be a "living thing." In August, he received a letter from Horace Liveright that asked for revisions of the biographical statement he had submitted for the promotion of the book. Liveright felt it should mention his "colored blood," because, he said, that was the "real human interest value" of his story. He urged Toomer to divulge his identity.[12]

In a complete turnabout from the equanimity with which he had met Barnett's inquiry on the matter of his race only a few months earlier, he responded to Liveright's suggestion with outrage. He asserted that his "racial composition" was of no concern to anyone except himself, and he pointed out that he was not a "Negro" and would not "feature" himself as such. He was willing, if he were forced to violate his principles on this, to lose the opportunity to publish his book.[13] Fortunately, such a drastic consequence did not follow, and the book was published on schedule.

However, the end result of his distress with Frank, Liveright, and himself that spring and summer was that by the time *Cane* was published in September 1923 Jean Toomer was no longer committed to excellence in literary art, and he was off on a new search for personal harmony. In his later writings on his emotional state during that fall, he noted how ironic it was that after he had worked so hard and so long for literary recognition, by the time it came—his book was well received and "talked about," and critics saw him as a new voice and praised his talent—it all seemed far away from his immediate concerns. He wrote: "I was in the rapids of the Relentless Stream. Sometimes I was up in the air, suspended between the solid ground and the blue sky. And then one day I asked myself a startling question—Who am I?"[14] He was in a state of internal fragmentation, his writing stopped, and he noted: "My disharmony became distressingly prominent. So it became clear that my literary occupations had not worked deep to make me an integrated man. . . . I became the champion of something non-literary, nonartistic. . . . I had come to the dead end of a direction and realized that the course of my life had led through mazes into a blind alley."[15]

Although the "facts" of Frank's foreword and Liveright's letter have been well-known parts of the Toomer saga for a long time, critics are often still not clear on why Toomer behaved as he did in late 1923 by rejecting the literary world (which some people insist was his turning away from fame) and turning to Gurdjieff's philosophy. For an understanding of these events, we must look back to Toomer's relationship to *Cane* and to his autobiographical writings relating to that time of his life.

Toomer's strong negative reactions to Liveright's request came at the climax of a brief but intense period in his life. Between the end of the spring and the middle of the summer of 1923 he had already lost the "wholeness" he had experienced during the writing of *Cane*. First, after he had given "birth" to the book, and he and it were separated, he lost both the sympathetic and symbiotic relationship he had had with it. For almost eighteen months the *writing* of *Cane* had offered him personal harmony; when it was done, the disharmony within himself that he had lived and struggled with for most of his life returned. Toomer had hoped that literary art would offer an "intelligible scheme" by which he could conduct his life with his soul, intellect, and body in harmony. *Cane* did not fulfill his expectations, for the painful reality he had discovered in his materials offered no vision of a future that would bring the individual closer to the harmony he was seeking. Nor was he willing to accept the burdens of a black identity.

Second, his confidence in Waldo Frank had been largely responsible for his literary aspirations. In conjunction with Frank, Hart Crane, and others, he had hoped to remake American literature, to help to create a world in which the development of the personal being could take place without the presence of such destructive elements as racial designations. Frank's insensitive foreword, which had been motivated by the distressed material of the book, reenforced Toomer's own ambivalence toward the book. The work had accomplished nothing to extricate human beings from the vulnerabilities of the human condition. He noted later that Liveright's interest in the racial angle came about because of the profit motive. This was just one more aspect of modern life he had thought that he and his friends had been struggling against.

He had been upset by his own personal feelings about *Cane* and by Frank's foreword, but he maintained his calm by rationalizing that he was not a "Negro" just because he was referred to as one. However, Liveright's request that he "name" himself as such was another matter, and one that he could not take lightly. His outward calm of the previous months shattered as he expressed outrage and refused to comply with the publisher. He was angry at Liveright, but more than that he saw *Cane* as a dead end because he could not and did not any longer identify with the book. His alienation from it made him see that the literature he had pursued in the hope of a vocation that would bring him internal harmony had betrayed his faith. Once again, the parts of him—his mind, body and intellect—were out of harmony.

In his opinion, his rejection of the literary world, as he knew it, was not capricious. In search of stability, he had looked at the people around him—his literary friends and colleagues—but what he saw had increased his frustration. He felt that their lives were as chaotic as his own but that they were unwilling or unable to face that truth. In fact, he concluded that his personal state of disorganization was no more than a reflection of the state of the world, which he saw as "uprooted . . . [and] breaking down," and he believed that it was not possible to escape the disintegration. Civilization could not move back to the life of an earlier time. The force of its forward motion had destroyed the "bridges" that might have connected it to the past. Although the natural world still existed, its influence was lost to modernization. The peasantry, such as he had portrayed in *Cane*, was swiftly passing, and industry had already devoured nature. He felt a great need for the creation of a "*human world*," one that would challenge the authority and power of technology, with something as "conducive to man's well-being and growth as . . . nature was . . . to . . . plant and animal life."[16] And he wanted to contribute to the building of such a world. Problems of race, nationality, and the like were outgrowths of the general conditions of the modern world, he stressed. But the real culprit was the economic system, which was "mutilating" all classes of people and draining away the spiritual and psychological strength of man. The "split and chaotic" shrinking human spirit and the empty soul were undergoing a slow death. To counteract this, the mind, body, and emotions of each person needed to be brought together in harmony.

The issue of internal harmony was of course an old one for Jean Toomer, but by 1923, he saw that solving one man's problems of chaos was not sufficient. Here was a problem for the entire modern world. He had felt in harmony with himself when he was working on the book, but when it was completed, because the world was the same, his disharmony had returned. The temporary wholeness he had experienced had come from the integration of his artistic self with his emotional identification with the small and clearly defined world of *Cane*. He could not have captured the power he put into the book had he not for that time put himself into the "son" of "The Song of the Son" and into Kabnis. But the extrinsic limitations of these roles only made him more acutely aware of his own fragmentation. The issues were beyond the scope of any individual's private solution. In the microcosm of himself and *Cane*, he could comprehend the entire modern world's chaos as he had not been able to do before, and as others could not. Such were his frustrations throughout the fall of 1923. *Cane* had illuminated the problems for him, but the professional and psychological milieu of which he was now a part offered no light on ways to counteract the negative forces that were increasing and destroying everything that was humane in the world.

These thoughts appear to have fully crystallized for Toomer during the fall of 1923. Horace Liveright's request for clarification of his racial origins came to him even as he must have been pondering their weighty implications for himself, for literature, and for the world. Liveright's assumption of racial separateness as an acceptable aspect of human existence was exactly the kind of thinking that fostered individual and group disharmony, and it was the competitive economic system that was responsible for such thinking. "To compensate for spiritual emptiness," he argued, human beings had "grown fangs and sacks of poison [which typified] man['s] insanity against [other men]."[17] He could not and would not be a Negro and continue to contribute to the human oppression implicit in racial designations. To do so was a violation of his moral principles and a repudiation of the mission he had hoped his writing would serve.

It is clear that race presented a psychological dilemma to Toomer for a long time before 1923, and important evidence of this dilemma begins to appear in concrete form in 1914. In fact, Jean Toomer may well have been trapped by his honest conviction that he had no African ancestry, by his unwillingness to accept the low status of blacks in America, and by his well-intentioned philosophical position that nonracial identity was a viable stance for all Americans. However, before he wrote *Cane*, his ambivalence about his racial identity, based on an intellectual conception of American racial practices, was in the main abstract. During the writing of *Cane*, he discovered, in a concrete way, to what extent black people are held hostage in America. He was then able to make the actual connection between racial oppression and the exercise of power that dehumanizes all of mankind. It is possible that his refusal to acquiesce to Liveright had its roots in a deeply felt personal desire not only to reject black identity but to reject all other oppressive elements of modern society. He tried to discuss the various aspects of the universal problem as he perceived them, but as far as he could ascertain, no one seemed to care or understand. The literati, for all of their antimaterialist claims, were uninterested in the issues he raised. He noted: "I distilled the essence of the literary and art worlds I came in contact with. With this result: that I saw with unmistakable clarity the truth that neither art nor literature were doing for the men and women who engaged in them what was most necessary in life—from my point of view—namely, providing them with a constructive whole way of living."[18] He saw people hopelessly entangled in "emotional snarls and conflicts." The people in art and literature were, in his opinion, in a "sorry state." Around him, and within him, he saw complete chaos, and he knew that he was searching for "a method, a way of living," that he was attempting to find an answer to the development of man.

By late fall 1923, Toomer was alienated from *Cane* and from most of his friends of the previous five years. As winter approached, only Gorham Munson, Hart Crane, and Margaret Naumburg remained within his social circle. Naumburg was Waldo Frank's wife and the founder of the progressive Walden School in New York City. She was interested in Eastern philosophy, and the two began studying together. He said that she came to mean many things to him, and "the fact that she was anti-social and largely negative towards people" was a positive factor in their relationship. This was a time when he did not wish to be sociable.[19]

Late that summer Toomer was a guest in the home of the Franks in Darien, Connecticut. The details of his visit were never publicly revealed, but there were rumors that an affair between Toomer and Naumburg had caused a rift between the men. What is certain is that they quarreled and separated after Toomer's visit. Toomer attempted a reconciliation later that fall, but it never came about. In

October, Frank left the United States for an extended European trip, and neither man ever renewed the bonds that had held them so closely in the early 1920s.

While it is true that Jean Toomer rejected "fame" as a man of letters because it was offered to him on the basis of his "Negro" blood, his rejection was fraught with a complex of emotional issues that have their roots in his search for personal harmony, and it must be understood in that light. It was inevitable that his rejection of *Cane* and the break with Waldo Frank and the world Frank represented had to take place at the same time. They were all of a piece, and symbolic of one phase of his life. The removal of one link in that chain meant the disintegration of the chain. He had rejected other things before, but the implications of this rejection were more far-reaching than any in his earlier life. By turning away from the literary world, he took a radical turn through which he discovered new qualities of temporary "wholeness," but he never found a secure haven for his searching soul.

In the fall of 1923, Toomer, Hart Crane, and Gorham Munson became interested in the ideas of P. D. Ouspensky and F. Matthias Alexander. Ouspensky, a Russian mathematical philosopher, was an early disciple of a Greek-Russian-Armenian mystic named George Gurdjieff. Before that, however, he had written a book, *Tertium Organum*, in which he posited the theory of a mystical understanding of the world. Alexander was a philosopher who stressed the artist's ability to integrate and develop his mind and body. It was during this time that Toomer and Crane discussed ideas for what became Crane's *The Bridge*.

In pursuit of the mysterious knowledge that was supposed to be the key to man's mastery of internal harmony and a harmonious existence in the world, in January 1924 Toomer met A. R. Orage, the New York representative of Gurdjieff. An Englishman with interests in literature, philosophy, economics, and occultism, Orage had become a disciple of Gurdjieff in 1919. Toomer had learned of the Gurdjieff movement from a pamphlet. He later said that on reading about it he "gave cries of joy," for here he found "statement after statement that said what [he] wanted to hear."[20] Orage was preparing the way for Gurdjieff to visit the United States, and Toomer eagerly awaited his arrival. His meeting with Orage severed conclusively any remaining links that he had with the world he had been a part of since 1919.

The American herald of Gurdjieff came with impressive credentials. Orage was apparently a brilliant man; T. S. Eliot once called him "the finest intelligence of his generation."[21] In 1906, having bought the *New Age*, a London literary and political weekly, Orage made journalistic history by using it to play a controversial role in British political and economic movements. He was critical of Fabianism and advocated national guilds. In 1919, Orage helped to found the Social Credit movement. Because his horizons had widened through reading Nietzsche, the *New Age* became a forum for Nietzscheans, and he wrote two small books on the philosopher. In 1922, at the age of forty-nine, Orage sold the journal, and to the chagrin of many of his friends and colleagues, moved to Paris to join Gurdjieff.

Gurdjieff, the embodiment of prophet, priest, king and/or devil, depending on whose view one takes, was a man with a mission to save those of mankind who wished to escape from their "waking sleep." His philosophy owed nothing directly to the great orthodox religions of the world, although he was known to have called it esoteric Christianity at times. In his early years, he had been fascinated by the ruins of Babylon; the Sarmoun Brotherhood, an order of dervishes considered by many to have been early shamans; and other decaying and lost makers of ancient and legendary wisdom. After years of travel in places where he claimed he secured information on these sources of knowledge, he put together a system for human development and set out to disseminate his findings to the world.

Hitherto unheard of in the West, he appeared in the early 1920s in post-World War Europe with its confusions and insecurities, attracted a great deal of attention, and influenced many people of diverse backgrounds to come to the Institute for the Harmonious Development of Man in Fontainebleau, outside of Paris. The time was right. The war to end all wars had only succeeded in making the world "unsafe" for democracy, and middle-class intellectuals in particular were in search of ways to find meaning in the chaos of modern civilization. Gurdjieff had a cosmic view that offered meaning to living through the attainment of higher consciousness. The English were especially intrigued with him; the French were the least impressed. But men and women from Europe and America flocked to the Institute to learn from the Master. However, his mission was only partially successful at best. By 1935, he had all but disappeared from public view and the Institute had been closed for years. He died in Paris in 1949 with little attention from the world at large, but a few days after his death, Frank Lloyd Wright, while accepting a medal in New York for his revolutionary architectural achievements, announced to the audience that Gurd-jieff, "the greatest man in the world," was dead.[22]

Over the years, two schools of thought have grown up around the Gurdjieff myth. His followers, of whom there are still many groups in London, Paris, and at least a half dozen cities in the United States, have always had only glowing praise for him. His presence was magnetic and hypnotic. He was physically dominant, and having seen them, no one ever forgot his eyes. P. D. Ous-pensky spoke of Gurdjieff's "piercing" eyes; others have described them as "unusual in depth and penetration," "the strangest eyes I ever saw"; still others spoke of their power and size.[23] Those who dispute Gurdjieff do so with vehemence. He has been called an inscrutable man, a charlatan, a demonic character, a libertine, and a rascal.[24] More than thirty years after his death, he is still a figure of controversy. Perhaps he was the sum of all of the things that have been said of him.

His writings consist of four books, of which only one, *The Herald of Coming Good,* an introduction to his ideas, was published in his lifetime, although a year after publication it was withdrawn from circulation. Since his death it has been reissued. *Beelzebub's Tales to His Grandson,* his magnum opus, is a critique of man's condition in the world and was published shortly after his death; *Meetings with Remarkable Men,* which describes his years of wan-derings, was issued ten years after his death; and *Life Is Real Only Then, When "I Am,"* a portrait of his self-development, was pub-lished twenty-six years after his death in 1975. Numerous biogra-phies, accounts, and impressions of him and his ideas have ap-peared over the years. Because of who he was, it is impossible to find an objective appraisal of either the man or his ideas or behav-ior. His detractors damn him as they highlight his inconsisten-cies, dishonesties, vulgarities, and crudities; his disciples ratio-nalize these aspects of his character and behavior as necessary manifestations of his ideas. Between a deliberate masking on his part and the mystery that surrounds his early life, Gurdjieff re-mains an enigmatic figure, ignored by mainstream philosophy. One critic described him thus: "His humor was Rabelaisian, his roles dramatic, his impact on people was upsetting. Sentimentalists came . . . and went away swearing that Gurdjieff was a dealer in black magic. Scoffers came, and some remained to wonder if Gurd-jieff knew more about relativity than Einstein. . . . Perhaps . . . "Py-thagorean Greek" is as short a way as any to indicate the strange-ness of Gurdjieff to our civilization."[25]

On his father's side, George Ivanovich Gurdjieff was a descendant of a Greek family, which traced its heritage back to ancestors who fled Byzantium when Constantinople fell to the Turks; on his mother's side, he came from an old Armenian family. According to his passport, he was born in Alexandropol in 1877, but he claimed to have been born in 1869. He grew up in the nearby city of Kars. This entire area, between the Black Sea and the Caspian, was on a heavily traveled route between Europe and Asia, and many languages and cultures came together in these towns. Gurdjieff heard Turkish, Greek, Armenian, Persian, and Arabic, in addition to a variety of dialects of these many languages. His father, who was a bard, told the young boy many stories to enrich his imagination and to teach him certain lessons through indication, indirection, and contradiction. Gurdjieff would use these methods with his own followers later. In addition, the father instructed the son so as to make him fearless and stoical. Among the townspeople, Gurdjieff not only learned languages but he also observed strange happenings connected to clairvoyance, telepathy, miraculous healings, and other psychic phenomena. From all of these influences, he emerged with a burning curiosity to seek out the sources of unknown knowledge and hidden wisdom.

One of the legends Gurdjieff heard as a child concerned the inner circle of humanity, a network of "evolved" human beings with special knowledge who watch over the destiny of the human race. One such group was called the Imastun, which is said to have existed from before the Flood. Another special group, the Buddhists, believe in the reincarnation of certain lamas. Sufis believe in a perpetual hierarchy headed by the Axis of the Age, who receives revelations of Divine Purpose and transmits them through special members of the sect. These special people include the Sarmoun Society, for which Gurdjieff searched for many years. The information he had was that the Sarmoun Brotherhood was a famous esoteric school founded in Babylon around 2500 B.C.; it existed openly in Mesopotamia up to the sixth and seventh centuries A.D., then disappeared. This school was supposed to have had the key to great knowledge and to know many secret mysteries.

For more than twenty years Gurdjieff journeyed through the Near and Middle East, Africa, Europe, and Asia in search of the Sarmoun Brotherhood, which he was convinced still existed but only in hidden places. In Mokara, an old trade and cultural center in central Asia, his quest ended in success, but during his wanderings he had visited and communicated with solitary dervishes, sheikhs, Sufi masters, and Christian monks. For two years of that time, he had studied the laws of hypnotism, suggestion, and the human unconscious, and he had developed extraordinary powers of telepathy and hypnotism. In the Sarmoun monastery he studied the sacred dances that he believed embodied symbols of universal truths that could be transmitted through generations, and he learned the concepts of the material nature of knowledge and of universal laws which became the basis for his cosmology. Gurdjieff later taught the dances to his followers in the 1920s. From his earliest operations—as hypnotist, healer, and wonder-worker in Russia until after he emerged from his travels—the stories told of him were rife with accounts that cast him in the role of a questionable character.

Beginning in 1915, Gurdjieff established himself as a forceful, original teacher. In Moscow and St. Petersburg, where he practiced, he spoke of the "Inner Circle of Humanity," of "schools" and "ways," and of his own version of the "Inner Circle." His package included dances, exercises, gymnastics, talks, lectures, and assignment of housework for groups that lived together from time to time under his supervision. The Russian Revolution intervened, and he and his followers moved through several Russian cities to Constantinople, Rumania, Hungary, Germany, and France. He would have liked to settle in England, but the government would not give him and his followers visas for more than a month. In July 1922, with financial help from a wealthy Englishwoman, Gurdjieff took possession of the Chateau du Prieuré, an abandoned mansion with a neglected park that was located in Avon outside of Fontainebleau. There he set up the Institute for the Harmonious Development of Man, where strenuous physical activities and rigorous exercises in emotional self-control were imposed on those who participated in the program.

The thing that was most striking about Gurdjieff to his Western followers was that when he appeared among them, although he had no knowledge of any European or other Western language, he did have a working knowledge of physics, chemistry, biology, and modern astronomy, and he could make insightful comments on the theory of relativity and the psychology of Freud. A careful examination of his ideas reveals that they constitute a union of selective tenets of Eastern philosophy with some Western theory. The aim of his teaching was to achieve harmonious development through a higher level of consciousness than human beings ordinarily experience. He believed that the higher the consciousness, the greater is man's ability to achieve his potential.

Gurdjieff's system is best described as a "work" with philosophical and psychological bases that engage the physical, mental, and emotional centers of human activity. To strengthen the physical condition, he prescribed work ranging from long hours of kitchen drudgery to felling trees in the chateau's forest to the dances and gymnastic exercises; to strengthen the mind, he prescribed mental exercises that were done simultaneously with the physical activities; and to strengthen the emotional life, he prescribed the stimulation of special music. To these requirements were added his lectures, discussions, and "situations" that created interpersonal friction and that motivated the public acknowledgment of personal problems. These situations were designed to counteract patterns of conditioning so that the "essential" nature of the individual would come to the surface. Together, these activities incorporated techniques of mind and body control that were to result in the development of higher consciousness. The people who have tried to explain Gurdjieff's system point out that it is too complicated and complex for the general unconvinced reader to understand and that Gurdjieff deliberately constructed an enigmatic philosophy. In addition, Western scholars are aware that Eastern thought lacks the logical coherence that is the foundation of Western thought. Eastern thought requires less attention to inconsistencies and discrepancies and focuses on basic concepts for their own merits. The abstruseness of Gurdjieff's philosophy confirmed his contention that self-realization is difficult, and the path that he outlined toward it was as difficult to comprehend as its achievement was to be won. To fully understand, his followers insist, one must be a Seeker.

However, it is possible to understand that the goal of the system was the achievement of higher consciousness so that man could participate in universal consciousness. Gurdjieff wanted his followers to see their suffering, their "nothingness," to know that it was a result of their unrealized potential, and then to sincerely wish to transcend that condition. These are the first steps toward the possibility of higher levels of consciousness, and they are available to everyone.

The Institute for the Harmonious Development of Man offered a program that promised those who followed it an opportunity to transcend the limitations of their ordinary human nature, to achieve different states of consciousness, to acquire new powers of understanding, and to move beyond the conditioning of earth's existence. Gurdjieff aimed to help his followers liberate themselves from the natural laws that separate human beings from cosmic consciousness and circumscribe man's place and function in the universe.

Gurdjieff felt that his system introduced a new approach to the human understanding of the cosmic purpose and offered an opportunity to those who wanted it to aspire toward a higher level of existence. His theory was that humans have latent powers that can be realized through special efforts. Under ordinary circumstances, he believed, no one has the powers of harmonious coordination, but anyone would be able to gain them through his system and eventually play a key role in determining the future of the biosphere. His techniques were united by the principle that the basic three sides of our nature can be developed in harmony, coordinated, and made subject to the discipline of the will.

A year and a half after the Institute for the Harmonious Development of Man went into operation in Fontainebleau, Gurdjieff and a group of forty of his Russian and English followers visited America to promote his school and teaching. They demonstrated the dances and gymnastics in New York, Boston, Philadelphia, and Chicago. Jean Toomer saw them and they moved him dramatically. He wrote the following about the experience: "[T]hey satisfied and exceeded anything [I] could have asked for. . . . [The] . . . gymnastic exercises . . . seemed to take hold of the body and literally recreate it. They were strangely beautiful and profound. . . . They involved the whole man."[26]

Some people who saw the dances were sure that they communicated an occult knowledge that could not be made manifest in other than physical terms. It was also apparent that the movements affected the psychological states of the performers. In place of conventionally graceful dance rhythms, these dances were often angular and included movements difficult to follow or reproduce. Special gestures represented letters of the alphabet, and intricate disjointed steps were connected to the mental exercises. A particularly impressive feat occurred in the "Stop Exercises," which became the trademark of the Institute. Gurdjieff would command his dancers, at any unexpected moment, to stop between positions, as though caught in a photograph, and without changing the tension of their facial muscles, their gaze, or any other vital center of themselves, they had to concentrate on the new grouping of muscles, block out all flow of feeling or thinking, and absorb the new command. These performers had developed a new and nonhabitual sense of balance in which different parts of the body could go in different directions at the same time.[27]

Although the French had been critical of the Gurdjieff dances when they were done in Paris late in 1923 and emphasized the strongly hypnotic rhythms of the music and the puppet-like quality of the performers, many Americans who witnessed the demonstrations were favorably impressed. One critic noted: "Nothing like these dances had ever been seen in New York, and they aroused intense interest. They called for great precision in execution and required extraordinary coordination. One could well believe they were, as claimed, written in an exact language, even though one could not read that language but only received an effect of wakefulness quite different from the pleasant sense of harmony most art produces."[28] The American tour was a financial success. It enabled the new guru to pay off the remaining debts on the Prieuré, and he returned to France with intentions of making another American visit in six months.

Toomer saw Gurdjieff and his knowledge as belonging to an extraordinary body of thought that was different from anything he had previously encountered. He believed that each part of the program belonged to the whole, and the exercises, dances, music, and ideas together evoked in him a world for which he had always yearned. He wrote: "Here was a discipline, and invitation to conscious experiment, a flexible and complete system, a life and way to which I felt I could dedicate my whole mind and heart and body and soul."[29] He thought that the method offered an escape from the chaos of modern civilization and an opportunity for the conscious individual to restore and replenish the starving human spirit.

The goals that Gurdjieff proposed were the ones that Toomer had been seeking unsuccessfully for more than a decade. Toomer had read Eastern writings, including some about Theosophy, before he went to Georgia in 1921, and his excursion into the works of Ouspensky and Alexander—after his disillusionment with *Cane* and Frank's world but before he had ever heard of Gurdjieff—demonstrates an already-serious interest in Eastern thought and the occult. The small sales of his book, contrary to what some critics have suggested, was unrelated to his leaving the literary world. Four months after the book was published, he discovered the system that offered him not merely American identity but full citizenship into the cosmos. The fact that groups of disciples had already formed with the intent of pursuing a higher consciousness made this philosophy even more suitable for Toomer's needs at this time.

During the summer of 1924, Toomer went to Fontainebleau, where he participated in the work of rebuilding and refurbishing the Prieuré. In July, under circumstances that remain mysterious, Gurdjieff drove his car at almost sixty miles an hour into a large tree. He was not killed, but he came close to death, and he had a painful recuperation that lasted for many months. In the meantime, the program at the Institute was thrown into confusion. The Russian students were bewildered and paralyzed with fear about what would become of them. They were foreigners in a strange country, and most of them did not know the language. They had regarded Gurdjieff as superhuman, but they discovered too late that he was not. Many of the English left. By the time Gurdjieff recovered sufficiently to take stock of the situation, he felt forced to abandon his original plans for work and life at the Institute. Instead, he set out to write about his "work," something he had not thought of doing before. Toomer returned to America after a month at Fontainebleau, and by then he considered himself sufficiently knowledgeable to begin to teach the Gurdjieff method himself.

Late in the fall of 1924, Toomer went to Harlem to try to establish a Gurdjieff group there. Orage, who remained the leading Gurdjieff representative in the United States, is reported to have been pleased by this move on Toomer's part because he thought it was significant that Toomer was in Harlem not as an exponent of black or white culture but of human culture.[30] The group did not last long, as Langston Hughes explains in *The Big Sea*. Although Gurdjieff claimed that his philosophy required no change in the external patterns of one's life, it did involve an appreciable investment of time for contemplation and study. Such an expenditure of time was impractical for black people—even the intellectuals—because most of them had to work for a living. Thus Toomer's efforts resulted in little success until he went to Chicago's Gold Coast district, where he did well for a number of years in leading groups from among people in that area.

Between 1925 and 1930 a good deal of Toomer's time was spent in his involvement with the Gurdjieff movement. He had lost contact with almost all of his old friends and acquaintances, and it was only with Gorham Munson and his wife that he remained close. They had also joined the Gurdjieff work. Toomer had visited Gurdjieff at the Prieuré in the summers after 1924 and had also been with Gurdjieff during his later visits to America. In the years following his automobile accident, Gurdjieff had abandoned his original plans for the Institute and, instead, was writing about his program in *Beelzebub's Tales to His Grandson*. No one dared interrupt him. The Institute was closed and there was no direct teaching. However, people came and went—many of them were Americans—and they discovered new ideas for themselves. Orage and Toomer sent money regularly to France to enable the Prieuré to sustain itself, as did many wealthy and generous sympathizers of the movement.

Toomer's efforts to expand Gurdjieff's influence led to what came to be known as the Cottage Experiment. For two months in the summer of 1931, six people lived together in a farmhouse called Witt Cottage in Portage, Wisconsin, and participated in an experiment that was a simulation of life at the Institute for the Harmonious Development of Man. Toomer ran the program. The members of the group did all the work that was necessary for their living and shared what they considered to be spiritual growth. The cottage was near a lake, surrounded by woods, and the group enjoyed rustic isolation. Most of these people had known one another for as long as five years, and some had previously taken part in Gurdjieff groups led by Toomer.

The days were spent mostly out of doors to take full advantage of the fresh air and sunlight. For exercise, the group walked, swam, sunned, and played tennis and croquet in addition to doing whatever manual work was necessary to meet the needs of their living. The evenings were devoted to serious discussions. As Toomer described the experiment later in a manuscript he called "Portage Potential," it was a clean, healthy life that combined psychological effort and outdoor activity. He worked very hard to make the effort a success. He wrote: "I was building a world. I was creating a form. It was to be my own; and I was putting into it a quantity and quality of functional energy greater and finer than I had ever before experienced. I saw the cottage life as an entity, as a single living organism—at least as a potential one."[31] Each person was responsible for his or her own awareness and for working with the others to make the whole experience positive. In the limited space it was expected that there would be interpersonal frictions and conflicts. People were also forced to do particular tasks that they disliked in order to reproduce the procedures that had been practiced at the

Prieuré. These tasks were techniques for learning to control both the body and the mind. Toomer wrote that he was "convinced . . . that the sharing of a common existence for purposes of self-development and group development was not only possible but fruitful."[32] He married Margery Latimer, a member of the group, a few days after the experiment ended.

Probably the success of the Witt Cottage Experiment in 1931 gave Toomer the confidence to launch a second experiment along the same lines after he moved to Pennsylvania in 1934. This time he had hopes for an extended life for this kind of work. His second attempt at communal living was called the Mill House Experiment, and it lasted roughly from 1936 to 1940. A group of people— Toomer's friends and neighbors—were invited to restore an abandoned gristmill and to bring back to life a semiabandoned farm that was a part of the Toomer estate. This work met the physical requirements needed for personal development. "The real goal was development, the development of the Man, specifically the development of each man and woman. The dynamics were affirmation and denial, the basic Yea and Nay of human life. The means were explicit and psychological tools to get the job done," one participant wrote later.[33]

The Mill House Experiment ended in early 1940. By then Toomer was suffering from health problems that robbed him of energy. His anxieties over internal harmony were also debilitating, and he lacked the funds to put the operation on a solid footing. Later, a member of the group attempted to articulate what had been achieved:

> We tried to see what and where we were; we made effort, when we could, towards catharsis development; we strove as best we could to do *it*, to become.
> Mill House was not simply a place. It was a work and a life and a spirit. And the building of Mill House as a place, fine as that was in its own right, was itself really a frame-work, a means in the building of a work and life and spirit.[34]

The participants seemed to believe that it was a worthwhile episode in their lives.

However, by the time Toomer had set up the Mill House Experiment, the close relationship he had shared with Gurdjieff for many years was almost all over. While it is impossible to be sure about the exact reasons for his turning away from the man he held in such high regard, a number of incidents can be cited that may have been partly responsible. For one, on a trip to the United States in 1930 Gurdjieff and Orage had had a public disagreement that resulted in the breakup of the Orage groups in the United States and in Orage's return to England. Toomer had been close to Orage and no doubt had reacted against Gurdjieff's crude handling of such a faithful disciple. Another matter that affected Toomer personally concerned his having raised money for the purpose of publishing some of Gurdjieff's manuscripts. To his chagrin, however, Gurdjieff appropriated the funds for his personal use and handled the matter in such a way as to leave Toomer open to accusations of mishandling them. A third contributing factor to the rupture might have been Toomer's enthusiasm over the success of the Cottage Experiment in 1931, which could have given him the confidence to become independent of Gurdjieff. People who knew him well believed that he hoped for a long time to be able to secure sufficient capital to establish an institute on his farm in Pennsylvania that would be like the one at Fontainebleau. Many of his activities at the farm were diminutive representations of life at the French institute. Marjorie Content Toomer, his second wife, who never joined the movement, has pointed out that everything her husband did during their lifetime together reflected Gurdjieff's influence.[35]

Toomer's break with Gurdjieff the man was less dramatic or definitive and more gradual than his rupture with Waldo Frank and the other writers of the early 1920s had been. In the early 1930s, Toomer became increasingly critical of Gurdjieff and expressed open disapproval of his drinking habits and rumors of his sexual promiscuity. During this time, he noted: "Gurdjieff is doing nothing at the present time that I want to participate in or that I want to bring others to participate in. . . . I am saturated, I have been saturated for several years—there is nothing that he is doing that promises to enlarge my capacity."[36]

His official separation from Gurdjieff came in 1934 shortly before he married Marjorie Content. In a letter to Gurdjieff, he explained that his new roles of husband and father were going to demand a great deal of his energy, and he intended to make them his primary priority. For that reason, he would no longer be able to commit his time to as many activities as he had in the past. But even then, he assured Gurdjieff that his "center of gravity" for many years had been a result of Gurdjieff's teachings, which he was convinced was "the one thing that can make man man."[37] He saw Gurdjieff last in 1934, and at the time of his death in 1949, Toomer expressed ambivalent feelings toward him: "My feelings are pretty mixed. . . . In some ways, it seems far removed from me, quite far, as if it were something experienced in a former life. But if I go down under the surface I find feelings there, quite strong ones pro and con."[38]

It is interesting to speculate about the father-son relationship in Toomer's experiences with the older man. Many years later, when he was in Jungian psychoanalysis and was recording his dreams as part of the therapy, a recurring figure in those dreams was Gurdjieff.[39] Had Gurdjieff and his philosophy offered the framework of a father's discipline to Toomer? Was Jean Toomer's lifelong search for a "system"—one that he hoped would offer him all things all of the time—a journey in search of the father he never had?

## I I

At the same time, in the late 1920s and early 1930s, during the years when Toomer was most involved with the Gurdjieff work and was intent upon developing an identity that excluded his experiences of the early 1920s, the success of *Cane* continued to make an impact on his life. Black writers and critics in particular did all they could to keep Toomer's achievement alive for almost a decade by taking advantage of the publishing establishment's new liberal attitudes toward black writing in the 1920s. In 1925, although Toomer claimed he never gave permission for it, selections from *Cane* appeared in Alain Locke's *The New Negro*, which became a kind of handbook for the Harlem Renaissance; in 1927, *Balo* was anthologized in *Plays of Negro Life*, edited by Locke and Montgomery Gregory; and in that same year, other selections from *Cane* were published in Countee Cullen's *Caroling Dusk*. While these events were taking place, Toomer remained publicly silent about his racial identity, but in the early 1930s he was forced to take direct measures to separate himself from the black experience.

In 1930, James Weldon Johnson wrote to Jean Toomer and asked his permission to reprint selections from *Cane* in his forthcoming edition of *The Book of Negro Poetry*, an anthology Toomer later called "one of the best" of its time. Toomer refused to grant the request on the grounds that he was not a Negro. In the correspondence that ensued between the men on this issue, Toomer stood firm. He said he had no anti-Negro feelings, but he wished in his work to deemphasize racial or cultural divisions among groups of people who were all Americans because he wanted to align himself with things that stressed common experiences, forms, and spirit. "My main energies and allegiances," he wrote, "are directed towards the building of a life which will include all creative people of corresponding type."[40]

Shortly after this incident, the National Association for the Advancement of Colored People asked permission to translate some of his work into German. To this request, he replied:

> The publication of my book several years ago gave rise to the impression that I was a Negro—and this impression has grown. . . . I have since found, however, that it has caused confusion and misunderstanding of my later writings. . . . In America there is forming a new race which, for the present, I will call the American race. In so far as I affiliate with any group less than the entire human group, I am a member of this race.[41]

Finally, in November of 1930, in accepting a speaking engagement in Canada, he noted:

> I am of French and English descent. . . . I have been associated in New York and Paris with some of the men who have been trying to bring about a renaissance in American art and life. . . . I have become known particularly because of my use of psychology as a means of understanding art and letters. . . . I am a psychologist as well as a creator and aesthetic critic.[42]

There is a progression to Toomer's responses to these three events. In the first case, although he separates himself from "Negro" identity, he places his emphasis on wanting to contribute to the building of the new group that is forming in the country, in which "corresponding type" and not racial background plays the more important role. In the statement to the National Association for the Advancement of Colored People, he more strongly asserts that he is not a Negro. In his final statement, the absence of any mention of minority-group representation in his background is striking. From all three responses, it is clear that Toomer's position on his race had evolved into open denial of his "Negro" heritage. He had considered the matter and was determined to erase, as much as possible, his connections to the Afro-American experience.

In 1931, a privately printed pamphlet of Toomer's carried the title "A Fiction and Some Facts," and in it he boldly stated his racial position. Here he pointed out that P. B. S. Pinchback's political ambitions, and not his lineage, governed Pinchback's decision to declare himself a Negro and join the struggle for black rights. However, Toomer himself had neither reason nor motive to do the same, and he did not wish to claim Negro blood. Denying that he might have believed that Negro heritage was inferior to that of other groups, he went on to say:

> If Negro blood is among the blood that make me what I am, then Negro blood, along with others, shares in producing whatever virtues I may have, and also shares in producing whatever vices I may have. Blood is blood. . . . As for being a Negro, this of course I am not—neither biologically nor socially. . . . In biological fact I am . . . all American. . . . In sociological fact I am also an American. I live as an American, always have and always will, except as I develop beyond national bounds and become a citizen of the world.[43]

The wish to disassociate himself from black heritage became an overriding passion; he was convinced of a "fiction" in his grandfather's racial self-designation, and by now it was anathema to him.

For all his protestations, he was unable to put an end to the general assumption that he was a Negro. In 1933, Nancy Cunard, a wealthy English woman with interests in the arts and in black people, asked him to collaborate with her on an anthology on Africa and the question of color in the United States. He did not accept the offer, but he noted that while he was not a Negro he was "interested in and deeply value[d] the Negro . . . and [had] written about the Negro." He explained that he was working on a theory that all Americans belonged to one race, and in order to establish that theory, it was necessary for him to take an "extreme position" and not associate with any race other than the American group.[44]

These events must have irritated Jean Toomer in his search for nonracial universal identity, but the storm that broke around him later in 1933 overshadowed them all. When it occurred, Toomer and his first wife, Margery Latimer, were living in Carmel, California, awaiting the birth of their first child. The cause of the disturbance was the result of repercussions from the Cottage Experiment of 1931. One male participant in the Portage Toomer-led group was sued for divorce by his wife on grounds of adultery that she claimed took place during the experiment. Newspapers called the activities at Witt Cottage a "love cult." The story was carried by the *Milwaukee Sentinel*, the *Wisconsin News*, the *San Francisco*

*Chronicle,* the *New York World-Telegram,* the *New York Herald,* and by *Time.* By the time it reached the national news media, the emphasis was no longer on the alleged sexual activities of the group at Witt Cottage but largely on the fact that Toomer was a Negro and that he was married to a white woman. The publicity was crude and cruel. Nor did Toomer help his cause as he tried to reiterate his by now often-repeated racial position. He and his wife were helpless in the face of the onslaught. He tried to turn the incident into something positive for himself by attempting to write a novel with the "scandal" as its basis. He called it "Caromb," a title derived from combining the first three letters of Carmel with three from the word somber.

After this event Toomer ironically had few difficulties with racial identity for the remainder of his life. Many years later, when he and his second wife, Marjorie Content Toomer, moved to Pennsylvania, no one seemed to know of either his fame or his notoriety, and no one questioned his race. He was ostensibly a middle-class white man among neighbors like himself, given to contemplation and discussion of the purpose of man in the universe. In the 1940s, he joined the Society of Friends, and over the years he wrote many essays and gave lectures for that group. Many of his pieces, often published in the *Friend's Intelligencer,* addressed issues concerning the Negro in society as a whole and among the Quakers in particular. Years later, Arna Bontemps, remembering the Harlem Renaissance, noted that the most productive judgment that could be made on Toomer's racial views was to accept the idea that he rejected the myth of race as it is fostered in our culture and that he appeared "to have reached a point in his thinking at which categories of this kind tend to clutter rather than clarify."[45] There can be little doubt that Toomer's conflicts as he struggled with who he was reflected the destructive qualities of attitudes about race in American culture.

# After *Cane*: Polemic versus Art

**I**

Although by the end of 1923 Jean Toomer had turned away from the lyrical, artistic expression that had been the signal achievement of *Cane*, he did not give up writing, and some of the works he published in the following decade must be judged by their literary merits. "Easter," a story that appeared in the *Little Review* in the spring of 1925, and "Mr. Costyve Duditch," which was published in the *Dial* in 1928, are his best post-*Cane* works of the 1920s and illustrate all of the major qualities of his writing of the later period.

"Easter" presents Jean Toomer in transition, still holding on to new currents in literary styles, but breaking away from some of the patterns of thought that characterized his work between 1922 and 1923. With this story, he severs the emphasis on the Afro-American experience that had distinguished his writing. Although in the 1940s he would write essays for the Society of Friends on questions of the "Negro" in society, it was only in "Blue Meridian," published in the 1930s, that he made any reference to black Americans in his creative work, even though "Blue Meridian" is not *about* black America.

Like all of Toomer's work of this late-1920s period, "Easter" embraces a universal vision. It is a surrealistic piece, with images that are absurd, grotesque, and influenced by Eastern thought. The title of the story is ironic. In place of the serious thoughtfulness associated with the time and events immediately preceding the Christian Easter, Toomer presents a background of bedlam against which he superimposes images that are bizarre, absurd, and even repulsive. No triumphant redeemer appears at the end, only a creature that causes such consternation that the faithful watchers flee in alarm. "Easter" is the satiric portrayal of the failure of Western thought and religion to effect the spiritual regeneration that the modern world desperately needs and for which it seeks.

In "Easter," the world is a house in which 666 living creatures come together and await a spiritual rebirth. The house is a modern-day representation of Noah's ark, except that its inhabitants have not been saved. Through the uneasiness of the crowd, the fragmentation of thoughts and activities, and the absurdity and repulsive quality of many of the images in the opening scene, the narrator establishes the chaotic condition of the modern world. A great deal of energy emanates from this gathering, but very little that is positive occurs. Many people talk, but the sound is "like flies buzzing in a monkey house." People fear that "the odor of tame animals might condense and pelter everyone with grafted monsters," for such a happening would "set eyes in permanent wry angles, or turn hair white instantly." The modern world is ludicrous, spiritually sterile, agitated, and rife with fears and anxieties. "Only a slim chance of a dove's descending," notes the narrator.[1]

Against this world which epitomizes disharmony, the author offers an "aside": "The landscape was vernal. Young tender things like blades of grass were pushing sunward. Spring guided fresh winds along the course of brooks and rivers and through the curly hair of children. For you, dear lambs, we bend, embrace, and give what wealth we have. Their curls were golden. The odor they gave off was sweet. The prophets knew them, and, for the marvel of their hands, yielded to be led to heaven" (E, p. 3). The contrast between the industrial world and the natural world is sharp. A house that "totters" when a woman blushes at the wholesome sight of animals mating gives way to the openness of nature: springs, brooks, rivers, children, growing things, and a sweet odor, unlike the foul odor that causes deformities. Situated within the disharmonious world, the natural world represents a choice that offers harmony, health, and peace. Yet the narrator points out, men, birds, and animals prefer the other and find a "lyric . . . binding" in their shared confusion. The scene ends when 466 of the inhabitants grow impatient and walk away in haste.

From the undifferentiated "buzzing" talk of the 666, we move to the 200 who remain. The group is "passionately given to the discussion of diverse topics." But the conversations are meaningless: "[T]heir words, strings, that wound fat balls about the subjects.

The balls were set up like tenpins and bowled over" (E, p. 4). When 194 of the inhabitants leave, the reader follows their activities.

A dreamlike quality pervades the atmosphere. Houses spin around helplessly, and men and women cry out against outrages directed against them or the world in general. Against this backdrop, Toomer draws realistic portrayals. He describes a preacher who goes to Bethlehem to post a proclamation calling for the unity of all Christians. He gives us a young man who finds himself at the corner of 125th Street and 7th Avenue in New York (a place famous for street preachers and politicians), where three corners are already occupied by the Salvation Army, the Mormons, and an advocate for liberty bonds. The young man takes the remaining corner and calls for the adoration of the mollusk. And Toomer tells of the poet who goes underground to write a verse in a subway station. In all of these events, which take place everywhere from New York to Los Angeles to the Holy Land, there is the suggestion of a historical global consciousness in which America, the most advanced nation in the modern world, is linked to the Judeo-Christian heritage.

The six inhabitants who remain in the house make up a group that huddles together, each finding the waiting almost intolerable. Finally, when they are at the limit of their endurance, the vigil ends. "The earth split open and he arose and shook himself like a dog from water" (E, p. 6). The group "gasped and fled the place," and the unidentified "he" was left alone in the house. His thoughts were a jumble of activity onto which all of the people and all of the birds and animals of the number of 666 impinge and intrude, making it impossible for logic or coherence to take shape in his mind. In the end, the single thread of rationality links him to the preacher who posted the proclamation in Bethlehem.

Time is an important element in this portrayal, and the passing of time is notable. The narrator makes it clear that it is time for a revitalization of the spiritual resources that are available to human beings. The world is in a state of utter disharmony, energy dissipates itself in meaningless ways, and people need and want to find the way back to harmony. The importance of time is reenforced throughout the portrayal. The story begins, "The scene started slow enough," and the first scene ends, "things dragged on . . . over many hours" (E, p. 3). The state of disharmony in the world developed over a long time, and while it is clear that the motion that it generated was full of negative energy, people were slow to awaken to their situation. Toward the end of the narrative, when the watchers check their calendar, we learn that the date is April 3 and that there are ten days more to wait. This information, linked to the title of the piece, impresses on us that it is time for rebirth and awakening.

Toomer's concern with time as an agent of change became apparent during his association with the avant-garde writers of the early 1920s. He left that group in part because it became clear to him that a more immediate and radical approach to the problems of the world was needed than that which his friends advocated. Time became much more important to him when in late 1923 he began to believe that the way to find internal harmony was through Eastern teachings. The swiftness with which he gave himself fully to the Gurdjieff work in 1924 is symptomatic of his heightened awareness of the pressing needs of time.

The symbolism of the numbers that appear in "Easter" bear most directly on the intellectual and philosophical changes in Toomer. The most prominent number is 666, which has been a cause of much discussion among numerologists. The genesis of this number comes from the book of Revelation (13:18) in the Christian Bible, and experts suggest that it refers to Nero Caesar, the powerful Roman emperor who persecuted early Christians. In the context of the story, Toomer seems to suggest that the group as a whole—all 666—represents the antithesis of the high ideals of true spiritual rebirth.

The two other numbers that clearly have symbolic meaning in "Easter" are three and six. Both of these numbers are prominent in Judeo-Christian theology. God created the world in six days and enjoined man to work only on six days of each week, and on Good Friday, the veil of the temple was rent without the help of man or natural phenomenon at the sixth hour of the day. Christ suffered three temptations; the cock crowed three times during the Gethsemane ordeal; Peter denied his Master three times; and, finally, Christ was in the grave for three days before the resurrection. In his use of both three and six, Toomer doubtless was making connections with the Judeo-Christian religious heritage as the force to which Western man looks for salvation. But it is a salvation that has failed. Toomer's burlesque of the resurrection scene in "Easter," the running away of those who had waited to the end presumably because of the fearsomeness of "his" appearance, and the inability of the risen one to find a focus beyond the scene of the incarnation are Toomer's symbols of that failure.

"Easter" is interesting because of its language and because of what it tells us about Jean Toomer's thinking at this time in his life. In this story, he calls on a variety of conventional literary forms—ambiguity, puns, and satire among them—and also uses surrealistic techniques to great advantage with the absurd and grotesque elements of the story. He shows great skill in combining these various forms and succeeds in producing another verbal portrait, almost as powerful in its own way as *Cane.* Here is an image of the disharmonious nature of the world and the helplessness of the traditional spiritual resources. Thematically, the work shows him moving away from the concerns that are peculiar to any one group of people by attempting to illuminate a world situation. As he began to explore the possibilities of cosmic consciousness, ordinary consciousness and its spiritual components took on new meanings for him, and it is these new meanings that begin to bear on his writings and which first show up in "Easter."

"Mr. Costyve Duditch," published in the *Dial* in 1928, shows Toomer more secure in his mission as a Gurdjieff teacher than he was in "Easter." Here is the story of one day in the life of the title character, a man who, although he appears individualistic in his society, wastes all of his potential for real living. Costyve Duditch is a world traveler by occupation; he travels not as a means of making money but purely to please himself. In fact, he is a world wanderer who rationalizes that travel "grooms" the person. He has no permanent ties of family or friends, but he maintains an apartment in Chicago and visits it periodically as he crisscrosses the globe.

Having arrived in Chicago on the previous night, Duditch wanders into Marshall Field's the next morning and accidentally drops and breaks an exquisite glass bowl that he has been admiring and examining. A wealthy man, Duditch can easily pay for the cost of the damage. Nevertheless, he is emotionally shaken by the experience. He feels that the event is only the physical manifestation of his true relationship to the world, and his inner turmoil discomforts him. His reflexive impulse is to escape, and he would have left the city immediately had he not had a prior commitment to meet a group of friends for tea that afternoon.

At the social gathering, where he is lionized as a celebrity, he regains his equilibrium for a time as he relates his adventures to an admiring group of listeners. A second "shattering" occurs when he responds to a question concerning the manner in which his body would be disposed of were he to die in a foreign country. Duditch, who considers no place foreign to himself, answers unhesitatingly that the customs of that country would suffice. The listeners are shocked that he would not want his body returned to America, and the party soon breaks up because of their discomfiture. Shortly after, a thoroughly frantic Duditch is on a train speeding away from Chicago for far-flung destinations. By the next morning, his spirits have revived, and he can "bounce from [his] berth, bowl up the aisle, and out-beam all the men in the shaving room."[2]

Costyve Duditch and his life and actions represent many of the qualities of modern man as Toomer saw them reflected in the light of the Gurdjieff philosophy. One of Duditch's main characteristics is that he is a mechanical man. We see him first in the early morning, hurrying down the street as blustery winds make it difficult for pedestrians to get to work at that hour. His friend, watching the approaching figure of Duditch, does so "as one does when viewing a racing auto draw near," and as Duditch moved past him "with a velocity which was extraordinary in the face of such uncertain winds," he had in fact seen "the approach and passing of a speedy mechanical object." When Duditch hears his friend call his name, he stops dead, "with haunched shoulders . . . neither turned nor budged . . . holding himself in blankness. . . . Then [he] wheeled around" (CD, p. 183). His physical actions in negotiating his way around the crowded streets, as well as his struggle against the wind (nature), have a robot-like effect.

But Duditch's mechanization goes beyond his walking habits on city streets, and his externally visible actions are also a pattern of inflexible habits. Wherever he is in the world, the pattern never changes. Although he has many suits of various fabrics, "two items [of dress] . . . [are] indispensable and unchangeable: his spats —his gray spats—and a standing collar" (CD, p. 187). He gives the impression that he is always "perfectly dressed." At 9 A.M. each morning he leaves his lodgings and heads to the financial district of whatever town or city he is in. Here he inquires about the state of his personal finances and his business investments. Later he goes to lunch, after which he applies himself to his literary work. This work, which has been in progress for a long time, concerns three books he hopes to write: "The Influence of Travel on the Personality" or "How Travel Grooms the Person," "When Love Was Great" or "Finesse in Love," and "There Is No Life without Creation." So regular are his habits in arranging the events of his life that his day usually goes "off like clock-work."

There are other ways in which Duditch is a mechanical man.

His friend observes that Duditch's tone of voice has no relation or connection to the content of his conversations. He maintains both an unchanging, pathetic pleading quality and an apologetic, persuasive quality that give the impression that his voice is disembodied, "pleading and delighted, pleading for no one, delighted with no tangible thing" (CD, p. 194). His face has only three expressions. He is "bright-eyed" when an idea is forming in him, he has a vacant look as soon as he articulates it, and he is "silent [but] anticipatory" when the idea is gone. Costyve Duditch is always building "houses of cards" that collapse on him, and his emotional interests give him only brief opportunities for outbursts of enthusiasm and activity. When he loses this energy, he is full of pathetic disillusionment and eagerly tries to find a new attachment. In all of these ways, Duditch displays a sterility of imagination, a lack of genuine feelings and emotions, and a superficial attitude toward his internal development.

Nevertheless, people are often attracted to Duditch, for here is a man who is not confined by the boundaries of conventional social mores. He loves to travel and is extremely proficient in describing the various places in which he has sojourned. He remains free from the burdens and demands of family, or even the more traditional ties of friendship. He is independent and intelligent and is free to grow and develop.

Unfortunately, his ability to travel, instead of providing this potential for human growth, gives him a way to escape it. Gurdjieff would have said that Duditch is ruled by his moving center, that part of his brain that directs his life toward outward show and material considerations.[3] Consequently, as he fears, he is the proverbial rolling stone that gathers no moss. Toomer demonstrates Duditch's fragmented life by describing certain of Duditch's idiosyncrasies, which his friends find amusing. For example, wherever he travels, he has an insatiable need to be recognized by doormen, clerks, porters, elevator operators, and other lower-echelon workers with whom he comes into contact. But instead of staying at any one place often, he makes infrequent visits to each hotel in order to test the help and make sure that he is really remembered. He prefers not to converse with people whom he meets for he is interested only in knowing that in the vast metropolises of the world people recognize him. Duditch, "a product of the sky-scraper age, . . . was up-rooted and he had to be blown about, rootlessly from place to place" (CD, p. 190). In his rootlessness and mechanical behavior, he is unaware of the possibilities of his potential.

The books that Duditch proposes to write—on travel and on love—have ironic implications for his life and general psychology. Travel has made no meaningful impression on him. He has been to every part of the world and seen all the great manifestations of various cultures, but he is unable to find spiritual guidance in any place to enrich his inner self. Even more ironic than his proposed travel book is the one he thinks he will write on love, for Duditch, we are told by the narrator, is a "gelding," having no capacity for the emotions of genuine sexual love or profound human attachments. Similarly, his uncreative life makes it impossible for him to write of the imagination or of originality. The people who know him best feel a sense of pity for him, but the greatest tragedy of his life is his unconsciousness of the sterility of his existence. Toomer presses the reader to see the barrenness of Duditch and, through him, of the modern human condition.

The most powerful symbol in the narrative is the broken bowl. Duditch admires the bowl and appreciates it because of its exquisite design and workmanship. He thinks he would like to give it to someone as a gift. Then, as he contemplates this idea, it slips from his nervous fingers, "sending glittering splinters in all directions" (CD, p. 189). The precious bowl is a representation of Duditch's life, which he allows to slip away from him in a thousand broken fragments. Just as he uses money to pay for the broken bowl, he uses it—through extraordinarily large tips to service people in hotels and railway stations, for example—to purchase the illusion of other people's respect and recognition in place of genuine caring relationships. When Duditch reaches the street after the hubbub in the store, it is as though the city is in the same condition as the bowl, and he feels that he is responsible for shattering the finest things in the world. Later, after tea, Duditch's friend wonders if his attitude toward death is caused by his lack of imagination or his "considered unwillingness to place more value on his body than its worth" (CD, p. 196). For his part, poor Duditch sees only that his world is once more smashed to bits, and he wants nothing more than to leave Chicago as soon as the earliest train can bear him away.

Duditch travels not to gain knowledge and to seek self-development but to escape from the responsibilities of a life that often means trying to mend the broken pieces. The ease with which he recovers from internal turmoil each time an experience forces him to feel it attests to his superficiality. That modern man is rootless and mechanical is Toomer's message. He sees a desperate need for the reversal of these qualities so that people can become aware of and begin to seek their natural potential.

Jean Toomer published several other works during the 1920s. "Winter on Earth" appeared in the *Dial* in 1923 and "York Beach" was published in the *New American Caravan* in 1929. "White Arrow," a poem, and "Reflections," a small group of aphorisms, both appeared in the *Dial* in 1929. "Winter on Earth" is primarily a philosophical discourse on man's need to strive toward greater individual and collective union with the powers of the universe. Toomer contends that because man in society has created a world that is opposite to nature, individuals must develop greater awareness of their spirituality and their innate connections to the universe. His message in "York Beach" is similar. The goal of human life, he says, is to develop potential, and he discusses the roles of materialism, alienation, and the ever-present need for spiritual development in the modern world. The central character in "York Beach" is a thinly disguised Jean Toomer, no longer terrified, uncertain, or ambivalent as Kabnis was, but confident in the knowledge that he has found the way to achieve self-realization.

In 1929, Toomer collected a group of ten of the stories he had written between 1924 and 1929 and offered them, unsuccessfully, for publication under the title "Lost and Dominant." "Easter," "Mr. Costyve Duditch," and "Winter on Earth" were included in the group. None of the others has ever been published. The preface to the collection summarizes his perspective on the world at that time. He will give us, he says, "the skyscraper world, our modern world with its power, speed and vivid activity" in the pages of this book. He will show us "Power in New York, Activity in Chicago, and Love on the way between," as well as a view of man as he exists in the wider earth.[4]

Toomer also wrote plays in the later years of the 1920s, none of which was published or produced. "A Drama of the Southwest" (1926) is an incomplete work, and "The Sacred Factory," written in 1927, is included in *The Wayward and the Seeking*. "The Sacred Factory" uses nonrepresentational techniques to explore themes concerning the dullness and sterility of ordinary life and the social repressiveness of the modern world. Through an examination of the life cycle of both a working-class family and a middle-class family, Toomer projects the thesis that "human existence [under ordinary circumstances] is stripped of wish, of hope, of possibility, reduced to a dull maintaining of itself."[5] Occasionally, an individual has a "sense of possibilities," but life around that person crushes it out.

Toomer's unpublished fiction from the later 1920s until 1936 includes three full-length novels—"Transatlantic" (ca. 1929), revised as "Eight Day World" (1933 or 1934), "Caromb" (ca. 1932), and "The Gallonwerps," first written as a play in 1927 and revised as a novel in 1933. The first two of these are based on events that occurred in Toomer's life during these years, and although "The Gallonwerps" is less connected to his personal experiences, he plays an important role in the action.

"Eight Day World," a 436-page work, was Toomer's longest manuscript. It is the fictionalized account of his shipboard experiences on his first trip to Fontainebleau in 1924. The action focuses on the relationships between a group of people who are fellow passengers on the ship for eight days. For this period the ship is the world, and for the passengers it is a life distinct from all other experiences. The thesis of the work is that life should be continuous growth toward Being. Toomer remained convinced for a long time that this was his best manuscript, but no one agreed to publish it. He even expressed fears that his future as a writer might have been tied to its fate. Unfortunately, that was sound prophetic judgment on his part.

"Caromb" is the novel Toomer wove out of the unpleasant racial confrontation that he and Margery Latimer Toomer had in California in 1932. In this work, he contrasts the physical beauty of the place with the ugliness of racial attitudes in America and offers a touching image of children who play but do not laugh or sing and who seem to live in a haunting, brooding atmosphere.

"The Gallonwerps" or "Diked," which Toomer called "A Satiric Farce for Marionettes," was a work that he devised for teaching his Gurdjieff groups. Its theme is the power of human suggestibility. To be diked is to be manipulated, and as he saw it, negative manipulation is one of the great evils of the modern world. He contended that education—including literary and religious teaching—is part of the communications network by which this negative process occurs and that advertising is the most often-used method of social manipulation. Toomer was not against manipulation as such, but he wanted to reverse the prevailing negative aspects of the practice in favor of a more positive mode. He hoped to expose the futility of false illusions and the destructive quality of selfish behavior. "The Gallonwerps" was popular among his Gurdjieffian friends, many of whom recognized themselves among its characters.[6]

Although most of Toomer's writings between 1923 and 1930 are too slight for purposes of any satisfactory literary analysis—they are flawed by thinness of plot, weak characters, lack of development or dramatic impulse, moralizing, and his irresistible need to be an undisguised Gurdjieffian proselyte—the major themes in these works are like those of many other social works of the period. Many other people with insight and imagination, facing the human situation, also expressed their concern for increasing materialism, industrialization, and the growing alienation between human beings and basic social values. These were considerations that were apropos to the times.

Toomer wrote a great deal but could generate no enthusiasm or interest among publishers for most of this effort. For one thing, having severed his connections with the literary world of his pre-*Cane* years, he was no longer able to find anyone in that world to champion his cause or express confidence in his work. On the contrary, many of the intellectuals who could have been helpful to him were skeptical of and even hostile to Gurdjieff and his philosophy. Consequently, the promotion of Toomer's writings, touting this questionable dogma, was not something they would have cared to do. In the highly selective world of publishing, he was on his own, and he did not fare well.

Had Toomer's break with Waldo Frank and other members of that coterie been only a matter of changing friendships because of personal matters and had Toomer continued to develop the potential that *Cane* had expressed, his career as a writer might have been different. In spite of *Cane*'s small sales, Toomer had gained recognition from it and could have helped publicize it had he wanted to do so. But he consciously and deliberately gave up the goals that would have advanced the writer's career he wanted to have. One of his friends noted: "Jean gave up the sort of writing that he did in *Cane*, that beautiful . . . sensual and lyrical writing. He gave up the kind of subject that he had been interested in. . . . [He] continued to write short stories . . . published here and there, but it wasn't the beautiful stuff he had been writing hitherto."[7]

Toomer's later writings were intended to explain a discipline and a body of thought, and, as a result, they were not literary. The goal of a writer who tries to articulate a philosophy is to convince the reader of the merits of the system; in so doing, the writer does not necessarily offer the reader a work that is imaginatively rich. For all of its limited landscape, the "imagination" of *Cane* gives it an inherent breadth that takes the reader beyond the obvious content of oppression and confinement. In his work of the late 1920s, Toomer pulls his sights inward, and his horizon ends at the identity-giving absolute of the Gurdjieff philosophy as that directs its followers toward self-realization. These writings lack the imagination of *Cane,* and in addition to their other stylistic limitations, they bog down in the mire of a single idea. Toomer's failure to continue to publish in the creative arena is a result of his inflexible position on nonracial identity and of the inappropriate quality of the Gurdjieff philosophy as material for the making of literature.

But if his career as a writer had sunk into oblivion in these years, in other ways Toomer was doing very well. He was in Chicago for most of this time, and, as a successful disciple and teacher of the Gurdjieff method, he was second in the country only to Orage. If he had felt any doubts about the movement when he joined it in 1924 (and that seems unlikely), they were dissolved by 1926 through his own experience of higher consciousness.

In April 1926, Jean Toomer was standing on an elevated platform in New York, waiting for a train, when he underwent a mystical experience. While it lasted, he was conscious of his mind and body separating from each other and becoming entities independent of each other. In this condition, he said, he was able to see clearly the true relationship between men and the universe. The experience gave him a new identity and made him aware that he was an "integral part of . . . [a] greater consciousness." In writing about it, he said, "I saw inner events as clearly as one sees outward forms in the luminosity of dawn or twilight."[8] At this time he believed that he had discovered conclusive proof that people "could awake and be." Now he saw objectively and in sharp outline that his life was only a part of a greater life that is actual "being." As a result of this experience, his concepts of "Life" and "Existence" altered. He felt that until then he had been "in exile." Now he had achieved "birth above the body," had discovered his astral body that could separate from his physical self, and had emerged into "incredible Consciousness."[9] Toomer records this event in a number of manuscripts but not until almost a dozen years after it had occurred.[10] This incident no doubt confirmed his hopes for the achievement of even greater degrees of higher consciousness and internal harmony that he had been seeking for a long time.

**I I**

Jean Toomer's career as a creative writer ended in 1936 with the publication of "Blue Meridian," second in significance among his works only to *Cane*. In *Cane*, Toomer had looked at the past and discovered the tragic consequences of racial distinctions and separations on human relationships; in "Blue Meridian," he attempted to redeem the past and envision an America that would evolve into the prototype of a society that had achieved universal humanity. These two works not only measure his success as a writer, but they form the frame of those years that are most important to an examination of the connection between Toomer as an unfulfilled artist and the world in which he lived and worked.

As we have seen, *Cane* was written and published within two years of its conception and was well received by writers and critics. Yet Toomer felt little enthusiasm about the book once it was completed and called it a "swan song." What no one knew then was that his prophecy was accurate not only for the black folk culture but also for Toomer's future as a man of literature. What Jean Toomer did know at the time, however, was that he intended to direct his imaginative energies into avenues other than the ones that had produced *Cane*.

The story of the genesis and reception of "Blue Meridian" is different from that of its illustrious predecessor. This poem was not a spontaneous response to deeply felt emotions, but a well-considered, carefully reasoned, idealistic statement about racial homogeneity in America which combines literary merits with social concerns. Toomer spent more than ten years writing this poem, and when it was completed, he had achieved his "poetic zenith . . . [in the] quest for [a positive] identity"[11] for himself and his fellow countrymen. However, although it appeared in the prestigious *New Caravan*, it received no critical attention, did nothing to influence reluctant publishers to accept any of his other works, and marked the end of his published career in imaginative literature. On a very deep and basic level, Jean Toomer and America marched to different drummers: when America was ready to receive him—albeit on its own terms—he renounced it; when he was ready to be received—on his own terms—he was spurned.

"Blue Meridian" brings together those philosophical and literary elements of Toomer's pre-*Cane* years with the goals that he articulated at the height of his involvement with Gurdjieff. Recent critics have noted the influences of Whitman, Hart Crane, and Gurdjieff on the poem. Its symbolist framework and thematic concepts have much in common with Whitman's "I Hear America Singing" and Crane's *The Bridge*, while many of its references and allusions come from the Gurdjieff philosophy. In his study of the poem,

Bernard Bell has identified it as an "eclectic yet harmonious blend of Darwinian evolution and Gurdjieffian mysticism."[12] This unlikely blending most closely describes the Toomer ideal of human potential, which, he believed, could rise above socially imposed limitations and thus participate in the energy and wisdom of the total universe. The poem focuses on the human family, which has evolved to the point at which race, class, religion, sex, and creed recede into meaninglessness, leaving essential beings to inherit a repossessed natural earth, one joined to the stars.

"Blue Meridian" is first, and above all else, a poem about America. It sings America for Americans of all races, tribes, kingdoms, and religions that have become gloriously one in the cultural/aesthetic melting pot. Such a state is not easily won, but rather it is the result of a painful evolution in which all Americans have participated:

> It is a new America,
> To be spiritualized by each new American.[13]

The heart of the poem, as Carolyn Taylor points out, lies in the twenty-four italicized lines that are scattered throughout the verse, and which, when put together, form a poem within the poem:[14]

> *Black Meridian, black light*
> *Dynamic atom-aggregate,*
> *Lay sleeping on an inland lake.*          (p. 214, ll. 3–5)
>
> *To be taken as a golden grain*
> *And lifted, as the wheat of our bodies,*
> *To matter uniquely man.*          (p. 218, ll. 190–93)
>
> *Crash!*          (p. 221, l. 278)
>
> *White Meridian, white light,*
> *Dynamic atom-aggregate,*
> *Lay sleeping on an inland lake.*          (p. 223, ll. 393–95)
>
> *It is a new world,*
> *A new America*          (p. 229, ll. 632–33)
>
> *To be spiritualized by each new American*          (p. 229, l. 642)
>
> *Each new American—*
> *To be taken as a golden grain*
> *And lifted as the wheat of our bodies,*
> *To matter superbly human.*          (p. 230, ll. 660–63)

*Blue Meridian, banded light,*
*Dynamic atom-aggregate,*
*Awakes upon the earth;*
*In his left hand he holds elevated rock,*
*In his right hand he holds lifted branches,*
*He dances the dance of the Blue Meridian*
*And dervishes with the seven regions*
    *of America, and the world.*            (pp. 233–34, ll. 809–16)

This is the myth of the evolution of a new America, seen through the eyes of a Gurdjieffian/utopian visionary. Here is ideal humanity, which materializes when the barriers that separate people are destroyed and all become as one. Dormant potential comes to life with outstretched arms and dancing feet in a new America, of which the spiritual energy of all Americans will be a part.

The twenty-four lines of the internal poem are distributed among the more than eight hundred lines of the total work, making their import as a unit less readily detected, although no less effective. Strategically, this arrangement disperses the power of the impact of these particular lines throughout the whole, preserves the unity of purpose for the entire piece, and reenforces the relationship between all of the poem's parts. These are the most powerful lines of the work and define, most explicitly, the role and function of the Blue Meridian, which is to merge the Black Meridian and the White Meridian.

Many of the ideas here come from the influence of Gurdjieffian thinking. Meridian is man without differentiation of sex, class, or religion and, at the end of the poem, is of no now-recognizable human color. But Meridian is at the center of thought and action, a "dynamic atom-aggregate," representative of the universe because he includes matter from all worlds. One of Gurdjieff's main ideas was that it is possible to study the universe through studying human beings. He contended that man, in his ordinary state, was asleep and in need of awakening. In the new America of the poem, a spiritual infusion causes man to rise from the stagnant waters of alienation and fragmentation and to evolve into harmony and oneness with the universal order. Toomer uses the number seven—the number of perfection as well as the number of representations on the Ray of Creation—to imply that all of the country and the world is drawn into the circle of perfection by the new American.[15]

The body of the poem explains the process by which the circle of perfection is drawn. The sequence of events in the development of the country is clearly stated. In the beginning,

> When the spirit of mankind conceived
> A New World in America, and dreamed
> The human structure rising from its base[,]
>
> (p. 217, ll. 142–44)

there was no time to select the right people for this land. Instead, "vast life" was brought to a "vast plot," and the peoples of the earth produced "waves of inhabitation." The hopes for a harmonious world rested on a "vision of the possible."

First came the "great European races"—the White Meridian—which built a materialistic and technological world. When they arrived, they found "the great red races," whom they swiftly "serpentined" into pueblos and Christianized in order to maintain complete control of them. In a short time, "pueblo, priest and Shalakos / Sank into the sacred earth" (p. 217, ll. 129–30) and, with the "ghosts of buffaloes, / A lone eagle feather, / An untamed Navajo" became fertilizer for the land (p. 217, ll. 134–36).

Western images of loss and death move from the European treatment of Native Americans to the Black Meridian:

> The great African races . . . [came]
> . . . singing riplets to sorrow in red fields,
> Sing a swan song, to break rocks
> And immortalize a hiding water boy.
>
> (p. 216, ll. 106–9)

A slave—and oppressed because of his race—the African could not rise to be an ideal. He spoke of "leaving the shining ground" without knowing where he was going, of singing because he ached:

> He moaned, O Lord, Lord,
> This bale will break me— (p. 217, ll. 118–19)

In their sweep across the continent, the dominant Europeans built "giant cities, / Made roads, laid silver rails, / Sang of their swift achievement / And perished, displaced by machines" (p. 216, ll. 73–76). The civilization they developed came to an end in a chaos of "crying men and hard women / . . . Baptized in finance / . . . Winnowing their likenesses from synthetic rock / Sold by national organizations of undertakers" (p. 216, ll. 80, 82, 85, 86). In surveying this past, the poet points out its hopelessness:

> Of what avail that with neon lights
> We make gas-tanks look like Christmas trees?
> Of what avail the battle
> Of the school-books and the guns?     (p. 221, ll. 279–82)

The extent to which this old America failed is evident in the blight on humans and nature:

> On land are shadows not of trees or clouds,
> On materials marks not made by Nature,
> On men and women ravages no animal can make,
> On children brands,
> On life a blight not put by God—     (p. 222, ll. 351–54)

However, this is not the end, and to change the course of death and destruction, there is a detour that can be taken on

> . . . a highway just beyond where all roads end,
> Along which, despite the prowlers of this planet,
> Men and women can love one another,
> Find their plot, build their world,
> Live this life with unstreaked dignity
> And lift a rainbow to the heavens.     (p. 223, ll. 388–93)

It is for this that the poet evokes the "waking forces" and pleads for the energy to crash "the barrier to [raise] man . . . to the higher form":

> O thou, Radiant Incorporeal,
> The I of earth and of mankind, hurl
> Down these seaboards, across this continent,
> The thousand-rayed discus of thy mind,
> And above our waking limbs unfurl
> Spirit-torsos of exquisite strength!     (p. 214, ll. 18–23)

Through the repetition of words and/or lines from the first part of the poem—with differences that suggest changes in motivation and results—Toomer achieves in the second part a verbal representation of the psychological and spiritual evolution he attempts to portray. The European settlers of the earlier action, "dear defectives / Winnowing their likenesses from synthetic rock" (p. 216, ll. 84–85) die in the second part, but then come "alive again / To demonstrate the worth of individuals, / The purpose of the commonwealth" (p. 230, ll. 682–84). Similarly, the great African races, "singing riplets to sorrow in red fields," evolve to find that

> Love does not brand as slave or peon
> Any man, but feels his hands,
> His touch upon his work,
> And welcomes death that liberates
> The poet, American among Americans,
> Man at large among men.          (p. 231, ll. 701–6)

As for the "red race,"

> . . . pueblo, priest, and Shalakos
> Sank into the sacred earth
> To resurrect—
> To project into this conscious world
> An example of the organic;
> To enact a mystery among facts—
> The mime-priest in the market place,
> Daubed with mud to grace the fecund,
> Clown, satirist, and innovator,
> Free dances—
> In the Corn Dance, the Koshare.   (p. 231, ll. 715–25)

Evolution breaks down the barriers that separate groups of peoples, and Universal Man finds the "center of gravity" and becomes the "compelling ideal." "We are the new people," says the poet:

> The man of blue or purple,
>
> .    .    .    .    .    .    .    .    .    .
>
> Foretold by ancient seers who knew,
> Not the place, not the name,
> But the reluctant of yes and no
> Struggling for birth through ages.
> We . . . are the new people,
> Born of elevated rock and lifted branches,
> Called Americans—
>
> .    .    .    .    .    .    .    .    .    .
>
> And we are the old people; we are witnesses
> That behind us extends
> An unbroken chain of ancestors,
> Ourselves linked with all who ever lived.
>                     (p. 232, ll. 733, 735–42, 747–50)

This, in Toomer's estimation, is the triumph of man over nonman, of birth over anti-being. The restrictive peculiarities of geographical regions, classes, occupations, religions, sexes, and all else that blocks human beings from brotherly coexistence with one another are no longer operative.

The evolution of the new American is a mystical/spiritual process that leans heavily on Toomer's belief in symbolic birth outside of the body, his use of religious symbols, and his evocation of forces more powerful than human beings. His belief in symbolic birth is a result of both the mystical experiences that he reported having had three times in his life and his faith in an intellectual rebirth in which an individual accepts his oneness with all other people regardless of racial, social, sexual, or cultural differences.

Toomer uses a full panoply of religious symbols throughout the poem. The Mississippi is one such image that frames the work. Introducing the river at the beginning as the "sister of the Ganges," the poet notes that in the "spirit" of America she waits to become a sacred river. At the conclusion of the evolution of the new American, the great Mississippi, "Main artery of earth in the western world, / Is a sacred river / In the spirit of our people" (p. 233, ll. 772–74).

Objects of worship play an important part in both the chaotic and evolved America. In the former, the old gods were led by an "inverted" Christ, a "shaved Moses," a "blanched Lemur," and a "moulting Thunderbird" (p. 215, ll. 62–64), symbols aimed at the subversion of conventional religious ideology from Judeo-Christian theology to American capitalism. Other traditional symbols of worship and religion in the poem include the human being as a "cracked crock" or an "aged receptacle," the white-robed priest, and the waterwheel. In addition, Wall Street, The Loop, and the human soul as denim, tight after the wash of experience and needing to be mended and stretched, find their way into the poem. In "Mankind is a cross, / Joined as a cross irrevocably," Toomer creates a variation on the traditional use of that symbol in the Christian world. The perpendicular portion, he says, is the stream that flows from the remote past and ends in the distant years ahead, while the horizontal section is the "planetary wash of those now living" (p. 232, ll. 764–67).

Another important symbol in the work is grain—the source of human and animal nourishment—and that with which Toomer identifies human beings. A growth period between the old America and the new America preserves "the great granary intact." The sterility and impotence of civilized man in the first part of the work is evidenced by his inability to mix blood "with the stuff upon . . . [the] boards / As water with flour to make bread" (p. 216, ll. 88–89). Having neither "yeast nor fire," the population becomes "angel-dough" and dies beating pavements and filling space with automobiles. In contrast, the new Americans do mix blood with "the stuff upon their boards / As water with flour to make bread"; they have both yeast and fire "to implement [themselves] by things." They eat, breathe, move, circulate, can "love and bear love's fruit," for they are living men and women (p. 230, ll. 684–94).

Although the mysticism and spirituality throughout the poem are not exclusively Gurdjieffian in nature, many of Toomer's images link them to Gurdjieff's body of thought. In his address to the ultimate powers, Toomer refers, for instance, to the "Big Light," the "Radiant Incorporeal," and the "I of earth and of all mankind." His request for "Spirit-torsos of exquisite strength" is a call for a development of the astral body that grows within but is able to separate from the physiological body. "Blue Meridian" acknowledges the supremacy of spirituality, and it is within the "spirit" of America, Toomer suggests, that all Americans will eventually become one.

The combination of conventional imagery and Gurdjieffian language and ideas, as demonstrated below, is one of the artistic strengths of the poem:

> The eagle, as you should know, American,
> Is a sublime and bloody bird,
> A living dynamo
> Capable of spiritualizing and sensualizing,
>
> .   .   .   .   .   .   .   .   .
>
> Of affirming and denying—        (p. 219, ll. 212–15)
>
> .   .   .   .   .   .   .   .   .
>
> The eagle is a flying machine
> One wing is broken,
>
> .   .   .   .   .   .   .   .   .
>
> There is a force gone wrong.    (p. 219, ll. 223–24, 225)

The eagle and the airplane—emblems of American strength and achievement—convey the tension between spiritualizing and denying, and the negative will that evolves from these connect Eastern thought and Western symbology. Toomer shows how even signal achievements can be transformed into negative patterns through attitudes toward power and materialistic gains.

Throughout the poem, Toomer uses concrete images to convey the life of the spirit. Not only is the Absolute the "Radiant Incorporeal," but it also possesses a "thousand-rayed discus of . . . [a] mind," which it is asked to "hurl" down across the breadth and expanse of America in order to bring about the awakening to a higher consciousness. "Whoever lifts the Mississippi," says the poet, "Lifts himself and all Americans" and thus "Makes the great brown river smile. / The blood of earth and the blood of man / Course swifter and rejoice when we spiritualize" (p. 233, ll. 775–80).

The notion of the materiality of all things in the universe, even of knowledge, is a Gurdjieffian idea that provides the basis for many of the metaphors in the poem. Toomer describes these abstract ideas, too, through concrete images, as in the following lines, which show how the old America has evolved into the new spiritualized America:

> To the depression
> The stock of debris descends,
> Down go its greed-events,
> Control by fear, prejudice, and murder.
>
> (p. 224, ll. 397, 400)

> . . . . . . . .
>
> What value this, paper of the past,
> Engraved, ingrained, but meaningless?
>
> (p. 244, ll. 401–2)

> . . . . . . . .
>
> In another Wall Street of the world
> The stock of value ascends.
> What then am I bid,
> By what free arm and yielding hand,
> Offering what currency,
> For this—
> (p. 226, ll. 520–25)

The evocation of the spirit of the Absolute, which begins the poem, also ends it. Throughout, mankind is linked to the cosmos: The force "Of brain and heart and limbs / Moving on and on / Through the terms of life on earth / And then beyond / To aid the operations of the cosmos" (p. 234, ll. 821–25). The combination of elements that connect the East and the West, the ancient and the modern worlds, technology and nature, and dream and reality reflect the universal basis of the philosophy that underlies the structure of the cosmos.

The poet evokes the universal spirit to "Blend our bodies to one flesh, / And blend this body to mankind" (p. 218, ll. 165–66). Man —particularly American man—is asleep. The actions of his past prove how unaware he is of how he has denied his humanity and his oneness with the universe. To redeem himself from the destructiveness that diminishes his existence, he must crash through the many laws that keep him earthbound. He must free himself from the limitations of his past and gain the higher regions of consciousness. Then there will be a new America for new Americans and harmony in each man and in all men. This is the message of the poem, and it is Gurdjieff's philosophy localized into American hopes, dreams, and prophetic thinking.

"Blue Meridian" is a public statement from Jean Toomer in which he offers America a philosophical and moral solution to the problems of race, sex, religion, and class in our society. In addition, it also presents a private resolution to his search for a positive identity. The personal journey delineated in "Blue Meridian" began for him with "The First American" in 1914, just before his first venture into the college world. His course was diverted by *Cane* in 1923, but it culminated in the completion of this poem in the early 1930s. And it was Gurdjieff's philosophy that gave him the tools with which he could hammer out the pragmatic structure of the reality he had been seeking. Two voices dominate the text— the poet speaking for all humankind of like mind and the poet speaking for himself:

> I stand where two directions intersect,
> At Michigan Avenue and Walton Place,
> Parallel to my countrymen,
> Right-angled to the universe.    (p. 218, ll. 184–87)

Nor is there a question that "The poet, American among Americans, / Man at large among men" (p. 231, ll. 705–6) is Jean Toomer, the first among his group to recognize the American race. Toomer believed unquestionably in the position that he stated in this work, and he turned his creative energies to convincing others of its merits in everything that he wrote after the publication of

*Cane.* The ideas in "Blue Meridian" enabled him to feel wholly human, neither inferior nor superior to others, but fully integrated into the stream of all living beings.

All of America is taken into the sweep of "Blue Meridian." The Mississippi, which has already played such an important role in the development of this country, becomes, like its Eastern sister, the Ganges, a sacred river. Its flow becomes the wash of spirituality that energizes its people. All other areas of the country are given similar functions. The East and West coasts become the masculinity and femininity of the new America, and the middle regions are likened to children, the "generator[s] of symbols." Plains, mountains, stately trees, and rising cities also share in the spiritual transformation. But the blue man, a synthesis of the separate racial groups in this country and in the world, is the dominating symbol of unity in this poem.

Jean Toomer produced no creative works that were accepted for publication after 1936 although, in addition to the novels he tried to write until early in the 1940s, he wrote different versions of autobiography, several of which exist only as fragments, and some poetry. The story of the rejections he received from editors and his frantic appeals to have his voice heard during this period is well told in Darwin Turner's "Jean Toomer: Exile," and need not be repeated here. Suffice it to say that these were the years during which his primary identity was that of a frustrated writer.

# The Man—the Artist:
# An Evaluation

## I

From the beginning, Jean Toomer's life was marked by a number of unfortunate events that must have had significant impact on him. His father's desertion when he was an infant and his mother's death six months before his fifteenth birthday were major factors that determined the environment in which he grew up and matured. He had an active aversion to the domineering influence of his grandfather and disliked his stepfather. His physical and social anxieties as a teenager developed within a family structure that had been severely disrupted.

Toomer's autobiographies, in their various states of incompleteness, are interesting, informative, and valuable assets to the study of his life and work. As a writer, he considered the autobiographical form extremely important for its insights about the past. He often imposed autobiographical elements on his fiction and drama. Among his writings, "Earth-Being," "A New Identity," "On Being American," "Outline of an Autobiography," and "Why I Entered the Gurdjieff Work" offer a variety of critical perspectives on his family and his life between 1894 and the late 1920s. All were written between 1928 and the early 1940s.

In looking at these autobiographical writings, it is helpful to keep in mind the major events in Toomer's life during these years. In the late 1920s, he had begun his Gurdjieff work. Writing autobiography during this time provided him with a way to observe and analyze his progress as he sought to become identified as a "universal" person. After the mid-1930s, autobiography gave him a chance to sharpen his self-definition. In "Earth-Being," in particular, he aims to show how his life, even from the beginning, had dimensions that foreshadowed his becoming an "extraordinary" being. As the title suggests, the emphasis falls on his relationship to the earth, but the account directs us to the higher purpose of human existence and links Toomer to behavioral habits that will make him seek the "transcending orbit." "A New Identity," "On Being American," and "Why I Entered the Gurdjieff Work" are less concerned with his early life and family relationships, and they focus on his internal motivation and his development toward an acceptance of the Gurdjieff philosophy. "Outline of an Autobiography," the most comprehensive draft, gives the best example of how Toomer wanted to present himself to the world.

Toomer had submitted one draft of his autobiography for publication as early as 1929, but it was rejected. As far as the records indicate, in 1946 he received his final rejection for a version of his life story that he called "Incredible Journey." In selecting the aspects of his life that he wished to explore and reveal, Toomer often aimed to show Gurdjieff's influence on his evolution from waking-sleep to self-consciousness.

In "Earth-Being," more than in any of the other versions, Toomer sets the stage for the unfolding story of a more than "ordinary" being.[1] Much of the language is infused with a Gurdjieffian mode of expression. "I see myself as one of countless millions of human beings. . . . I am trying to record the essential experiences of one of those beings born and existing on earth," says the writer.[2] There is nothing unusual here, but the voice and the tone of the writer draw us to recognize the influence of Gurdjieff's thought on him. "I will take my own life as material because my understanding of it exceeds my understanding of other material," he explains.[3] That all things in the universe are weighable and measurable is one of the first of the Gurdjieffian precepts.

In the preface to "Earth-Being," Toomer speaks of himself as a "tiny cosmic speck . . . not yet crystallized [with] the universal." He thinks that at his birth "some cells [in him] heard [his] birth-cry . . . [and rebelled against submission] to the laws which govern the growth and development of human beings on this earth." His childhood was a period in which he "began to develop and differentiate spiritually, as [he] became psychologically individualized."[4] He claims to be "building a world" that will "progressively" correspond to his developing needs and functions. He finds "building" a suitable word for his activities, for he has been influenced, he tells us, by the word since early childhood, when he lived on a street and in a neighborhood where building was changing the face of field and farm into city.

Toomer's voice is authoritative, knowledgeable, independent, and confident. It is difficult, from what he reveals about himself, to see him as an "ordinary" man. We are struck with the ease with which he tells us that he "knows" about his entrance into life, not merely from his mother's womb into the "next larger world," but even from that "magic darkness—of the source behind the womb."[5] He reflects a special independence by disassociating himself physically (which is, for him, spiritually and psychologically) from his family. When family and friends discuss his physical resemblance to his forebears, he dismisses their findings: "If I could have spoken for myself I would have told them that I resembled myself," he notes.[6] "Earth-Being" introduces a man—that is, a microcosm of the world of human beings—who has a mission to explore the emotional and spiritual complexities of his being as these are manifest in his life and to help others understand themselves in their oneness and separateness from the universe as a whole.

Toomer tended to be indulgent and romantic about his early life, and this stance is perhaps responsible for his belief that his "center of gravity" had settled in his emotions. His descriptions of the various members of his family and of his life on Bacon Street are idealistic. It is curious, for instance, that he describes the father whom he may never have seen, and whose name was rarely mentioned in his grandfather's house while he was growing up, with great surety. He talks confidently of the man's height and build, his "presence," and his "way with people." How did Jean Toomer know that his father wore his clothes "carelessly" even though they were "carefully selected, in good taste, and from the finest materials"? Or that "he got petty and cross when things went wrong"? From a photograph of Nathan Toomer that his son had, the latter constructed a charming portrait: "He had a fine head on his broad shoulders, well-modeled features. . . . his lips and chin were not particularly strong, not noticeably weak. His eyes, generously spaced apart, were level-looking, quick with feeling."[7]

Two events relating to the father and son are worth mention here. Toomer recalled, more than thirty years after it would have occurred, that he had seen his father once during his early childhood. He had been on the street playing when a large man took him up in his arms and kissed him: "I liked him very much. He said things to me which I didn't understand, but I knew he was my father and that he was showing how much he loved me and what a fine little man I had grown to be. . . . He lowered me, pressed a bright silver dollar in my hand, kissed me again, and told me to run back to her [his mother]."[8] He was sure that this person was his father, although no one had told him so. The accuracy of the details of this recollection is of much less importance than the fact that decades later Toomer recorded it among his remembrances of childhood. Also, we recall that when Toomer went to Sparta, Georgia, in 1921, he made inquiries concerning the whereabouts of Nathan Toomer, who had lived in that area. In addition to learning of the elder Toomer's death, he surmised that people were reluctant to talk about the man because of issues surrounding his racial identity. Nathan Toomer had lived like a white man, Jean Toomer was told, but behind his back his enemies called him "nigger."[9] With this information, the son seemed to have refrained from further open curiosity about the life and fate of his father.

Toomer's most interesting portraits, however, are of his grandfather, and, from the inconsistencies in different versions of the autobiographies, it is clear that Toomer both admired and rejected P. B. S. Pinchback as his model. Also clear are his feelings of rivalry with the older man: "Not until I was three could I rule my nurse. Not until I was seven could I rule my mother and grandmother. Not until I was twenty-seven did I finally conquer my grandfather."[10] He was twenty-seven years old when Pinchback made the deal with him that led to the trip to Georgia in 1921. There are times in the autobiographies when he claims that he had an extremely compatible relationship with Pinchback; at other times, he focuses on Pinchback as an autocrat who made life almost intolerable for everyone around him. The young Toomer seemed to be divided in his loyalties between the father he never knew and the grandfather who inspired him to affection and rebellion.

By the time Toomer came to know his grandfather, Pinchback was well advanced in age, and his hair and beard were turning silver white. He was even then a hearty man, whom his grandson said dressed well and went "downtown" every day to business, acting the part of the "grand old man." One rumor about him was that he had, on occasion, been mistaken for Andrew Carnegie, an error he never took the time to correct. Young Toomer found him exciting even as he disliked his tyranny. Later, the bitter fights between the two centered around the older man's disappointment in his grandson's inability or refusal to settle into a career.

Many people have commented on how often Toomer uses women as central characters in his work and on his understanding of and sympathy toward the role of women in society. His recollections of the two women who figured most prominently in his early life—his mother and grandmother—offer insights into his perceptions of women, as do *Cane* and *Natalie Mann*. He recalls that his mother's life was full of unhappiness and disappointment primarily because of her father and her two husbands. Born into privilege and refinement, she nevertheless exhibited strong will, a quality that also characterized her father; in a woman, however, such a quality was considered unladylike and socially unacceptable. In marrying the fifty-two-year-old Nathan Toomer, Nina Pinchback, who was twenty-six at the time, committed an act of open defiance against her domineering father. She had claimed her right to autonomy. But both her freedom and her satisfaction were short-lived, for when Toomer deserted her, only months later, she was forced to return to her father's house, now with her infant son. Her unhappiness is not difficult to imagine. Jean Toomer recalled that Pinchback treated her like a child during the years immediately following the collapse of her marriage and even regulated her social activities. He noted that she must have felt trapped.[11]

Toomer remembered that his mother was graceful and quick in motion, not beautiful, but poised and distinctive. She loved poetry, sang, read novels, and sometimes wrote light verse. She instilled the love of music in him, and from her he also learned to love to dance. Toomer loved her, and her death in 1909 was a severe blow to him. He identified with her helplessness and her unhappiness, and the portrayals of many of his women characters express the sympathy he felt for her. Nor did he overlook the quiet strength of his grandmother. Nina Emily Hethorne Pinchback was temperamentally her husband's opposite, but she was strong in her own way. Jean Toomer described her as having a "soft gentle face, sensitive and delicate, touched with a strain of timidity or meekness." Her appearance was deceptive. Her obvious domain was the management of an orderly and well-organized home that was a haven for her husband during his political career, and she stood by him and supported his ambitions throughout his life: "She saw the rise of the family and, outliving her husband and all but one of her children, she endured its rather tragic fall. She was the one person in my home who sustained her faith in me . . . who supported me through thick and thin."[12]

One of the most important people in the life of the young Jean Toomer was his Uncle Bismarck, the second son of the family. While he was growing up in his grandfather's house, Toomer learned to admire this man increasingly as the years went by, perhaps because the younger Pinchback had a quality of understanding and affection that was lacking in his father. Bismarck had had medical training at Yale but was unable to make a successful living in medicine. After a brief stint in backcountry Mississippi and on an Indian reservation in the West, he returned to Washington and secured a job with the government. As long as he lived in his parents' house, he and Jean spent many evenings together, and the young Toomer learned many things from him. Bismarck loved to read, and sometimes he "tried his hand at fiction." To his nephew, he was a literary man who read him stories and introduced him to literature when he was very young. Bismarck had other interests, too, and Jean Toomer learned about history and geography from him as well. "My imagination took flight," he wrote, "and I was thrilled to follow it into those worlds of wonder."[13] This wonderful fraternity between man and boy came to an end when Bismarck married and moved away. For Toomer, his leaving was a serious loss.

Two grandparents, a mother, an uncle, and a stepfather were the people who made up, at different times, the family in which Jean Toomer grew up until he was fifteen years old. After that, for the next five years, he lived only with his aging grandparents. The inconsistencies in the family makeup, the many homes to which he had to adjust (there were at least seven different places called home between 1895 and 1914), and Pinchback's financial reversals made for a very unstable situation for the sensitive boy. In addition, Pinchback was not a happy man during the years Jean Toomer knew him. His failing resources, his daughter's inability to make a financially comfortable marriage, and his sons' failures to succeed in their careers weighed heavily on him. The once dashing, adventurous Pinchback, who rose from having been a cabin boy on a Mississippi riverboat to become a controversial political figure in Louisiana through initiative, will, and daring, was terribly disappointed in the lives of his children. Toomer was a young child when he became aware of the conflicts between his grandfather and other members of the family. In particular, his mother's unhappiness and his grandfather's dominance over her life made a special impression on him.

Yet in his early years, when they all lived on Bacon Street, he felt that he was growing up in what seemed to be a center of activity. Bacon Street was still little more than a short dirt road where carriage wheels made deep "furrows in the rich mud" when it rained.[14] Close by, there were trees and fields, but buildings were going up rapidly and changing the landscape. For Toomer and his young friends

> the seasons came to our small piece of the surface of the earth, each with its own unique gifts—turning leaves and russet sunsets; white frosty days and snow and ice; thawings, blossoms, fragrance and blue skies; the full ripe days of heat and drowsy droning opulence—each to evoke from children corresponding moods and rounds of activity. . . . the world of children was sufficiently close to natural forces to respond to the rich variety of the earth's logically changing moods. . . . children, still harmoniously within the universe, and behaving accordingly, grew into the new days of the new seasons, and in a year they had a complete cycle of experience.[15]

With the adaptability of youth, Toomer did not dwell wholly on the unhappiness of his family environment but also extracted from it those things that enriched his development. He loved the stories his Uncle Bismarck told him or read to him, and he enjoyed school, where he was mischievous and disruptive but where he was able to have fun in spite of the drawbacks of what he later called an archaic educational system imposed on the young. His greatest handicap was finding reading difficult, and he did not master that skill as early as some of his peers. He compensated by being the best fighter in the neighborhood. His love of sports and the outdoors were important parts of his energetic life at this time. Toomer called this period of his life a "comparatively free and open world, subject to but few of the rigid conventions and fixed ideas which contract the human psyche and commit people to narrow lives ruled by narrow preferences and prejudices."[16]

In the fall of 1905, when he was eleven, he was very ill. His illness followed a summer during which his mother had gone off by herself for an extended time, something she continued to do periodically. Years later, he understood that she was expressing her need to break away from the "iron grip" of her father. Her independence and intelligence had been subverted by dependence on men, and her periodic trips alone were her only expressions of individuality and full personhood. But in 1905 Toomer felt only rejection, and his illness later in the year helped him to take vengeance against her for her deed. He loved the attention he received at the time and reveled in the "subjects-to-king" relationship in which his mother and grandparents tended to his needs: "My illness had been a means of securing through sickness what I consciously feared I would not be able to secure in any other way; namely, the complete concerned attention of my mother. . . . I had obtained what I wanted. I had made mother concern herself with me to the at least seeming exclusion of all else. More, I had compelled the whole family to group about and attend me."[17] In retrospect, Toomer saw this illness as the climax of the tension he had internalized, beginning with his father's desertion and culminating in his fears and premonitions about his mother's impending marriage. This childhood experience can also be seen as an expression of the inordinate need for attention that Toomer would have all of his life.

During the years that Toomer had attended the M Street High School in Washington, he had had his first full view of the black world and, in particular, of the black middle class. From their life on Bacon Street in the 1890s and early 1900s, the Pinchbacks had moved progressively into poorer and blacker neighborhoods. By 1909, when Jean Toomer returned from New Rochelle, they lived in an all-black community, in which the resident families were working people who held government or professional jobs. The young people from these families were Toomer's friends, and he noted later that he had then observed that they were no different from the white friends he had known in New York. They were not conscious of their race, he said, and had no active prejudices against whites or blacks, as far as he could tell: "They lived within their world, not on the antagonistic periphery of it where clashes are most likely to occur. . . . These youths had their rounds of activity, parties and interests—and were self-sufficient. . . . They seldom or never came in contact with members of the white group in any way that would make them racially self-conscious."[18]

What Toomer did not understand, or chose not to recognize even after many years, was that this way of life was imposed on the black middle class by the rigid system of segregation that existed in Washington and kept the races separate until recent times. These young people grew up and matured in a wholly segregated world, not by their free choice, but through the dictates of forces beyond their control. Fortunately for them, opportunities for education and social advantages within their group protected them from the worst abuses of racial prejudice and gave them a comfortable world within the boundaries of the restrictions. They were the ones who, in the 1920s, created and participated in the Harlem Renaissance and who left a heritage of artistic black pride for their heirs—the black rebels who stormed the barricades of racial segregation in the 1960s and 1970s.

But neither the racial tolerance that reigned in his grandfather's house (for in the years of his prosperity, Pinchback chose his friends from among men of all colors, and he loved to entertain them in fine style in his grand abode on Bacon Street) nor the indifference to race that Toomer reported among his high school friends saved him from anxieties about his racial identity. Later, in writing about the effect these concerns had on his thinking during early adulthood, he claimed that his unique childhood and adolescence gave him the advantage of knowing both groups intimately, so that he was aware that much of what was said by each group about the other was incorrect and irrational. Yet this knowledge did little to allay his fears when he decided to go to the University of Wisconsin, and, instead, motivated him to formulate his earliest theory of the "American" identity.

Toomer's career through various universities, during which time he expected financial support from his aging, indigent grandfather, the events leading up to the writing of *Cane*, and his subsequent rejection of the literary world have been discussed in detail. In reading the story of those years, we are struck by the audacity of Toomer's financial demands on his grandfather at the time. Yet Pinchback had always showed that he wanted the best for his daughter's son. We learn from Toomer, for example, that the old man took his last job with the Department of Revenue for the purpose of sending Toomer to a preparatory school, and Toomer had considered going to Andover or Exeter. Pinchback's failing health had thwarted that plan.[19] Yet Toomer, as he went from one university to another, accomplishing very little at each, responded to his grandfather's refusal to finance his explorations by blaming the old man for the bad judgment he had used with his investments.

Toomer had never considered the making of money as one of the goals of his life, although he expected to enjoy its amenities. His major priorities were for internal harmony and the development of higher consciousness, and his cavalier attitude toward financial matters made it possible for him to concentrate on the things that were important to him. In his early manhood, his lack of emotional involvement with money enabled him to give up each failed vocational idea without worrying about what it had cost and to expect his grandfather to finance each new idea despite the fact that the older man disapproved of his vacillations. He never lost this attitude. After the death of his grandfather, in the years before he married Marjorie Content, he appears to have been just as nonchalant about providing for his financial security. It was said of him, not in a derogatory way, that he was "successful in getting people to support him . . . because [they] thought he was worth supporting."[20] After his marriage in 1934, financial security was no longer an issue.

Temperamentally, Toomer's ideas about the purpose of life were antimaterialistic and prohumanitarian. He lost no opportunity to articulate his views. Furthermore, he made his professional decisions based on this philosophy. When he embarked on the project to spread socialism among dockworkers in New Jersey in 1918, he did so with missionary zeal. These were people whom he perceived were suffering in ignorance because of the exploitation of the capitalist system which placed industrialization and technology above intrinsic human values. His inability to convince these men of their deprived condition was a blow to him, and it represented a personal crusade that had failed. When he began to write, he hoped and intended to change the nature of American society. He did not achieve his intention with *Cane* because, he believed, it provided no system for universal harmony and because the issue of racial conflict was too closely identified with the center of its meaning. When Toomer became a Gurdjieff disciple, he finally discovered the means to wholeness. His primary goal for living became not making money or cultivating the life of the mind but converting souls to the fullness of higher consciousness.

Underlying all of this was his intrinsic mysticism. The notion that it was possible for all aspects of a human being to function in harmony was one that he appropriated very early in his life. He was completely convinced that internal harmony was necessary for peace of mind and an understanding of the purpose and workings of the universe, which were the highest goals a human being could seek. He believed that the person who achieved higher consciousness would achieve full human potential and, as a consequence, would know full happiness.

Toomer's conviction that the Gurdjieff philosophy was the true way to internal harmony and higher consciousness led him to commit himself fully to it. He became a teacher and writer in the interests of the movement. Although he separated himself from Gurdjieff in 1934, he carried many of the ideas of the Gurdjieffian philosophy into his life and writing for many years thereafter, even as he explored other avenues toward his goal. Toomer refused the fame of a disharmonious world, preferring to await the rewards of an integrated world. He died disappointed. He had devoted his life to unlocking spiritual secrets of the universe for the use of man, and his efforts had failed. He had also missed the call to fame.

Readers have been curious about the nature of the "internal disruptions" about which Toomer complained for most of his life. His earliest allusions to this distress go back to his high school years. At that time, he had an "avalanche of sex indulgences," which frightened him, and he saw himself falling apart. Without telling anyone, he took himself "in hand" and set out to rescue himself. This was the beginning, for him, of self-imposed discipline. The discipline was physical—regular exercises in a program of muscle-building and endurance—as well as dietary. In spite of at least one regression in which he feared he was going into "decline," the danger passed, and he developed into a "healthy young man," who was actively involved in all the affairs of young people of his age and station.[21]

While the descriptions of his state are dramatic and were of grave concern to him at the time, the causes of these disruptions, in actuality, were no doubt less distressful than he believed. Toomer had returned to Washington at a crucial time in his physical development, most likely with no preparation for or responsible knowledge of the changes that were taking place in his adolescent body. More important, there was no one to whom he could confide his anxieties about the process of growing up. Subsequently, whenever life was not going as smoothly for him as he hoped, Toomer complained of internal disruptions. The periods between his changes from one system of thought to another in search of internal harmony are rife with these agonies. One especially acute period occurred between the time he rejected the literary world and accepted the Gurdjieffian philosophy, when he described himself in a state of extraordinary chaos. Toomer's need for internal harmony was the constant theme of his life, and it made him vulnerable to psychological distress whenever he perceived that a course he was following toward wholeness was leading him to another dead end.

On the whole, Toomer presents himself in his early years as

a multifaceted human being. While he was capable of deep affection for others, especially for his mother, his Uncle Bismarck, his grandmother, and several of the friends of his youth, he also cultivated an aloofness from almost everyone at some time in his life. His brand of egocentrism appears to have combined the qualities of sociability and gregariousness with those of withdrawal and introspection. Throughout his life, he was intent upon being both the participant and the observer.

From Jean Toomer's autobiographies, we derive the image of a man who perceived a seriousness in human existence that neither he nor other "ordinary" men could readily understand. All things were connected for him, and he wanted to understand and ultimately control the connectedness of experience. In this sense, he did not consider himself an "ordinary" man. He understood that he was a being of earth, but his existence, he thought, was fundamentally connected to the larger forces of the universe. He saw all of life and existence as a continuum and believed that a human being's highest achievement would be the comprehension of that continuum. He spent his life in search of that knowledge. His strong mystical nature was expressed most profoundly in *Cane* and in his involvement with Gurdjieff's philosophy and work. "From Exile into Being," which was revised as "The Second River" and is sometimes called "Awake and Be," is an autobiographical account of his spiritual journey to higher consciousness in 1926. This document of the experience of bodily transcendence gives useful insights into Toomer's thoughts on a life above the pale of waking-sleep.

Writing autobiography not only gave Jean Toomer the opportunity to examine his personal experiences for his own self-knowledge, but it enabled him to present himself as he wished to be seen. As literary materials, Toomer's autobiographical writings are engaging, and they embody a serious attempt to examine and define his experiences. As Darwin Turner has pointed out, in these writings above all others, he is a "delightful personality—candid, self-assured, persuasive, witty, poetic, and informative."[22]

**I I**

With the works of Charles W. Chesnutt in fiction and Paul Laurence Dunbar in poetry, black writers became familiarly known in literary circles by the end of the nineteenth century. In 1903,

W. E. B. Du Bois's *The Souls of Black Folk* announced in emphatic tones that black writers intended to claim a place of recognition in the new century, and James Weldon Johnson's *The Autobiography of an Ex-Colored Man* in 1911 was a fitting example of the new black literature that Du Bois had promised. Yet Johnson, Chesnutt, Dunbar, and others made only limited imprints on both the black and the white literary worlds. *Cane*, on the other hand, resounded across racial lines in 1923 when it was published, and Afro-American literature became an essential member in the household of American literature. Had Jean Toomer chosen to exploit what his achievement offered, there is little doubt that he would have become one of the most important spokesmen for black American letters in the twentieth century.

The literary career of Jean Toomer conforms to a pattern of birth, death, and rebirth. From 1930 until 1967 he was almost unknown except to literary historians with an interest in Afro-American literature. Then in 1967, the year of his death, a new reprint of *Cane*, still with Waldo Frank's foreword, appeared, and in 1969 a Harper and Row paperback, with a new introduction by Arna Bontemps, thrust the book and its author into the literary spotlight for the first time since its initial publication forty-six years earlier. Since then, *Cane* has held the place it rightfully deserves in the world of American letters, and Toomer's motivation for rejecting the world of literature, and possibly fame, has been the source of much speculation among new scholars in the field.

Praise for *Cane* was notable in the year of its first publication. White critic John Armstrong of the *New York Tribune* wrote the following in October 1923: "It can perhaps be safely said that the Southern negro, at least, has found an authentic lyric voice in Jean Toomer; a voice and a heart, likewise, that is synchronized with [his] aspirations, . . . hopes and fears. . . . The author of 'Cane' has created a distinct achievement wholly unlike anything of this sort done before."[23] Montgomery Gregory, in the December issue of *Opportunity*, noted that

> "Cane" is not to be classified in terms of the ordinary literary types, for the genius of creation is evident in its form. Verse, fiction, and drama are fused into a spiritual unity, an "aesthetic equivalent" of the Southland. . . . No previous writer has been able in any such degree to catch the sensuous beauty of the land or of its people or to fathom the deeper spiritual stirrings of the mass-life of the Negro.[24]

Gregory goes on to say that the "matchless beauty of the folk-life" and its "discordant and chaotic human elements" are woven into the "mysterious, subtle and incomprehensible appeal of the South" so as to make the book "not Of the South, . . . not Of the Negro; it Is the South, it Is the Negro—as Jean Toomer has experienced them."[25]

Most black critics gave Toomer and the book their unqualified endorsement. W. E. B. Du Bois, who admitted in print that he did not fully understand it, nevertheless said that Toomer had created a painting of black life, "not with Dutch exactness, but rather with an expressionist's sweep of color," and he called him an "artist with words." Expressing the patience and wisdom of an elder, Du Bois continued that he would be "watching for the fullness of his [Toomer's] strength and for that calm certainty of his art which undoubtedly will come with years."[26]

William Stanley Braithwaite, the poet, writing for the *Crisis* of September 1924, added that Toomer was the first black writer who portrayed black people "without the surrender or compromise of the artist's vision." Pointing to the new writer's genius, he noted that "he could write just as well, just as poignantly, just as transmutingly, about the peasants of Ireland, had experience brought him in touch with their existence." And looking toward the future, he called *Cane* a "book of gold and bronze, of dusk and flame, of ecstasy and pain, and Jean Toomer . . . a bright morning star of a new day of the race in literature."[27] Du Bois and Braithwaite were joined by such other voices as Langston Hughes, Jessie Fauset, Countee Cullen, and Claude McKay in voluminous praise of the emergent artist. This unanimous expression of tribute to and admiration for Jean Toomer from contemporary black writers proclaimed their recognition of the value of his achievement for them and for Afro-American literature.

By the time *Cane* was rediscovered by scholars and critics in the late 1960s, the exotic Negro of the 1920s had passed out of vogue, and in his place were black men and women asserting an identity they had chosen for themselves. Not seeking to forget the pain of the past, they wanted to understand its meaning in order to forge stronger selves in the future. *Cane* offered the foundations of a usable past for black writers and critics and new perceptions of the black experience for the angry black voices of the era.

New black scholars have done much to reestablish the reputation of *Cane* and to determine its position in black American and in American literary art. Houston Baker's assertion that this book is "the journey towards genuine, liberated black art, a protest novel, a portrait of the artist, and a thorough delineation of the black situation" is accurately expressive of the stand that most of these scholars have taken.[28] Baker claims that Toomer uses the combination of "awe-inspiring physical beauty, human hypocrisy, restrictive religious codes . . . frustrated ambitions, violent outbursts and tragic death at the hands of white America" to create a sense of the black southern heritage as "the spirit of a people . . . [who] cannot be denied."[29] To this end, he notes:

> Toomer knew—and did not attempt to sublimate—the pains and restrictions of a black Southern heritage [even as he left] the pristine loveliness and indomitable spirit of the folk to be discovered and extolled by the sensitive observer. . . . [And he] moves . . . toward the freedom that always accompanies deeper self-knowledge and a genuine understanding of one's condition in the universe.[30]

*Cane* brings the search for black identity to a positive conclusion through confirmation and newly discovered psychological freedoms. The book established Jean Toomer as a literary artist and as the first American writer to present a composite vision of the black American experience.

As a work of art, *Cane* ranks in the highest echelons of American literature. For a long time, its style presented a difficulty many people resolved by trying to fit it into a conventional genre. As a result, critics have called it everything from a "hodge-podge" of forms to a novel. Toomer did not consider it a novel, nor did he admit to its belonging to any of the convenient categories into which most literature fits. In keeping with the ideas that he and his friends of the early 1920s were trying to put into practice, the book creates its own form through the combination of many forms, but it comes closest to being, as Du Bois suggested, an expressionist painting of words and forms. Toomer rejected the finished portrait, but the work remains a testimony to his creative accomplishment.

Although a lesser work than *Cane*, the much-neglected "Blue Meridian" deserves to be acknowledged more widely because it is a significant artistic achievement. In *Cane*, Toomer had looked back in the hopes of finding answers to the questions of the past, but in "Blue Meridian," he looks to the future by assuming the mantle of a poet-prophet-priest. "Blue Meridian" literally completes the personal portion of Toomer's artistic search for a confirming identity, and figuratively it completes the unfinished circle that appears on the page preceding "Kabnis" in *Cane*. There is a sharp contrast between the ambivalence of the narrator at the end of "Kabnis" and the jubilation of the personified hero at the conclusion of "Blue Meridian." The full realization of the pain, the joy, and the strength in the meaning of the black past is not an end that satisfies the narrator of *Cane*. Kabnis may well be, as Baker suggests, "the fully emergent artist-singer of a displaced 'soil-soaked beauty' and an agent of liberation for his people,"[31] but his song holds no promises that assure us of the end of the terrors of the blood-burning moon, the feelings of alienation from middle-class pretensions, and the social rejection felt by the Paul Johnsons of the world. On the other hand, the poet-prophet-priest sings with unambiguous joy in "Blue Meridian" because his journey sets him truly free. In projecting the unity of all Americans of all races, creeds, and classes, his poem offers a solution to one of the most grievous problems of the nation and makes of art a humanizing force. In "Blue Meridian," Jean Toomer offered to transcend the world of *Cane*, but like the biblical prophet, he found himself crying in the wilderness and unheard.

"Blue Meridian," as a work of literature, is as sophisticated as *Cane*; it also follows in the tradition of no less an ancestor than Walt Whitman and in the path of Toomer's eminent contemporary, Hart Crane. Yet it met a critical fate that was as disappointing as *Cane*'s was heartening. If Jean Toomer was out of step with the world in his unhappiness with the ultimate meaning of *Cane*, then so was he with his elation about the possibilities of "Blue Meridian." The world chose not to get the point, and it chose to ignore the work. The reasons are not difficult to understand. Most black writers accept their black identity without distress and use their art to fashion larger freedoms for themselves and all black people, while white America, on the whole, is not interested in eliminating racial conflict in the lives of Americans. Black writers were too realistic to imagine a dream in which all races would be blended into one, and white America could not concede the possibility of such a world. Toomer simply was not willing to accommodate his life and his art to anything else, and while black writers and critics claimed him as their own, in spite of his protestations, political considerations made it impossible for the white publishing establishment to ignore his race.

*Cane* and "Blue Meridian" are Toomer's best literary works, but they stand at opposite ends of his literary career, both in time and in their philosophical significance. They weave Toomer's life and art together and also demonstrate how deeply embedded are the roots of the racial problems in America. They also make an Ishmael of Toomer and become a symbol of how racial struggle functions most ironically in its negative connotations—despite Toomer's discomfort with *Cane*, he received rewards from society (he might have had fame had he wanted it), but in his personal triumph with "Blue Meridian," he was a man ignored. Even now, with a wealth of other available information about him, it is on *Cane* that the literary critic places the greater emphasis in seeking to interpret the man and his art.

This study of Jean Toomer's life and literary works takes as its premise the idea that *Cane* embodies two journeys—one, the meaning of the black identity in America through the vision of the artist, and the other, Jean Toomer's search for a connection between his personal, individual self and the spirit of the black folk culture as he experienced it in Georgia in the fall of 1921. The first journey ended positively and brought a greater awareness of freedom to many black people. The second journey ended with Toomer's significant discovery of an identity that he was unwilling to assume.

Throughout his personal journey for self-definition, Toomer recognized both male and female aspects of himself, and he made frequent use of gender-defined qualities in his characters to explore his relationship to the black folk culture. In "Fern" and "Avey," the male narrator of *Cane* makes his most persistent attempts to claim the black "female" folk culture as his own. But he does not understand this culture and cannot partake of its nurturing qualities, on one hand, and it refuses to be controlled by male Jean Toomer, representative of the dominant white culture of art and literature, on the other. Viewed from this angle of vision, the narratives demonstrate the psychological distance between Jean Toomer and the culture he encountered in backcountry Georgia. He could listen to the folk women at sunset and appreciate and feel deeply moved by their songs and spirituals. Yet, even had he wanted to remain physically in the rural South, he would have been emotionally and psychologically incapable of doing so. He could only admire and respect the humane and aesthetic—and female-nurturing—qualities of this culture, but he could not claim it for his own.

Compared with the folk culture, the urban culture is anti-humane and incapable of nurturing. The acquisitive materialism of "Rhobert," the alienation expressed in "Theater," and the oppressive restrictiveness of "Box Seat" reveal characteristics opposite to those of the Georgia women. Dan Moore, with his sexuality and his rejection of middle-class social values, parallels Barlo in the southern stories, but Dan has lost the self-assuredness and the charisma of his counterpart. Instead, he is insecure, crude, and often out of control. The preeminent "femaleness" of the folk culture has eroded into the dominant "maleness" of the urban culture.

Esther in the South and Paul Johnson in the North come closest to the consciousness of the questing Jean Toomer. Esther and Paul function symbolically as the counterparts of Fern and Avey in the bid by Toomer-turned-narrator to identify with the black folk culture. In Esther's alienation from and rejection by the community, one can see Toomer's relationship to the black folk culture. Here the "femaleness" in him—his most tender sensibilities and sensitivities—seeks nurturing, but his whiteness, of which his physical manifestation is only a metaphor, irrevocably separates him from the intimacy of blacks, even as his unseen blackness excludes him from the fellowship of whites.

Paul Johnson is the bastard son of white America, indistinguishable from that part of his heritage in his appearance; nevertheless, he is the disinherited son of the South, who claims the rights for which the battle of Seventh Street was won. He wants to explore human relationships without being reminded of the social significance of his "darkness." Paul brings the Georgia sun and slanting roofs of unpainted cabins to the glass-and-asphalt jungle of Chicago, as Toomer brings the humanizing portraits of *Cane* to a dehumanized, industrialized America. Both Paul Johnson and Jean Toomer fail, because the racial barriers are impregnable against the assaults of humanitarian ideals.

Toomer's personal journey culminates in "Kabnis," as he searches for human solutions to the dilemmas of black life in the South and in the North. He sees that education and political activism—pragmatic channels to social change—do not hold solutions to problems buried deep within the human soul. For black people, art in life—the spirituals, work songs, slave narratives, and folk tales—has been, from the beginning, a source of survival. Poet-Kabnis, in the tradition of his forebears, will sing a new-old song of the strengths and weaknesses, the joys and pains, and the burdens and freedoms of a people's history that will heal the embattled soul. For the soul of the black American culture, *Cane* was effective; for the soul of Jean Toomer, it was not.

Although *Cane* proved the strength and aesthetic value of Afro-American culture as well as its intrinsic worth to the larger American culture, it described the journey of every black American much more than it did that of Everyman. Thus, as Toomer saw it, *Cane* was not a work of redemption for him—it held no universal identity, and Kabnis emerged with no vision that promised relief from the painful realities of the world.

Yet Toomer's emotional identification with the materials of the black experience, as he wrote the book, gave him his history. So successfully had he woven his feelings into the fabric of the work that early in 1923 Claude Barnett confidently wrote the following to him: "There have been several arguments contending that your style and finish are not Negroid, while I . . . felt certain that you were—for how else could you interpret 'us' as you do unless you have peeked behind the veil?"[32] Liveright's request for a more explicit statement from him on this same matter was additional proof that his race was "showing." He had succeeded too much with *Cane*, and the end results were not what Jean Toomer wanted. The book must have seemed to have assumed the characteristics of a double-edged sword. It had demolished his early fears of never being able to organize himself sufficiently to write, but it also stripped him of the cloak of racelessness he craved as his identity.

It would be a mistake to think that Toomer's affirmative response to Barnett's inquiry in April 1923 meant that he had accepted an exclusive black identity at that time and then capriciously changed his mind when confronted by Liveright in August of the same year. Rather, the explanation of the seeming contradiction in his behavior lies in the fact that the artist of *Cane* and the person of Jean Toomer, as hopelessly entangled as they were with each other for a while, were also separate from each other. While he worked on the book, Toomer's deep mysticism and intent search for spiritual connections made the experience almost supernatural. The essence of black culture enveloped and filled him. He even wrote to Waldo Frank describing times when he felt that he was losing all sense of an identity separate from the materials of his writing. Barnett's inquiry, made on the basis of his early works in the *Crisis* and other journals, touched that part of his consciousness that had responded to the spirituals as he had heard them in

Georgia. The speculations of this editor and his friends were a tribute to the harmony Toomer could feel evident between himself and the work at hand. But although the Georgia experiences and the writing of *Cane* had these powerful dimensions, they were not strong enough to neutralize the meaning that evolved or to convince him to willingly link his whole future to the Afro-American identity. For Jean Toomer never lost sight of the awareness that he wanted and needed a larger identity. By the time Liveright asked him for the racial statement, he had already disengaged himself from the close relationship he had shared with *Cane* for almost two years. The harmony it had appeared to crystallize in him between the end of 1921 and the early part of 1923 had already dissipated. His refusal to comply with Liveright's request was a statement denying that the materials of his book were an adequate representation of his identity.

It is not possible in a study limited to Toomer's artistic achievements to make a definitive statement on the factors that first propelled him to his position on the American race and eventually to a denial of African heritage. Nor can one say what motivated him to maintain this stand for so many years despite the fact that it led to the loss of his chances to further his literary career. Perhaps a full-life biography of him will hold the answers to such questions. However, it is possible to speculate on some of the factors that were involved in his position. Certainly, the low status of black people in American society played an important role in his decision. Yet it would be a mistake to see his attitude as the result of racial trauma alone and not attempt to locate his actions in his overall approach to life. Toomer had desired to achieve internal harmony early on and to help other people do so as well. He believed that racial differences, as they are experienced in the modern world, are divisive elements that perpetuate disharmony in everyone. Hence, he rejected all racial categories. The fact is that he refused to be a "Negro," but he never claimed to be a white man. He was convinced that in the melting pot of America, the people of this nation were evolving into a racial mixture that would make it not only inaccurate but impossible to select out strains of racial or ethnic heritage eventually. As he saw it, it was also only a matter of time before this fact became evident to all Americans. But in the meantime, holding onto racial distinctions was causing an enormous waste of energy and human potential. As Toomer perceived it, he wanted to dispense with racial classifications not only for his own sake but for all those who wanted a humane society. He was distressed that others failed to comprehend the importance of this stand.

Jean Toomer was a true son of America in search of the dream of America. However unrealistic it might have been, his solution to the dilemma of racial struggle was a sincere effort to strike at the nation's most shameful predicament. He was echoing the words and pleas of a black man before him, who, unafraid of his blackness, had declared the "color line" the problem of America for the twentieth century to resolve.[33] The factors affecting Toomer's life are complicated, but the question of race in American society figures prominently in his failure to achieve self-fulfillment.

It is also not possible to know if Toomer would have remained in the literary world if the issue of race had not surfaced when and in the way that it did. The pattern of his life—the various beginnings and endings—and his internal feelings of disharmony when the book was completed, suggest that he could have become vulnerable to Gurdjieff and his philosophy for other reasons as well. However, it was the racial issue that served as a catalyst for his separation from the literary world. His rejection of the limitations he perceived in the "Negro writer" label calls attention to the relationship of the artist to his society, a matter that goes well beyond Jean Toomer and the problems of any single artist, from a minority group or otherwise. History has proved that when a society attempts to place limits on the creative will of the artist, there is a tragic loss of cultural vision, and all are poorer for that loss.

Some of the blame for Jean Toomer's failure rests with him. In his embrace of Gurdjieff and his philosophy, in his single-minded search for a system to provide a blueprint for absolute and complete internal harmony, and in his wish to transcend all boundaries that limit human potential, his vision lost touch with reality. He was not an "ordinary" man, and he did not ask the ordinary questions of existence nor seek the ordinary answers. He was a visionary who reached outside of himself to the stars and the universe in his search for answers to the most fundamental and profound questions of human life.

But Toomer also wanted to write, and that was not a passing fancy. He continued to work at it until well into the 1940s. He was given the ear and eye of a poet, became an artist, and perhaps was a genius. *Cane* and "Blue Meridian" are proof of his immense artistry, and "Easter" and "Mr. Costyve Duditch" hold rich kernels of potential. But he turned away from the literary world because he refused to be racially labeled. When he began to follow Gurdjieff and to write in the tradition of the philosopher-teacher, he gave up the desire to nourish and cultivate his artistic gifts. His rejection of the literary world proved to be a great loss for American literature as well as for his own creative life. In his life and literary works, Jean Toomer represents a "universal" man, after all, because although he was often wounded, he never gave up his struggle to become an autonomous human being.

# NOTES

## Introduction

1. Toomer, "Outline of an Auto-
biography," Jean Toomer Special
Collection, Box 18, Folder 15, unpaged
notes (hereafter cited as Toomer
Collection).

2. Toomer did not support the war as
a matter of general principle, and he did
not think that the Allies were any more
right than their enemies. He felt during
World War I, as he did during World War
II, that people in power had made great
errors and that those without political
decision-making power were called
upon to fight and die.

3. Information taken from letters be-
tween Jean Toomer and Margaret Mead,
Toomer Collection, Box 1, Folder 7.

4. For a detailed discussion of the
Mill House Experiment, see Taylor,
"'Blend Us with Thy Being': Jean
Toomer's Mill House Poems," pp. 47–81.

5. Ibid., p. 35.

6. Letter from Jean Toomer to Harri-
son Smith, September 27, 1932, cited in
Turner, "Jean Toomer: Exile," p. 53.

7. Ibid.

8. Letter from Jean Toomer to Paula
Elkirsch, June 7, 1949, Toomer Collec-
tion, Box 1, Folder 3.

9. Toomer, "Dianetics," Toomer Col-
lection, Box 42, Folder 12, p. 8. Also dis-
cussed in an interview with Gorham
Munson by India M. Watterson at the
Wellington Hotel, New York, June 28,
1969, Amistad Research Collection, Dil-
lard University (hereafter cited as the
Munson-Watterson Interview).

## Chapter 1

1. Toomer, "Earth-Being," Toomer
Collection, Box 19, Folder 3, p. 1. Also
cited in Toomer, *The Wayward and the
Seeking*, p. 15.

2. For information on Pinchback, see
Du Bois, *Black Reconstruction*; Sim-
mons, *Men of Mark*; and *Dictionary of
American Biography*, s.v. "Pinchback,
Pinckney Benton Stewart." Pinchback
was born on May 10, 1837. He is re-
ported to have been the son of a white
Mississippi planter and a mixed-blood
slave, Eliza Stewart, who appears to
have had Indian and African blood. Her
master, the father of her children,
emancipated her and them, and she
took them to Ohio to be educated.
Pinchback later returned to the South,
led a battalion of black soldiers during
the Civil War, and then made political
fame and a sizable fortune after the war.

3. Toomer, "Outline of an Autobiogra-
phy," Toomer Collection, Box 14, Folder
9, pp. 13–14. Most of what Toomer
knew of his father was hearsay, and he
put together his opinions from frag-
ments of information. About three years
after the death of his mother, his mater-
nal grandfather discussed Nathan
Toomer with him. From the older man
he heard that Nathan had inherited
property from his father in Georgia and
that he had been married twice before
his marriage to Nina Pinchback.
Toomer also suggests that Nathan
Toomer could have provided well for
Nina Pinchback had they lived in Geor-

gia but that he would have been unable to support her in Washington in a style acceptable to her father.

4. Ibid., Box 15, Folder 2, p. 52.

5. Toomer, "Earth-Being," Toomer Collection, Box 19, Folder 3, p. 1.

6. Toomer, "Outline of an Autobiography," Toomer Collection, Box 15, Folder 5, p. 3.

7. Ibid., Box 15, Folder 6, p. 15.

8. Toomer, "Autobiography," Toomer Collection, Box 19, Folder 1, chap. 4, pp. 34–35. Although Toomer realized that his mother was unhappy and although he withheld his sympathies from her, he was extremely sensitive to her disappointments and especially wanted to help her to preserve her pride. On one occasion, shortly before her death, he arrived home from school to find her on the dining-room floor "writhing in pain." Judging that this was something she wanted to conceal, he "backed out of the room, moved by fear of what she would feel if she knew" that he had seen her. Toomer repeats the story of his unsympathetic attitude toward his mother during those years in different versions of his autobiographies. Also see Lewis, *When Harlem Was in Vogue*, p. 61.

9. Toomer, "Autobiography," Toomer Collection, Box 19, Folder 1, chap. 4, pp. 29–30.

10. Ibid., p. 35. Toomer claims that his mother's surgery was successful and that she died of postoperative complications. He blamed his grandfather for this unfortunate event, insisting that Pinchback's dominant attitudes drove Nina Pinchback to an unsuitable, unhappy second marriage.

11. Ibid., p. 36. Toomer explains that during this time he had a feeling that life was "shooting" at him, and he took the "attitude towards the world that there was menace in it." This made it necessary for him to "keep the outside out."

12. Ibid., chap. 10, p. 28. Toomer says that he bought the entire set of MacFadden's encyclopedia of physical culture and read every page of these books. He said that he learned a great deal about the human body and its functions from them and gained useful knowledge and respect for natural as against medical cures. Many years later, during his college years, he went to Chicago to visit MacFadden's house, which at that time was no longer a residence and was used as a center for natural cures. He was impressed by what he saw there.

13. Toomer, "Why I Entered the Gurdjieff Work," Toomer Collection, Box 66, Folder 8, p. 2.

14. Ibid., p. 4.

15. Toomer, "Outline of an Autobiography," Toomer Collection, Box 14, Folder 2, p. 6. Toomer repeats this story in several of his autobiographies and in *A Fiction and Some Facts* (1931). He claimed that Pinchback's political ambitions led to the error in the racial identification of his family.

16. Toomer, "Outline of an Autobiography," Toomer Collection, Box 15, Folder 11, p. 18.

17. Ibid., p. 13.

18. Ibid., Box 16, Folder 1, p. 116.

19. Toomer, "Autobiography," Toomer Collection, Box 19, Folder chap. 19, p. 11.

20. Toomer, "Outline of an Autobiography," Toomer Collection, Box 14, Folder 1, p. 25(a).

21. Toomer, "Why I Entered the Gurdjieff Work," Toomer Collection, Box 66, Folder 2, pp. 13–14.

22. Toomer, "Outline of an Autobiography," Toomer Collection, Box 14, Folder 1, p. 29.

23. Toomer, "Why I Entered the Gurdjieff Work," Toomer Collection, Box 66, Folder 8, p. 12.

24. Toomer, "Outline of an Autobiography," Toomer Collection, Box 18, Folder 15, unpaged notes.

25. Jean Toomer to Sherwood Anderson, December 29, 1922, Toomer Col-

lection, Box 1, Folder 1. Also see Benson and Dillard, *Jean Toomer*, p. 23.

26. Toomer, "Outline of an Autobiography," Toomer Collection, Box 14, Folder 1, p. 56.

27. Toomer, "Why I Entered the Gurdjieff Work," Toomer Collection, Box 66, Folder 1, p. 26.

28. Ibid., p. 28.

**Chapter 2**

1. Munson-Watterson Interview, Amistad Research Collection.

2. Toomer, *Cane* (1975), p. 17. Subsequent references to *Cane* are from this edition unless otherwise specified. References will be identified by page numbers in the text.

3. Toomer, "Why I Entered the Gurdjieff Work," Toomer Collection, Box 66, Folder 2, p. 26.

4. Du Bois, *The Souls of Black Folk*, p. 187.

5. Toomer, "Why I Entered the Gurdjieff Work," Toomer Collection, Box 66, Folder 2, p. 30.

6. Toomer, "Outline of an Autobiography," Toomer Collection, Box 16, Folder 1, p. 16.

7. Jean Toomer to Waldo Frank, 1922, Toomer Collection, Box 1, Folder 3. Also see Benson and Dillard, *Jean Toomer*, p. 29.

8. Holmes, "Jean Toomer, Apostle of Beauty," p. 253.

9. Toomer, "Outline of an Autobiography," Toomer Collection, Box 16, Folder 1, p. 56. Also see Trachtenberg, *Memoirs of Waldo Frank*, p. 102.

10. John McClure to Jean Toomer, 1922, Toomer Collection, Box 1, Folder 7. Also see Benson and Dillard, *Jean Toomer*, p. 20.

11. Benson and Dillard, *Jean Toomer*, p. 20.

12. Ibid.

13. Sherwood Anderson to Jean Toomer, 1922, Toomer Collection, Box 1, Folder 1.

14. Ibid.

15. Jean Toomer to Sherwood Anderson, December 28, 1922, Toomer Collection, Box 1, Folder 1. Also see Benson and Dillard, *Jean Toomer*, p. 23.

16. Benson and Dillard, *Jean Toomer*, p. 23.

17. Ibid.

18. Ibid.

19. Turner, "An Intersection of Paths: Correspondence between Jean Toomer and Sherwood Anderson," p. 461.

20. Jean Toomer to Waldo Frank, 1922, Toomer Collection, Box 1, Folder 3.

21. Jean Toomer to Waldo Frank, 1922, Toomer Collection, Box 1, Folder 3. Also see Benson and Dillard, *Jean Toomer*, p. 29.

22. Jean Toomer to Waldo Frank, April 1922, Toomer Collection, Box 1, Folder 3.

23. Jean Toomer to Waldo Frank, May 1922, ibid.

24. Jean Toomer to Waldo Frank, August 1922, ibid. Also see Benson and Dillard, *Jean Toomer*, p. 28.

25. Jean Toomer to Waldo Frank, August 21, 1922, Toomer Collection, Box 1, Folder 3. Also see Benson and Dillard, *Jean Toomer*, p. 26.

26. Jean Toomer to Waldo Frank [ca. May 1922], Toomer Collection, Box 1, Folder 3.

27. Jean Toomer to Waldo Frank [ca. 1922], ibid.

28. Ibid.

29. Trachtenberg, *Memoirs of Waldo Frank*, p. 103.

30. Ibid., p. 105.

31. Toomer, unpublished poem, Toomer Collection, Box 50, Folder 1.

32. Jean Toomer to Waldo Frank [1922], Toomer Collection, Box 1, Folder 3.

33. Jean Toomer to Mae Wright [1922], Toomer Collection, Box 1, Folder 10.

34. Ibid.

35. Ibid.

36. Ibid.

37. Ibid.

38. Jean Toomer to Waldo Frank [1922], Toomer Collection, Box 1, Folder 3.

39. Ibid.

40. Sylvander, *Jessie Fauset, American Writer*, p. 60.

41. Jean Toomer to Waldo Frank [1922], Toomer Collection, Box 1, Folder 3.

42. Ibid.

**Chapter 3**

1. Turner, "The Failure of a Playwright," p. 309. Reprinted in Durham, ed., *Studies in "Cane,"* p. 90.

2. Ibid.

3. Locke and Montgomery, eds., *Plays of Negro Life*, pp. 271–72.

4. Ibid., p. 283.

5. Toomer, "Why I Entered the Gurdjieff Work," Toomer Collection, Box 66, Folder 1, chap. 2, p. 28.

6. Toomer, *The Wayward and the Seeking*, p. 253.

7. Ibid., p. 269.

8. Ibid., p. 295.

9. Ibid., p. 299.

10. Ibid., p. 267.

11. Ibid., p. 262.

12. Ibid., p. 315.

13. Ibid., p. 274.

14. Ibid., p. 272.

15. Ibid., p. 296.

16. Ibid., p. 290.

17. Ibid., p. 306.

**Chapter 4**

1. Toomer, "Why I Entered the Gurdjieff Work," Toomer Collection, Box 66, Folder 8, p. 29.

2. Ibid., p. 29.

3. Ibid.

4. Ibid., pp. 31–32.

5. Jean Toomer to Waldo Frank, Toomer Collection, Box 1, Folder 3.

6. From the dust jacket of the first printing of *Cane*, 1923.

7. Jean Toomer to Waldo Frank, Toomer Collection, Box 1, Folder 3.

8. Jean Toomer to Sherwood Anderson, Toomer Collection, Box 1, Folder 1.

9. Jean Toomer to Gorham Munson, Toomer Collection, Box 1, Folder 7.

10. Ibid.

11. Jean Toomer to Waldo Frank [1922], Toomer Collection, Box 1, Folder 3.

12. Ibid.

13. Jean Toomer to Horace Liveright, March 1923, Toomer Collection, Box 1, Folder 6.

14. Ibid.

15. In 1923, after *Cane* was published, Toomer joined the Poetry Society of South Carolina as a nonresident member. Founded in 1920, the society had no written rules against admitting non-Caucasians as members, but evidently it had not expected any other people to join. The discovery that one of its members, Jean Toomer, was the author of a book about Negroes, and that he was designated a Negro, created consternation among the members. Also see Durham, ed., *Studies in "Cane,"* pp. 11–14.

16. Bismarck Pinchback to Jean Toomer, September 28, 1923, Toomer Collection, Box 1, Folder 8.

17. Allen Tate to Jean Toomer [1923], Toomer Collection, Box 1, Folder 9.

18. Du Bois and Locke, "The Younger Literary Movement," p. 161. Reprinted in Durham, ed., *Studies in "Cane,"* pp. 35–40.

19. Alain Locke to Jean Toomer [1923], Toomer Collection, Box 1, Folder 6.

20. Countee Cullen to Jean Toomer [1923], Toomer Collection, Box 1, Folder 1.

21. Toomer, "Why I Entered the Gurdjieff Work," Toomer Collection, Box 66, Folder 8, p. 14.

*There are no notes to Chapters 5 and 6.*

## Chapter 7

1. Frank, Foreword to 1923 edition of *Cane*, pp. i–iii.

2. Jean Toomer to Waldo Frank [1923], Toomer Collection, Box 1, Folder 3.

3. Toomer, *The Wayward and the Seeking*, p. 125.

4. Toomer, "Why I Entered the Gurdjieff Work," Toomer Collection, Box 66, Folder 1, p. 52.

5. Toomer, *The Wayward and the Seeking*, p. 126.

6. Toomer felt that the reader of *Cane* would become interested in his racial identity after reading Frank's foreword. This had been an issue he had hoped to avoid in his efforts to produce American literature that ignored racial divisions. Also see Toomer, *The Wayward and the Seeking*, p. 125.

7. Ibid., p. 126.

8. Ibid., p. 128.

9. Claude Barnett to Jean Toomer, April 23, 1923, Toomer Collection, Box 1, Folder 1. Also in Benson and Dillard, *Jean Toomer*, p. 33.

10. Jean Toomer to Claude Barnett, April 29, 1923, Toomer Collection, Box 1, Folder 1. Also in Benson and Dillard, *Jean Toomer*, p. 33.

11. Toomer, *The Wayward and the Seeking*, p. 126.

12. Horace Liveright to Jean Toomer, August 29, 1923, Toomer Collection, Box 1, Folder 6.

13. Jean Toomer to Horace Liveright, September 5, 1923, Toomer Collection, Box 1, Folder 6.

14. Toomer, "Why I Entered the Gurdjieff Work," Toomer Collection, Box 66, Folder 1, p. 52.

15. Toomer, *The Wayward and the Seeking*, p. 129.

16. Ibid.

17. Ibid., p. 130.

18. Toomer, "Outline of an Autobiography," Toomer Collection, Box 14, Folder 1, p. 63.

19. Ibid., pp. 63–64.

20. Toomer, "Why I Entered the Gurdjieff Work," Toomer Collection, Box 66, Folder 8, p. 23.

21. Munson, "Black Sheep Philosophers: Gurdjieff-Ouspensky-Orage," p. 22.

22. Ibid., p. 20.

23. Perry, *Gurdjieff in the Light of Tradition*, pp. 60–61.

24. For different opinions on Gurdjieff's integrity, compare Perry with J. G. Bennett's *Gurdjieff—Making a New World*. Also see Munson, "Black Sheep Philosophers."

25. Munson, "Black Sheep Philosophers," p. 25.

26. Toomer, "Why I Entered the Gurdjieff Work," Toomer Collection, Box 66, Folder 1, p. 43.

27. Gordon, "Gurdjieff's Movement Demonstrations," p. 39.

28. Munson, "Black Sheep Philosophers," p. 22.

29. Toomer, "Why I Entered the Gurdjieff Work," Toomer Collection, Box 66, Folder 1, p. 43.

30. Munson-Watterson Interview, Amistad Research Collection.

31. Toomer, "Portage Potential," Toomer Collection, Box 41, Folder 1, p. 64.

32. Ibid.

33. Davenport, "Mill House," p. 7.

34. Ibid.

35. Conversation between Nellie McKay and Mrs. Marjorie Content Toomer, August 1976.

36. Toomer, "Outline of an Autobiography," Toomer Collection, Box 17, Folder 1, p. 12.

37. Jean Toomer to George Gurdjieff, November 26, 1943, Toomer Collection, Box 1, Folder 4.

38. Jean Toomer to Paula Elkirsch, June 7, 1949, Toomer Collection, Box 1, Folder 3.

39. Toomer, "Dianetics," Toomer Collection, Box 42, Folder 12, pp. 14–15.

40. Jean Toomer to James Weldon Johnson, 1930, Toomer Collection, Box 1, Folder 4.

41. Jean Toomer to Georgia Johnson, 1930, Toomer Collection, Box 1, Folder 4.

42. Jean Toomer to Mrs. Beardsley, November 1, 1930, Toomer Collection, Box 1, Folder 1.

43. Toomer, *A Fiction and Some Facts* (1931), Toomer Collection, Box 23, Folder 28. Also in Benson and Dillard, *Jean Toomer*, pp. 41–44.

44. Jean Toomer to Nancy Cunard, February 8, 1932, Toomer Collection, Box 1, Folder 1.

45. Bontemps, "The Negro Renaissance Remembered," pp. 22–36. Reprinted in Durham, ed., *Studies in "Cane,"* pp. 75–78.

## Chapter 8

1. Toomer, "Easter," p. 3 (hereafter cited in the text as E plus page number).

2. Toomer, "Mr. Costyve Duditch," p. 196.

3. Gurdjieff claimed that three "brain centers" are responsible for human behavior—the intellectual center, the emotional center, and the "moving" center. A person's pattern of behavior depends on which of the centers is dominant and on which is his or her "center of gravity." The person whose center of gravity is in the moving center likes pomp and ceremony, and he or she is ruled by the physical self and considerations that are materialistic; the person in whom the emotional center dominates is moved by prayer and devotion and trusts feelings above material considerations; and the person who is governed by the intellect tends to be abstract and thrives on theory and argument and less on feelings. See Bennett,

*Gurdjieff—Making a New World,* p. 243.

4. Toomer, "Lost and Dominant," Toomer Collection, Box 50, Folder 51, p. 1.

5. Toomer, *The Wayward and the Seeking,* p. 330.

6. Conversation between Nellie McKay and Mrs. Marjorie Content Toomer, August 1976.

7. Munson-Watterson Interview, Amistad Research Collection.

8. Toomer, "Exile into Being," Toomer Collection, Box 20, Folder 1, p. 137.

9. According to the Gurdjieff philosophy, the person who achieves the highest level of inner unity and who is therefore able to know deeply and clearly and to act in the light of real understanding has a second body—the astral or *kesdjan* body. This highly intellectual, emotional, and spiritual body grows within the physical body and can last after the death of the physical body, but it is not immortal. The astral body has the ability to separate from the physical body and make contact with universal consciousness. When it reenters the physical body, it dissolves all conflicts, and the person, now in a state of harmony, can achieve his or her full potential. See Bennett, *Gurdjieff—Making a New World,* pp. 244–45.

10. This incident was one of three times in his life in which Toomer claims that he experienced a separation of his essence from his physical body. The first time this occurred was while he was a student in Madison, Wisconsin, in 1914. The second time was in the summer of 1919, when he worked at a settlement house in New York, and the final time was in New York City in April 1926. He discusses these happenings in a number of documents including "Awake and Be," "Earth-Being," and "Autobiography." There is no evidence that he revealed these occurrences to anyone before he began to write about them in the 1930s.

11. Bell, "Jean Toomer's 'Blue Meridian,'" p. 78.

12. Ibid.

13. Toomer, "Blue Meridian," p. 214 (hereafter cited in the text by page number and line number). All references are to the poem as it appears in *The Wayward and the Seeking: A Collection of Writings by Jean Toomer*, ed. Darwin Turner (Washington, D.C.: Howard University Press, 1980).

14. Taylor, "'Blend Us with Thy Being,'" p. 54.

15. In Gurdjieff's philosophy, man exists to serve nature by generating the energy to preserve the balance among the seven elements that make up the universe. Gurdjieff's cosmology was based on what he called the Ray of Creation, or the Absolute, which is the unity of the will of creation and all the laws that govern all possible systems of worlds. The two basic laws are the Law of Three, which governs creation, and the Law of Seven, which governs the succession of events. The Law of Three and the Law of Seven and the position of the earth on the Ray of Creation are responsible for man's inability to achieve higher consciousness unless he has knowledge beyond that which is ordinarily available to him. Speeth and Friedlander, *The Gurdjieff Work*, pp. 42–45.

## Chapter 9

1. "Ordinary" here means a person who is satisfied with his life in "waking-sleep," rather than one who consciously strives for higher consciousness.

2. Toomer, *The Wayward and the Seeking*, p. 15.

3. Ibid.

4. Ibid., p. 18.

5. Ibid., p. 16.

6. Ibid., p. 17.

7. Ibid., p. 32.

8. Ibid., p. 34.

9. Toomer, "Outline of an Autobiography," Toomer Collection, Box 14, Folder 9, p. 7.

10. Toomer, *The Wayward and the Seeking*, p. 17.

11. Ibid., p. 37.

12. Ibid., p. 23.

13. Ibid., p. 44.

14. Ibid., p. 28.

15. Ibid., p. 54.

16. Ibid., p. 61.

17. Ibid., pp. 73–74.

18. Ibid., p. 86.

19. Ibid., p. 87.

20. Munson-Watterson Interview, Amistad Research Collection.

21. Doubtless the "sex indulgences" about which Toomer wrote had to do with masturbation. See Darwin Turner's introduction to the 1975 edition of *Cane*.

22. Toomer, *The Wayward and the Seeking*, p. 9.

23. Armstrong, "The Real Negro," p. 26. Reprinted in Durham, ed., *Studies in "Cane,"* pp. 35–40.

24. Gregory, Review of *Cane*, pp. 374–75. Reprinted in Durham, ed., *Studies in "Cane,"* pp. 35–40.

25. Ibid., p. 37.

26. Du Bois and Locke, "The Younger Literary Movement," pp. 161–62. Reprinted in Durham, ed., *Studies in "Cane,"* p. 42.

27. Braithwaite, "The Negro in American Literature," p. 210. Reprinted in Locke, *The New Negro*, p. 44.

28. Baker, *Singers of Daybreak*, p. 54.

29. Ibid., p. 66.

30. Ibid., p. 80.

31. Ibid., p. 79.

32. Claude Barnett to Jean Toomer, April 23, 1923, Toomer Collection, Box 1, Folder 1.

33. Du Bois, *The Souls of Black Folk*, p. 54.

# BIBLIOGRAPHY

## Manuscript Sources

Nashville, Tennessee
  Cravath Memorial Library, Fisk University
  Jean Toomer Special Collection
New Orleans, Louisiana
  Will W. Alexander Library, Dillard University
  The Amistad Research Collection

## Works by Jean Toomer

### Books

*Cane*. New York: Boni and Liveright, 1923. Reprints. New York: University Place Press, 1967; New York: Harper and Row, 1969; New York: Liveright, 1975.
*Essentials*. Privately published. Chicago: H. Dupee, 1931.
*The Wayward and the Seeking: A Collection of Writings by Jean Toomer*, edited by Darwin Turner. Washington, D.C.: Howard University Press, 1980.

### Stories (not included in *Cane* and *The Wayward and the Seeking*)

"Easter." *Little Review* 11 (Spring 1925): 3–7.
"Of a Certain November." *Dubuque Dial*, November 1, 1935.
"York Beach." In *New American Caravan*, edited by Alfred Kreymborg, Lewis Mumford, and Paul Rosenfeld, pp. 12–83. New York: Macaulay, 1929.

### Poems (not included in *Cane* and *The Wayward and the Seeking*)

"As the Eagle Soars." *Crisis* 41, no. 4 (April 1932): 116.
"Banking Coal." *Crisis* 24, no. 2 (June 1922): 65.
"Brown River Smile." *Pagany* 3 (Winter 1932): 29–33.
"White Arrow." *Dial* 86 (July 1929): 596.

### Plays

*Balo*. In *Plays of Negro Life*, edited by Alain Locke and Montgomery Gregory, pp. 269–86. New York: Harper and Brothers, 1927.
*Natalie Mann*. In *The Wayward and the Seeking: A Collection of Writings by Jean*

*Toomer*, edited by Darwin Turner, pp. 243–325. Washington, D.C.: Howard University Press, 1980.

*The Sacred Factory.* In *The Wayward and the Seeking: A Collection of Writings by Jean Toomer*, edited by Darwin Turner, pp. 327–410. Washington, D.C.: Howard University Press, 1980.

## Autobiographies

Chapters form "Earth-Being." *Black Scholar* 2 (January 1971): 3–14.
*A Fiction and Some Facts.* Privately published (1931).
Selections from "Earth-Being," "Incredible Journey," "On Being an American," and "Outline of an Autobiography." In *The Wayward and the Seeking: A Collection of Writings by Jean Toomer*, edited by Darwin Turner, pp. 15–133. Washington, D.C.: Howard University Press, 1980.

## Essays

*The Flavor of Man.* William Penn Lecture, 1949. Published as a pamphlet by The Young Friend's Meeting of Philadelphia, 1949.
"Oxen Cart and Warfare." *Little Review* (Autumn–Winter 1924–25): 44–48.
"Race Problems and Modern Society." In *Man and His World*, edited by Baker Brownell, pp. 67–111. New York: D. Van Nostrand, 1929.

## Unpublished Novels

"Angel Begoria" (1943).
"Caromb" (1932).
"The Gallonwerps" (1927; revised, 1933).
"Transatlantic" (1929; revised as "Eight Day World," 1933; revised, 1934).

## Unpublished Plays

"A Drama of the Southwest" (incomplete, 1926).
"The Gallonwerps" (1927).

## Unpublished Stories

"A Certain November" (date uncertain).
"Drachman" (1928).
"Fronts" (date uncertain).
"Love on a Train" [1928].
"Lump" [1928].
"Mr. Limph Krok's Famous 'L' Ride" [1930].
"Pure Pleasure" (date uncertain).
"Two Professors" [1930].

## Secondary Sources

### Works about Jean Toomer

Armstrong, John. "The Real Negro." *New York Tribune,* October 14, 1923, p. 26. Reprinted in *Studies in "Cane,"* edited by Frank Durham, pp. 35–40. Columbus: Charles E. Merrill Publishing Company, 1971.

Baker, Houston. "Journey toward Black Art: Jean Toomer's *Cane.*" In *Singers of Daybreak: Studies in Black American Literature,* pp. 53–80. Washington, D.C.: Howard University Press, 1975.

Bell, Bernard W. "Jean Toomer's 'Blue Meridian': The Poet as Prophet of a New Order of Man." *Black American Literature Forum* 14 (Summer 1980): 77–80.

———. "A Key to the Poems in *Cane.*" *CLA Journal* 14 (March 1971): 251–58.

———. "Portrait of the Artist as High Priest of Soul: Jean Toomer's *Cane.*" *Black World* (September 1974): 4–19, 92–97.

Benson, Brian Joseph, and Dillard, Mabel Mayle. *Jean Toomer.* Boston: Twayne Publishers, 1980.

Bone, Robert. *The Negro Novel in America.* New Haven: Yale University Press, 1958.

Bontemps, Arna. "The Harlem Renaissance." *Saturday Review,* March 22, 1947, pp. 12–13, 44.

———. "The Negro Renaissance: Jean Toomer and the Harlem Writers of the 1920's." In *Anger and Beyond: The Negro Writer in the United States,* edited by Herbert Hill, pp. 20–36. New York: Harper and Row, 1966. Reprinted in *Studies in "Cane,"* edited by Frank Durham, pp. 75–88. Columbus: Charles E. Merrill Publishing Company, 1971.

Braithwaite, William Stanley. "The Negro in American Literature." *Crisis* 28 (September 1924): 210.

Davenport, Franklin. "Mill House." *Banc* 2, no. 2 (1972): 6–7.

Du Bois, W. E. B., and Locke, Alain. "The Younger Literary Movement." *Crisis* 27 (1924): 161–63.

Durham, Frank, ed. *Studies in "Cane."* Columbus: Charles E. Merrill Publishing Company, 1971.

Frank, Waldo. Foreword to *Cane.* New York: Boni and Liveright, 1923.

Fullinwider, S. P. "Jean Toomer, Lost Generation, or Negro Renaissance?" *Phylon* 27 (1966): 396–403. Reprinted in *Studies in "Cane,"* edited by Frank Durham, pp. 66–74. Columbus: Charles E. Merrill Publishing Company, 1971.

———. "The Renaissance in Literature." In *The Mind and Mood of Black America,* pp. 123–71. Homewood, Ill.: Dorsey Press, 1969.

Gregory, Montgomery. Review of *Cane. Opportunity* (December 1923): 374–75. Reprinted in *Studies in "Cane,"* edited by Frank Durham, pp. 35–40. Columbus: Charles E. Merrill Publishing Company, 1971.

Hill, Herbert, ed. *Anger and Beyond: The Negro Writer in the United States.* New York: Harper and Row, 1966.

Holmes, Eugene. "Jean Toomer, Apostle of Beauty." *Opportunity* 10 (August 1932): 252–54, 260.

Huggins, Nathan Irvin. *Harlem Renaissance.* New York: Oxford University Press, 1971.

Lewis, David L. *When Harlem Was in Vogue.* New York: Alfred A. Knopf, 1979.

Locke, Alain, ed. *The New Negro: An Interpretation.* New York: Albert and Charles Boni, 1925.

Rosenfeld, Paul. "Jean Toomer." In *Men Seen,* pp. 227–36. New York: Dial Press, 1925.

Sylvander, Carolyn. *Jessie Fauset, American Writer.* New York: Whitston Press, 1980.

Taylor, Carolyn. "'Blend Us with Thy Being': Jean Toomer's Mill House Poems." Ph.D. dissertation, Boston College, 1977.

Turner, Darwin. "And Another Passing." *Negro American Literature Forum* (Fall 1967): 3–4.

————. "An Intersection of Paths: Correspondence between Jean Toomer and Sherwood Anderson." *College Language Association Journal* 17, no. 4 (June 1974): 455–67.

————. "The Failure of a Playwright." *College Language Association Journal* 10, no. 4 (1967): 308–18. Reprinted in *Studies in "Cane,"* edited by Frank Durham, pp. 89–92. Columbus: Charles E. Merrill Publishing Company, 1971.

————. "Jean Toomer: Exile." In *In a Minor Chord: Three Afro-American Writers and Their Search for Identity,* pp. 1–59. Carbondale, Ill.: Southern Illinois University Press, 1971.

————. "Jean Toomer's *Cane.*" *Negro Digest* 18 (January 1969): 54–64.


## Other Works

Bennett, J. G. *Gurdjieff—Making a New World.* London: Turnstone Books, 1973.

*Dictionary of American Biography.* S.v. "Pinchback, Pinckney Benton Stewart."

Du Bois, W. E. B. *Black Reconstruction in America.* 1935. Reprint. Cleveland: World Publishing Company, 1968.

————. *The Souls of Black Folk.* 1903. Reprint. Greenwich: Fawcett Publications, 1961.

Gordon, Mel. "Gurdjieff's Movement Demonstrations: The Theatre of the Miraculous." *Drama Review* 22 (1978): 33–44.

MacFadden, Bernarr Adolphus. *The Virile Powers of Supreme Manhood.* New York: Physical Culture Publishing Company, 1900.

Munson, Gorham. "Black Sheep Philosophers: Gurdjieff-Ouspensky-Orage." *Tomorrow* 9 (February 1950): 20–25.

Ouspensky, P. D. *In Search of the Miraculous.* New York: Harcourt, Brace and World, 1949.

Perry, Whitall N. *Gurdjieff in the Light of Tradition.* Middlesex, England: Perennial Books, 1978.

Simmons, William J. *Men of Mark.* 1887. Reprint. New York: Arno Press, 1968.

Speeth, Kathleen Riordan, and Friedlander, Ira. *The Gurdjieff Work.* New York: Pocket Books, 1976.

Trachtenberg, Alan, ed. *Memoirs of Waldo Frank.* Amherst: University of Massachusetts Press, 1973.

# INDEX